Other Books in the Enduring
Issues Series:

Enduring Issues in Religion

John Lyden

David L. Bender, *Publisher*
Bruno Leone, *Executive Editor*

Bonnie Szumski, *Series Editor*

John Lyden, Assistant Professor of Religion,
Dana College, Blair, Nebraska,
Book Editor

Greenhaven Press, Inc., San Diego, CA 92198-9009

Greenhaven Press, Inc.
PO Box 289009
San Diego, CA 92198-9009

Library of Congress Cataloging-in-Publication Data

Enduring issues in religion / John Lyden, book editor.
    p.   cm.   — (Enduring issues series)
    Includes bibliographical references and index.
    ISBN 1-56510-260-6 (lib.) — ISBN 1-56510-259-2 (pbk.)
    1. Religions. 2. Religion [1. Religions.]   I. Lyden, John,
1959–   . II. Series.
BL80.2.E53   1995
200—dc20   94-16101
                                                            CIP
                                                            AC

Contents

General Introduction   91

Chapter 3: What Is the Sacred?

Chapter 4: How Can One Find Meaning in Life?

Chapter 5: What Lies Beyond Death?

Foreword

"When a thing ceases to be a subject of controversy, it ceases to be a subject of interest."

William Hazlitt

The Enduring Issues Series is based on the concept that certain fundamental disciplines remain interesting and vibrant because they remain controversial, debatable, and mutable. Indeed, it is through controversy that these disciplines were forged, and through debate that they continue to be defined.

Each book in the Enduring Issues series aims to present the most seminal and thought-provoking issues in the most accessible way—by pitting the founders of each discipline against one another in a pro/con format. This running debate style allows readers to compare and contrast major philosophical views, noting the major and minor areas of disagreement. In this way, the chronology of the formation of the discipline itself is traced. As American clergyman Lyman Beecher argued, "No great advance has ever been made in science, politics, or religion, without controversy."

In an effort to collect the most representative opinions of these disciplines, every editor of each book in the Enduring Issues Series has been chosen for his or her expertise in presenting these issues in the classroom. Each editor has chosen the materials for his or her book with these goals in mind: 1) To offer, both to the uninitiated and to the well read, classic questions answered by the leading historical and contemporary proponents. 2) To create and stimulate an interest and excitement in these academic disciplines by revealing that even in the most esoteric areas there are questions and views common to every person's search for life's meaning. 3) To reveal the development of ideas, and, in the process, plant the notion in the reader's mind that truth can only be unearthed in thoughtful examination and reexamination.

The editors of the Enduring Issues series hope that readers will find in it a launching point to do their own investigation and form their own opinions about the issues raised by these academic disciplines. Because it is in the continued contemplation of these questions that these issues will remain alive.

To the Instructor

Suggestions for Use of This Book

This book is for use in a course that introduces the student to the study of religion. To use it most effectively, the teacher should refer to the questions at the beginning of each selection and to discussion questions at the end of the book that refer to each chapter. The instructor may choose to structure class discussion around these in order to facilitate consideration of the various views presented. Students should be encouraged to compare the views and summarize similarities and differences in order to begin developing their own viewpoints on these issues.

One cannot study religion totally objectively, if this is taken to mean without personal bias. Everyone is biased about most issues, certainly on matters religious; what is important is to be aware of our biases, to question and critique them, and to see if one can defend one's views in dialogue with other viewpoints. In the process of this dialogue, one's views can be deepened and enriched or transformed into totally different views—but that is the risk involved in all critical thinking that is willing to question why one believes as one does. The teacher is encouraged to use this book to stimulate that type of critical self-examination and development in students.

To this end, the teacher might assign papers on each chapter in which the students are required to state and defend their own answers to the questions. They may utilize arguments from the selections but should also develop their own individual arguments and points of view. The teacher might also require students, at the outset of the course, to state their own religious beliefs in a short paper, by answering certain general questions; for example:

- What is your philosophy of life?
- How can one find meaning and purpose in life?
- Is there an ultimate reality, a god? Describe it.
- Is there a life after this one?

All students should be able to answer questions such as these, regardless of whether they are religious in a traditional sense, because everyone has some sort of "ultimate concern," in Paul Tillich's terms. At the end of the course the instructor may ask students to reevaluate their philosophies and write somewhat longer statements of beliefs based on critical assessment of the views studied in the course. They might be asked to reflect on questions such as the following:

- With which views did you agree and why?
- With which views did you disagree and why?
- Have you found truth in more than one religious tradition?
- How have your views or your understanding of religion changed?

This sort of reflection can help students see how their own views change as they reflect on the views of others and respond to them.

The teacher may also wish to use supplementary materials to give the students more background on these views, and bibliographies have been included at the end of each chapter for this purpose. For example, the selections in the last three chapters have been drawn mainly from contemporary authors to give the reader a picture of current views in these traditions, but if one wishes to focus on classic texts, one might turn to some of the anthologies mentioned. One might also wish to consult sources that supply historical background on the development of the religious traditions.

However one chooses to use this book, the selections included can help students understand and think about some of the most fundamental questions associated with religion.

INTRODUCTION

We live in a religiously diverse world. While this has always been the case, it is only in recent history that this fact has been fully acknowledged. Global communication has shrunk the world and increased contacts among diverse cultures, with their diverse religious traditions; in addition, the increase of pluralism within societies has made people more aware of those who hold religious views different from their own. It is no longer possible to ignore other religions, regardless of whether one views these religions positively or negatively.

At the same time, the academic study of religion has changed a great deal. Just a few decades ago in the United States, college courses on religion were much more likely to reflect a specifically Christian content and approach. Today, the study of religion reflects the pluralism of American society and the world at large; courses frequently focus on non-Christian religions as well as the religious experiences of groups that were marginalized by traditional Christianity, such as women and racial minorities. Scholars use a variety of approaches to study religion, borrowing from the disciplines of anthropology, psychology, sociology, history, philosophy, and other fields.

The contemporary study of religion has revealed that religion is so complex as to almost escape definition. It is not easy to define religion in a way that does justice to the variety of phenomena we usually classify under this heading. We may ask, indeed, why one should even attempt to define it, or why we should pull together the study of diverse religions and the various approaches to them. Is there anything that is common to all those things that we call religions?

A variety of answers can be given to this question (and the reader will find some of them in the first chapter). Perhaps at this point all one needs to note is that human experience seems to contain a religious dimension, however we may define that dimension. We cannot ignore the human desire to question our origins and our goals, the meaning and purpose of our existence, the reason for our lives. We wonder where we came from and where we are going. We strive for something more, even when we are unsure what it is. A mystery pervades our existence—a mystery we can only approach through means such as faith, hope, and courage.

Some have said that no answer can be found to the mystery, for humans have created it and no suprahuman or supranatural answer exists. Perhaps we long for a purpose to our existence, hidden in some other plane of reality and flinch at the idea that there may be no such transcendent purpose. But even if one chooses to see no purpose, one still acknowledges that the desire to find a purpose is part of human life. For better or worse, we almost instinctively seek meaning, and this is when we enter the religious realm.

Enduring Issues in Religion seeks to introduce the reader to religion as a phenomenon and to present some of the basic religious questions and the answers given to them by a variety of scholars of religion. The first two chapters deal with questions about how one should think about or study religion, and the last three chapters present some answers to religious questions supplied by representatives of a variety of religious traditions. One might say that the first two questions are methodological, for they ask about how one should define religion and how one should approach religious traditions that differ from one's own. It will be noted that the authors of the selections in the first two chapters are primarily Westerners of Christian background, so they do not represent the wide range of religious traditions discussed in the later chapters. This is not meant to narrow the range of views discussed; rather, the background of these authors simply reflects the fact that these questions have been of most interest to Westerners, and Christians in particular.

The selections found in the last three chapters, on the other hand, are organized in such a way that the views of eight religious traditions on three general questions are discussed. The religious positions represented include the religion of the Sioux peoples in addition to seven of the major world religions. The Sioux religion was selected as an example of what is sometimes called aboriginal or nonliterate religion. Religions classified in this way are found all over the world, but they are similar to the extent that they are based on oral tradition rather than written scriptures. They are small-scale religions that usually operate on a tribal level. Prior to contact with outsiders the people who practiced these religions tended to live at a simple level of technological development. There are many stereotypes about such peoples, who are frequently viewed negatively as primitives, or romantically as noble savages. It should be realized that these people are not evolutionary throwbacks and that their religious traditions coexist in the modern world alongside the other world religions. Also, the decision to use Sioux beliefs to represent this type of religion should not be taken to imply that all nonliterate religions are identical; rather, their beliefs are meant to show the reader one example of a modern religion based in nonliterate traditions.

The reader may also notice that the first chapter includes the views of atheists, whereas the later chapters do not. Their views of religion are important to include, and so they have not been omitted. The focus of this book, however, is on the phenomena usually classified as religions, so the eight positions represented in the last three chapters do not include atheism. One can argue convincingly that atheism is a religion according to certain definitions, but it does not usually regard itself as such, and it lacks other characteristics normally shared by religions such as a community that celebrates rituals. For these reasons, atheist answers to the religious questions have been omitted, but this should not be taken to imply a value judgment on them; it simply reflects the fact that only a limited number of viewpoints could be represented.

The viewpoints of the last three chapters have been selected from twentieth-century authors most of whom are adherents of the tradition about which they write. In some cases, the author is not a follower of the religion but has recorded the views of one who is. In either case, the selections give the reader a sense of how these religions are defended today. Each selection has also been juxtaposed with a quotation from the sacred scriptures of the religion to show the classical basis for the modern position. In the case of the Sioux religion, which has no written scriptures, the quotations are from John Neihardt's *Black Elk Speaks* (1932). Although this is a modern text written by a white man (and many have said it does not represent the Sioux viewpoint accurately) it has come to serve as a sort of scripture for many Native Americans as it was the first popular published account of a Native American holy man's life and visions.

Readers would also do well to note the diversity in views expressed by the various proponents of particular religions. An effort has been made to represent the diverse strands of tradition within each religion, so that one should realize that important differences exist among the Buddhists, the Taoists, etc. This will help readers to recognize that there is not one "Buddhist view"—there are only Buddhists, each of whom expresses a particular understanding of Buddhist doctrine. Although they would agree on many things, each will express himself or herself in a unique way.

Overall, this book is designed to take the reader on a quest into the study of religion so that one may begin to investigate one's own response to religious questions. As the reader will see, no clear consensus exists as to how one should answer these questions; individuals will have to decide for themselves how they will approach them.

CHAPTER

1

What Is Religion?

Chapter Preface

Religion is a difficult term to define. One must find a definition that is broad enough to include all the things normally considered to be religions, but also one that is not so general as to be meaningless. The definition that one chooses, whether consciously or unconsciously, will also affect how one views the various religions of the world. This is why it is important to consider how one should define the term before beginning serious study of religions.

Scholars have debated about the correct definition of *religion* and will surely continue to do so. But as the modern discipline of religious studies developed, certain classic definitions have emerged that remain the standards. Some of these definitions evaluate religion positively as a response to the ultimate, and others evaluate it negatively—for example, as a psychological illness or an attempt to escape personal responsibility. Paul Tillich's definition allows for both "true" religions, which respond to a true ultimate, and "false" or demonic religions, which exalt nonultimate things to a position of ultimacy. Karl Barth's view of religion is most unusual, as he views religion as the sinful human attempt to understand the ultimate—and yet, he views Christianity as a true religion insofar as it communicates God's revelation.

Whichever definition one uses, the way one defines religion will influence how one evaluates various religions and their beliefs and practices.

Religion Is the Feeling of Total Dependence

FRIEDRICH SCHLEIERMACHER

Friedrich Schleiermacher (1768-1834) is widely regarded as the founder of Liberal Protestant Theology. He sought to reconcile Christian doctrine with nineteenth-century science and philosophy, and made reflection on religious experience one of the primary bases for his theology. His 1799 work, *Religion: Speeches to Its Cultured Despisers*, described the essential aspect of religion as "feeling." He developed this definition of religion in his major theological work, *The Christian Faith*, published in 1821 and revised in 1830. His description of religion as "the feeling of ultimate dependence" has been among the most influential definitions in modern religious thought. Schleiermacher defends his view by arguing that while religion includes both knowledge and action, it is actually based

Excerpted from the English translation of the second German edition of Friedrich Schleiermacher's *The Christian Faith*, edited by H.R. Mackintosh and J.S. Stewart. Philadelphia: Fortress Press, 1976. Used by permission of the current publisher and copyright holder, T. & T. Clark Ltd., Edinburgh, Scotland.

in an "immediate self-consciousness" in which the self feels itself totally dependent on something infinitely beyond itself—something that the Christian calls "God."

QUESTIONS

1. Why does Schleiermacher believe that religion should not be viewed as primarily a matter of knowledge, or action?
2. How does he defend his view that the basis of religion is the "feeling of absolute dependence"?
3. Why is there no such thing as a "feeling of absolute freedom," according to Schleiermacher?

■ ■ ■

The piety which forms the basis of all ecclesiastical communions is, considered purely in itself, neither a Knowing nor a Doing, but a modification of Feeling, or of immediate self-consciousness.

[In] securing to piety its own peculiar province in its connexion with all other provinces, our proposition is opposing the assertions from other quarters that piety is a Knowing, or a Doing, or both, or a state made up of Feeling, Knowing, and Doing; and in this polemical connexion our proposition must now be still more closely considered.

If, then, piety did consist in Knowing, it would have to be, above all, that knowledge, in its entirety or in its essence, which is here set up as the content of Dogmatics (*Glaubenslehre*). . . . But if piety *is* that knowledge, then the amount of such knowledge in a man must be the measure of his piety. For anything which, in its rise and fall, is not the measure of the perfection of a given object cannot constitute the essence of that object. Accordingly, on the hypothesis in question, the most perfect master of Christian Dogmatics would always be likewise the most pious Christian. And no one will admit this to be the case, even if we premise that the most perfect master is only he who keeps most to what is essential and does not forget it in accessories and side-issues; but all will agree rather that the same degree of perfection in that knowledge may be accompanied by very different degrees of piety, and the same degree of piety by very different degrees of knowledge. It may, however, be objected that the assertion that piety is a matter of Knowing refers not so much to the content of that knowledge as to the certainty which characterizes its representations; so that the knowledge of doctrines is piety only in virtue of the certainty attached to them, and thus only in virtue of the strength of the conviction, while a possession of the doctrines without conviction is not piety at all. Then the strength of the conviction would be the measure of the piety; and this is undoubtedly what those people have chiefly in mind who so love to paraphrase the word *Faith* as 'fidelity to one's convictions.' But in all other more typical fields of knowledge the only measure of conviction is the clearness and completeness of the thinking itself. Now if it is to be the same with *this* conviction, then we should simply be back at our old point, that he who thinks the religious propositions most clearly and completely, individually and in their connexions, must likewise be the most pious man, If, then, this conclusion is still to be rejected, but the hypothesis is to be retained (namely, that conviction is the measure of piety), the conviction in this case must be of a different kind and must have a different measure. . . .

If, on the other hand, piety consists in Doing, it is manifest that the Doing which constitutes it cannot be defined by its content; for experience teaches that not only the most admirable but also the most abominable, not only the most useful but also the most inane and meaningless things, are done as pious and out of piety. Thus we are thrown back simply upon the form, upon the method and manner in which the thing comes to be done. But this can only be understood from the two *termini*, the underlying motive as the starting-point, and the intended result as the goal. Now no one will pronounce an action more or less pious because of the greater or less degree of completeness with which the intended result is achieved. Suppose we then are thrown back upon the motive. It is manifest that underlying every motive there is a certain determination of self-consciousness, be it pleasure or pain, and that it is by these that one motive can most clearly be distinguished from another. Accordingly an action (a Doing) will be pious in so far as the determination of self-consciousness, the feeling which had become affective and had passed into a motive impulse, is a pious one.

Thus both hypotheses lead to the same point: that there are

both a Knowing and a Doing which pertain to piety, but neither of these constitutes the essence of piety: they only pertain to it inasmuch as the stirred-up Feeling sometimes comes to rest in a thinking which fixes it, sometimes discharges itself in an action which expresses it. . . .

The common element in all howsoever diverse expressions of piety, by which these are conjointly distinguished from all other feelings, or, in other words, the self-identical essence of piety, is this: the consciousness of being absolutely dependent, or, which is the same thing, of being in relation with God.

1. In any actual state of consciousness, no matter whether it merely accompanies a thought or action or occupies a moment for itself, we are never simply conscious of our Selves in their unchanging identity, but are always at the same time conscious of a changing determination of them. The Ego in itself can be represented objectively; but every consciousness of self is at the same time the consciousness of a variable state of being. But in this distinction of the latter from the former, it is implied that the variable does not proceed purely from the self-identical, for in that case it could not be distinguished from it. Thus in every self-consciousness there are two elements, which we might call respectively a self-caused element (*ein Sichselbstsetzen*) and a non-self-caused element (*ein Sichselbstnichtsogesetzthaben*); or a Being and a Having-by-some-means-come-to-be (*ein Sein und ein Irgendwiegewordensein*). The latter of these presupposes for every self-consciousness another factor besides the Ego, a factor which is the source of the particular determination, and without which the self-consciousness would not be precisely what it is. . . . In self-consciousness there are only two elements: the one expresses the existence of the subject for itself, the other its co-existence with an Other.

Now to these two elements, as they exist together in the temporal self-consciousness, correspond in the subject its *Receptivity* and its (spontaneous) *Activity*. If we could think away the co-existence with an Other, . . . any self-consciousness could then express only activity—an activity, however, which, not being directed to any object, would be merely an urge outwards, an indefinite 'agility' without form or colour. But as we never do exist except along with an Other, so even in every

21

outward-tending self-consciousness the element of receptivity, in some way or other affected, is the primary one; and even the self-consciousness which accompanies an action (acts of knowing included), while it predominantly expresses spontaneous movement and activity, is always related (though the relation is often a quite indefinite one) to a prior moment of affective receptivity, through which the original 'agility' received its direction. To these propositions assent can be unconditionally demanded; and no one will deny them who is capable of a little introspection and can find interest in the real subject of our present inquiries.

2. The common element in all those determinations of self-consciousness which predominantly express a receptivity affected from some outside quarter is the *feeling of Dependence*. On the other hand, the common element in all those determinations which predominantly express spontaneous movement and activity is the *feeling of Freedom*. The former is the case not only because it is by an influence from some other quarter that we have come to such a state, but particularly because we *could* not so become except by means of an Other. The latter is the case because in these instances an Other is determined by us, and without our spontaneous activity could not be so determined. . . .

Accordingly our self-consciousness, as a consciousness of our existence in the world or of our co-existence with the world, is a series in which the feeling of freedom and the feeling of dependence are divided. But neither an absolute feeling of dependence, *i.e.* without any feeling of freedom in relation to the co-determinant, nor an absolute feeling of freedom, *i.e.* without any feeling of dependence in relation to the co-determinant, is to be found in this whole realm. If we consider our relations to Nature, or those which exist in human society, there we shall find a large number of objects in regard to which freedom and dependence maintain very much of an equipoise: these constitute the field of equal reciprocity. There are other objects which exercise a far greater influence upon our receptivity than our activity exercises upon them, and also *vice versa*, so that one of the two may diminish until it is imperceptible. But neither of the two members will ever completely disappear. The feeling of dependence predominates in the relation of children to their parents, or of citizens to their fatherland; and yet individuals can, without losing their relationship, exercise upon their fatherland not only a directive influence, but even a counter-influence. And the dependence of children on their parents, which very soon comes to be felt as a gradually diminishing and fading quantity, is never from the start free from the admixture of an element of spontaneous activity towards the parents: just as even in the most absolute autocracy the ruler is not without some slight feeling of dependence. It is the same in the case of Nature: towards all the forces of Nature—even, we may say, towards the heavenly bodies—we ourselves do, in the same sense in which they influence us, exercise a counter-influence, however minute. So that our whole self-consciousness in relation to the World or its individual parts remains enclosed within these limits.

3. There can, accordingly, be for us no such thing as a feeling of absolute freedom. He who asserts that he has such a feeling is either deceiving himself or separating things which essentially belong together. For if the feeling of freedom expresses a forth-going activity, this activity must have an object which has been somehow given to us, and this could not have taken place without an influence of the object upon our receptivity. Therefore in every such case there is involved a feeling of dependence which goes along with the feeling of freedom, and thus limits it. The contrary could only be possible if the object altogether came into existence through our activity, which is never the case absolutely, but only relatively. . . . As regards the feeling of absolute dependence which, on the other hand, our proposition does postulate: for just the same reason, this feeling cannot in any wise arise from the influence of an object which has in some way to be *given* to us; for upon such an object there would always be a counter-influence, and even a voluntary renunciation of this would always involve a feeling of freedom. Hence a feeling of absolute dependence, strictly speaking, cannot exist in a single moment as such, because such a moment is always determined, as regards its total content, by what is *given*, and thus by objects towards which we have a feeling of freedom. But the self-consciousness which accompanies all our activity, and therefore, since that is never zero, accompanies our whole existence, and negatives absolute freedom, is itself precisely a consciousness of absolute dependence; for it is the consciousness that the whole of our spontaneous activity comes from a source outside of us in just the

same sense in which anything towards which we should have a feeling of absolute freedom must have proceeded entirely from ourselves. But without any feeling of freedom a feeling of absolute dependence would not be possible.

4. As regards the identification of absolute dependence with 'relation to God' in our proposition: this is to be understood in the sense that the *Whence* of our receptive and active existence, as implied in this self-consciousness, is to be designated by the word 'God' and that this is for us the really original signification of that word. In this connexion we have first of all to remind ourselves that, as we have seen in the foregoing discussion, this 'Whence' is not the world, in the sense of the totality of temporal existence, and still less is it any single part of the world. For we have a feeling of freedom (though, indeed, a limited one) in relation to the world, since we are complementary parts of it, and also since we are continually exercising an influence on its individual parts; and, moreover, there is the possibility of our exercising influence on all its parts; and while this does permit a limited feeling of dependence, it excludes the absolute feeling. In the next place, we have to note that our proposition is intended to oppose the view that this feeling of dependence is itself conditioned by some previous knowledge about God. And this may indeed be the more necessary since many people claim to be in the sure possession of a concept of God, altogether a matter of conception and original, *i.e.* independent of any feeling; and in the strength of this higher self-consciousness, which indeed may come pretty near to being a feeling of absolute freedom, they put far from them, as something almost infra-human, that very feeling which for us is the basic type of all piety. Now our proposition is in no wise intended to dispute the existence of such an original knowledge, but simply to set it aside as something with which, in a system of Christian doctrine, we could never have any concern, because plainly enough it has itself nothing to do directly with piety. If, however, word and idea are always originally one, and the term 'God' therefore presupposes an idea, then we shall simply say that this idea, which is nothing more than the expression of the feeling of absolute dependence, is the most direct reflection upon it and the most original idea with which we are here concerned, and is quite independent of that original knowledge (properly so

called), and conditioned only by our feeling of absolute dependence. So that in the first instance God signifies for us simply that which is the co-determinant in this feeling and to which we trace our being in such a state; and any further content of the idea must be evolved out of this fundamental import assigned to it. Now this is just what is principally meant by the formula which says that to feel oneself absolutely dependent and to be conscious of being in relation with God are one and the same thing; and the reason is that absolute dependence is the fundamental relation which must include all others in itself.

Religion Is the Opium of the People

KARL MARX AND FREDERICK ENGELS

The names of Karl Marx (1818-1883) and Frederick Engels (1820-1895) are always associated with the beginnings of communist thought, and it was their *Communist Manifesto* (1848) and other works that they co-authored that defined modern communism. Both Marx and Engels criticized religion as an illusory hope for a better world which arises out of the experience of social inequality in this world. Religion is the "opium of the people," they claimed, a drug that gives people false happiness as a substitute for life in a just and equal world. It is important to realize, however, that in the Marxist view religion is not the cause of social oppression; it is only a by-product of it, and as such, will vanish once the social revolution eliminates inequality. The "intellectual weapon" for this revolution is his own philosophy, according to Marx, and the "material weapon" is the "proletariat," the urban working class which will finally reject its position of servitude and seize control. Part 1 is by Marx and Part 2 is by Engels.

Excerpted from Karl Marx's "Toward the Critique of Hegel's Philosophy of Law: Introduction." In *Writings of the Young Marx on Philosophy and Society*, trans. and ed. by Loyd D. Easton and Kurt H. Guddat. New York: Doubleday Anchor, 1967. Reprinted by permission of Loyd Easton and Mrs. Kurt Guddat. Excerpts from *On Religion* by Karl Marx and Friedrich Engels. Moscow: Progress Publishers, 1975.

QUESTIONS

1. In what sense is religion a "reflection" of the hopes of human beings, according to Marx and Engels?
2. Why do Marx and Engels view this hope as an illusory one?
3. What must happen in society in order for religion to "fade away," according to the authors?

■ ■ ■

Part 1

For Germany the *criticism of religion* has been essentially completed, and criticism of religion is the premise of all criticism.

The *profane* existence of error is compromised when its *heavenly oratio pro aris et focis* [defense of altar and hearth] has been refuted. Man, who has found only the *reflection* of himself in the fantastic reality of heaven where he sought a supernatural being, will no longer be inclined to find the *semblance* of himself, only the non-human being, where he seeks and must seek his true reality.

The basis of irreligious criticism is: *Man makes religion*, religion does not make man. And indeed religion is the self-consciousness and self-regard of man who has either not yet found or has already lost himself. But *man* is not an abstract being squatting outside the world. Man is *the world of men*, the state, society. This state and this society produce religion, which is an *inverted consciousness of the world* because they are an *inverted world*. Religion is the generalized theory of this world, its encyclopaedic compendium, its logic in popular form, its spiritualistic point d'honneur, its enthusiasm, its moral sanction, its solemn complement, its general ground of consolation and justification. It is the *fantastic realization* of the human essence inasmuch as the *human essence* possesses no true reality. The struggle against religion is therefore indirectly the struggle against *that world* whose spiritual *aroma* is religion.

Religious suffering is the *expression* of real suffering and at the same time the *protest* against real suffering. Religion is the sigh of the oppressed creature, the heart of a heartless world, as it is the spirit of spiritless conditions. It is the *opium* of the people.

The abolition of religion as people's *illusory* happiness is the demand for their *real* happiness. The demand to abandon illusions about their condition is a *demand to abandon a condition which requires illusions*. The criticism of religion is thus in *embryo* a *criticism of the vale of tears* whose *halo* is religion.

Criticism has plucked imaginary flowers from the chain, not so that man will wear the chain that is without fantasy or consolation but so that he will throw it off and pluck the living flower. The criticism of religion disillusions man so that he thinks, acts, and shapes his reality like a disillusioned man who has come to his senses, so that he revolves around himself and thus around his true sun. Religion is only the illusory sun that revolves around man so long as he does not revolve about himself.

Thus it is the *task of history*, once the *otherworldly truth* has disappeared, to establish the *truth of this world*. The immediate *task of philosophy* which is in the service of history is to unmask human self-alienation in its *unholy forms* now that it has been unmasked in its *holy form*. Thus the criticism of heaven turns into the criticism of the earth, the *criticism of religion* into the *criticism of law*, and the *criticism of theology* into the *criticism of politics*. . . .

The clear proof of the radicalism of German theory and hence of its political energy is that it proceeds from the decisive *positive* transcendence of religion. The criticism of religion ends with the doctrine that *man is the highest being for man*, hence with the *categorical imperative to overthrow all conditions* in which man is a degraded, enslaved, neglected, contemptible being— conditions that cannot better be described than by the exclamation of a Frenchman on the occasion of a proposed dog tax: Poor dogs! They want to treat you like human beings!

Even historically, theoretical emancipation has a specific practical significance for Germany. For Germany's *revolutionary* past is theoretical—it is the *Reformation*. As the revolution then began in the brain of the *monk*, now it begins in the brain of the *philosopher*.

Luther, to be sure, overcame bondage based on *devotion* by replacing it with bondage based on *conviction*. He shattered faith in authority by restoring the authority of faith. He turned priests into laymen by turning laymen into priests. He freed man from outward religiosity by making religiosity the inwardness of man. He emancipated the body from its chains by putting chains on the heart.

But if Protestantism was not the true solution, it was the

true formulation of the problem. The question was no longer the struggle of the layman against the *priest external to him* but of his struggle against *his own inner priest,* his *priestly nature.* And if the Protestant transformation of German laymen into priests emancipated the lay popes—the *princes* with their clerical set, the privileged, and the Philistines—the philosophical transformation of priestly Germans into men will emancipate the *people.* But little as emancipation stops with princes, just as little will *secularization* of property stop with the *confiscation of church property* set in motion chiefly by hypocritical Prussia. At that time the Peasants' War, the most radical fact of German history, came to grief because of theology. Today, when theology itself has come to grief, the most unfree fact of German history—our *status quo*—will be shattered by philosophy. . . .

Where, then, is the *positive* possibility of German emancipation?

Answer: In the formation of a class with *radical chains,* a class in civil society that is not of civil society, a class that is the dissolution of all classes, a sphere of society having a universal character because of its universal suffering and claiming no *particular* right because no *particular wrong* but *unqualified wrong* is perpetrated on it; a sphere that can invoke no *traditional* title but only a *human* title, which does not partially oppose the consequences but totally opposes the premises of the German political system; a sphere, finally, that cannot emancipate itself without emancipating itself from all the other spheres of society, thereby emancipating them; a sphere, in short, that is the *complete loss* of humanity and can only redeem itself through the *total redemption of humanity.* This dissolution of society as a particular class is the *proletariat.*

The proletariat is only beginning to appear in Germany as a result of the rising *industrial* movement. For it is not poverty from *natural circumstances* but artificially produced poverty, not the human masses mechanically oppressed by the weight of society but the masses resulting from the *acute disintegration* of society, and particularly of the middle class, which gives rise to the proletariat—though also, needless to say, poverty from natural circumstances and Christian-Germanic serfdom gradually join the proletariat.

Heralding the *dissolution of the existing order of things,* the proletariat merely announces the *secret of its own existence* because it *is* the *real* dissolution of this order. Demanding the *negation of private property*, the proletariat merely raises to the *principle of society* what society has raised to the principle *of the proletariat*, what the proletariat already embodies as the negative result of society without its action. The proletarian thus has the same right in the emerging order of things as the *German king* has in the existing order when he calls the people *his* people or a horse *his* horse. Declaring the people to be his private property, the king merely proclaims that the private owner is king.

As philosophy finds its *material* weapons in the proletariat, the proletariat finds its *intellectual* weapons in philosophy. And once the lightning of thought has deeply struck this unsophisticated soil of the people, the *Germans* will emancipate themselves to become *men*.

Let us summarize the result:

The only emancipation of Germany possible *in practice* is emancipation based on *the* theory proclaiming that man is the highest essence of man. In Germany emancipation from the *Middle Ages* is possible only as emancipation at the same time from *partial* victories over the Middle Ages. In Germany *no* brand of bondage can be broken without *every* brand of bondage being broken. Always seeking *fundamentals*, Germany can only make a *fundamental* revolution. The *emancipation of the German* is the *emancipation of mankind*. The *head* of this emancipation is *philosophy*, its *heart* is the *proletariat*. Philosophy cannot be actualized without the transcendence of the proletariat, the proletariat cannot be transcended without the actualization of philosophy.

Part 2

The social principles of Christianity justified the slavery of antiquity, glorified the serfdom of the Middle Ages and are capable, in case of need, of defending the oppression of the proletariat, even if with somewhat doleful grimaces.

The social principles of Christianity preach the necessity of a ruling and an oppressed class, and for the latter all they have to offer is the pious wish that the former may be charitable.

The social principles of Christianity place the Consistorial Counsellor's compensation for all infamies in heaven, and thereby justify the continuation of these infamies on earth.

The social principles of Christianity declare all the vile acts of the oppressors against the oppressed to be either a just punishment for original sin and other sins, or trials which the Lord, in his infinite wisdom, ordains for the redeemed.

The social principles of Christianity preach cowardice, self-contempt, abasement, submissiveness and humbleness, in short, all the qualities of the rabble, and the proletariat, which will not permit itself to be treated as rabble, needs its courage, its self-confidence, its pride and its sense of independence even more than its bread.

The social principles of Christianity are sneaking and hypocritical, and the proletariat is revolutionary.

So much for the social principles of Christianity. . . .

Christianity knew only *one* point in which all men were equal: that all were equally born in original sin—which corresponded perfectly to its character as the religion of the slaves and the oppressed. Apart from this it recognised, at most, the equality of the elect, which however was only stressed at the very beginning. The traces of common ownership which are also found in the early stages of the new religion can be ascribed to solidarity among the proscribed rather than to real equalitarian ideas. Within a very short time the establishment of the distinction between priests and laymen put an end even to this incipient Christian equality. . . .

All religion . . . is nothing but the fantastic reflection in men's minds of those external forces which control their daily life, a reflection in which the terrestrial forces assume the form of supernatural forces. In the beginnings of history it was the forces of nature which were first so reflected, and which in the course of further evolution underwent the most manifold and varied personifications among the various peoples. This early process has been traced back by comparative mythology, at least in the case of the Indo-European peoples, to its origin in the Indian Vedas, and in its further evolution it has been demonstrated in detail among the Indians, Persians, Greeks, Romans, Germans and, so far as material is available, also among the Celts, Lithuanians and Slavs. But it is not long before, side by side with the forces of nature, social forces begin to be active—forces which confront man as equally alien and at first equally inexplicable, dominating him with the same apparent natural necessary as the forces of nature themselves.

The fantastic figures, which at first only reflected the mysterious forces of nature, at this point acquire social attributes, become representatives of the forces of history. At a still further stage of evolution, all the natural and social attributes of the numerous gods are transferred to *one* almighty god, who is but a reflection of the abstract man. Such was the origin of monotheism, which was historically the last product of the vulgarised philosophy of the later Greeks and found its incarnation in the exclusively national god of the Jews, Jehovah. In this convenient, handy and universally adaptable form, religion can continue to exist as the immediate, that is, the sentimental form of men's relation to the alien, natural and social, forces which dominate them, so long as men remain under the control of these forces. However, we have seen repeatedly that in existing bourgeois society men are dominated by the economic conditions created by themselves, by the means of production which they themselves have produced, as if by an alien force. The actual basis of the reflective activity that gives rise to religion therefore continues to exist, and with it the religious reflection itself. And although bourgeois political economy has given a certain insight into the causal connection of this alien domination, this makes no essential difference. Bourgeois economics can neither prevent crises in general, nor protect the individual capitalists from losses, bad debts and bankruptcy, nor secure the individual workers against unemployment and destitution. It is still true that man proposes and God (that is, the alien domination of the capitalist mode of production) disposes. Mere knowledge, even if it went much further and deeper than that of bourgeois economic science, is not enough to bring social forces under the domination of society. What is above all necessary for this, is a social *act*. And when this act has been accomplished, when society, by taking possession of all means of production and using them on a planned basis, has freed itself and all its members from the bondage in which they are now held by these means of production which they themselves have produced but which confront them as an irresistible alien force; when therefore man no longer merely proposes, but also disposes—only then will the last alien force which is still reflected in religion vanish; and with it will also vanish the religious reflection itself, for the simple reason that then there will be nothing left to reflect.

VIEWPOINT

3

Religion Is an Experience of Awe and Mystery

RUDOLF OTTO

Rudolf Otto (1869-1937) studied religions around the world with the aim of finding some common essence shared by all of them. He concluded that all religions are a response to "the holy," his name for the mysterious transcendent dimension of existence which we all experience. His view is similar to Schleiermacher's and influenced by it, but he finds Schleiermacher's view too conceptual, and too far from the actual experience of the holy. It is more than a feeling of dependence, he argues, and more than a mode of self-consciousness: it is the depth of religious emotion, a paradoxical mix of love and fear, attraction to and repulsion from that to which all religions point, the "wholly other."

QUESTIONS

1. How does Otto describe the experience of "the holy" which is found in all religions?
2. What does Otto mean by the *"mysterium tremendum"*?

Reprinted from *The Idea of the Holy* by Rudolf Otto, translated by John W. Harvey (2nd ed., 1950) by permission of Oxford University Press.

3. What are some of the various ways in which the holy can be experienced, according to Otto?

■   ■   ■

'Numen' and the 'Numinous'

'Holiness'—'the holy'—is a category of interpretation and valuation peculiar to the sphere of religion. It is, indeed, applied by transference to another sphere—that of ethics—but it is not itself derived from this. While it is complex, it contains a quite specific element or 'moment', which sets it apart from 'the rational' in the meaning we gave to that word above, and which remains inexpressible in the sense that it completely eludes apprehension in terms of concepts. The same thing is true (to take a quite different region of experience) of the category of the beautiful.

Now these statements would be untrue from the outset if 'the holy' were merely what is meant by the word, not only in common parlance, but in philosophical, and generally even in theological usage. The fact is we have come to use the words 'holy', 'sacred' (*heilig*) in an entirely derivative sense, quite different from that which they originally bore. We generally take 'holy' as meaning 'completely good'; it is the absolute moral attribute denoting the consummation of moral goodness. . . .

But this common usage of the term is inaccurate. It is true that all this moral significance is contained in the word 'holy', but it includes in addition—as even we cannot but feel—a clear overplus of meaning, and this it is now our task to isolate. . . .

It is worth while to find a word to stand for this element in isolation, this 'extra' in the meaning of 'holy' above and beyond the meaning of goodness. By means of a special term we shall the better be able, first, to keep the meaning clearly apart and distinct, and second, to apprehend and classify connectedly whatever subordinate forms or stages of development it may show. For this purpose I adopt a word coined from the Latin *numen. Omen* has given us 'ominous', and there is no reason why from numen we should not similarly form a word 'numinous'. I shall speak, then, of a unique 'numinous' category of value and of a definitely 'numinous' state of mind, which is always found wherever the category is applied. . . .

Creature-Feeling

The reader is invited to direct his mind to a moment of deeply-felt religious experience, as little as possible qualified by other forms of consciousness. Whoever cannot do this, whoever knows no such moments in his experience, is requested to read no farther; for it is not easy to discuss questions of religious psychology with one who can recollect the emotions of his adolescence, the discomforts of indigestion, or, say, social feelings, but cannot recall any intrinsically religious feelings. We do not blame such an one, when he tries for himself to advance as far as he can with the help of such principles of explanation as he knows, interpreting 'aesthetics' in terms of sensuous pleasure, and 'religion' as a function of the gregarious instinct and social standards, or as something more primitive still. But the artist, who for his part has an intimate personal knowledge of the distinctive element in the aesthetic experience, will decline his theories with thanks, and the religious man will reject them even more uncompromisingly.

Next, in the probing and analysis of such states of the soul as that of solemn worship, it will be well if regard be paid to what is unique in them rather than to what they have in common with other similar states. To be *rapt* in worship is one thing; to be morally *uplifted* by the contemplation of a good deed is another; and it is not to their common features, but to those elements of emotional content peculiar to the first that we would have attention directed as precisely as possible. As Christians we undoubtedly here first meet with feelings familiar enough in a weaker form in other departments of experience, such as feelings of gratitude, trust, love, reliance, humble submission, and dedication. But this does not by any means exhaust the content of religious worship. Not in any of these have we got the special features of the quite unique and incomparable experience of solemn worship. In what does this consist?

Schleiermacher has the credit of isolating a very important element in such an experience. This is the 'feeling of dependence'. But this important discovery of Schleiermacher is open to criticism in more than one respect.

In the first place, the feeling or emotion which he really has in mind in this phrase is in its specific quality not a 'feeling of dependence' in the 'natural' sense of the word. As such, other domains of life and other regions of experience than the religious occasion the feeling, as a sense of personal insufficiency and impotence, a consciousness of being determined by circumstances and environment. The feeling of which Schleiermacher wrote has an undeniable analogy with these states of mind: they serve as an indication to it, and its nature may be elucidated by them, so that, by following the direction in which they point, the feeling itself may be spontaneously felt. But the feeling is at the same time also qualitatively different from such analogous states of mind. Schleiermacher himself, in a way, recognizes this by distinguishing the feeling of pious or religious dependence from all other feelings of dependence. His mistake is in making the distinction merely that between 'absolute' and 'relative' dependence, and therefore a difference of degree and not of intrinsic quality. What he overlooks is that, in giving the feeling the name 'feeling of dependence' at all, we are really employing what is no more than a very close analogy. Anyone who compares and contrasts the two states of mind introspectively will find out, I think, what I mean. It cannot be expressed by means of anything else, just because it is so primary and elementary a datum in our psychical life, and therefore only definable through itself. It may perhaps help him if I cite a well-known example, in which the precise 'moment' or element of religious feeling of which we are speaking is most actively present. When Abraham ventures to plead with God for the men of Sodom, he says (Gen. xviii. 27): 'Behold now, I have taken upon me to speak unto the Lord, which am but dust and ashes.' There you have a self-confessed 'feeling of dependence', which is yet at the same time far more than, and something other than, *merely* a feeling of dependence. Desiring to give it a name of its own, I propose to call it 'creature-consciousness' or creature-feeling. It is the emotion of a creature, submerged and overwhelmed by its own nothingness in contrast to that which is supreme above all creatures.

It is easily seen that, once again, this phrase, whatever it is, is not a *conceptual* explanation of the matter. All that this new term, 'creature-feeling', can express, is the note of submergence into nothingness before an overpowering, absolute might of some kind; whereas everything turns upon the *character* of this overpowering might, a character which cannot be expressed verbally, and can only be suggested indirectly through the tone and content of a man's feeling-response to it. And this response must be directly experienced in oneself to be understood. . . .

The Analysis of 'Tremendum'

We said above that the nature of the numinous can only be suggested by means of the special way in which it is reflected in the mind in terms of feeling. 'Its nature is such that it grips or stirs the human mind with this and that determinate affective state.' We have now to attempt to give a further indication of these determinate states. We must once again endeavour, by adducing feelings akin to them for the purpose of analogy or contrast, and by the use of metaphor and symbolic expressions, to make the states of mind we are investigating ring out, as it were, of themselves.

Let us consider the deepest and most fundamental element in all strong and sincerely felt religious emotion. Faith unto salvation, trust, love—all these are there. But over and above these is an element which may also on occasion, quite apart from them, profoundly affect us and occupy the mind with a wellnigh bewildering strength. Let us follow it up with every effort of sympathy and imaginative intuition wherever it is to be found, in the lives of those around us, in sudden, strong ebullitions of personal piety and the frames of mind such ebullitions evince, in the fixed and ordered solemnities of rites and liturgies, and again in the atmosphere that clings to old religious monuments and buildings, to temples and to churches. If we do so we shall find we are dealing with something for which there is only one appropriate expression, '*mysterium tremendum*'. The feeling of it may at times come sweeping like a gentle tide, pervading the mind with a tranquil mood of deepest worship. It may pass over into a more set and lasting attitude of the soul, continuing, as it were, thrillingly vibrant and resonant, until at last it dies away and the soul resumes its 'profane', non-religious mood of everyday experience. It may burst in sudden eruption up from the depths of the soul with spasms and convulsions, or lead to the strangest excitements, to intoxicated frenzy, to transport, and to ecstasy. It has its wild and demonic forms and can sink to an almost grisly horror and shuddering. It has its crude, barbaric antecedents and early manifestations, and again it may be developed into something beautiful and pure and glorious. It may become the hushed, trembling, and speechless humility of the creature in the presence of—whom or what? In the presence of that which is a *mystery* inexpressible and above all creatures.

It is again evident at once that here too our attempted formulation by means of a concept is once more a merely negative one. Conceptually *mysterium* denotes merely that which is hidden and esoteric, that which is beyond conception or understanding, extraordinary and unfamiliar. The term does not define the object more positively in its qualitative character. But though what is enunciated in the word is negative, what is meant is something absolutely and intensely positive. This pure positive we can experience in feelings, feelings which our discussion can help to make clear to us, in so far as it arouses them actually in our hearts.

Religion Is an Illusion Produced by Psychological Projection

SIGMUND FREUD

Sigmund Freud (1859-1939) created the modern discipline of psychology and developed a new way of looking at the human mind as a multilayered entity with conscious, subconscious, and unconscious levels of thought. He viewed human beings as creatures who wrestle with themselves, as their rational and irrational natures come into conflict. Neurosis, or psychological illness, develops when a person is unable to deal with reality and instead creates a false and unhealthy view of the world. In Freud's view, religion is a neurosis which develops when people refuse to give up the need for a father figure who watches over and protects them. Religion is both irrational and unhealthy, therefore, and people would be better off if they could accept a "scientific" view of the world which rejects religion and its unrealistic notions.

QUESTIONS

1. What are the main functions of religion, according to Freud?
2. How does religion develop in the individual's life, in Freud's view?
3. What reasons does Freud give for his view that science has demolished the religious worldview (*Weltanschauung*)?

■ ■ ■

If we are to give an account of the grandiose nature of religion, we must bear in mind what it undertakes to do for human beings. It gives them information about the origin and coming into existence of the universe, it assures them of its protection and of ultimate happiness in the ups and downs of life and it directs their thoughts and actions by precepts which it lays down with its whole authority. Thus it fulfills three functions. With the first of them it satisfies the human thirst for knowledge; it does the same thing that science attempts to do with *its* means, and at that point enters into rivalry with it. It is to its second function that it no doubt owes the greatest part of its influence. Science can be no match for it when it soothes the fear that men feel of the dangers and vicissitudes of life, when it assures them of a happy ending and offers them comfort in unhappiness. It is true that science can teach us how to avoid certain dangers and that there are some sufferings which it can successfully combat; it would be most unjust to deny that it is a powerful helper to men; but there are many situations in which it must leave a man to his suffering and can only advise him to submit to it. In its third function, in which it issues precepts and lays down prohibitions and restrictions, religion is furthest away from science. For science is content to investigate and to establish facts, though it is true that from its applications rules and advice are derived on the conduct of life. In some circumstances these are the same as those offered by religion, but, when this is so, the reasons for them are different.

The convergence between these three aspects of religion is not entirely clear. What has an explanation of the origin of the universe to do with the inculcation of certain particular ethical precepts? The assurances of protection and happiness are more intimately linked with the ethical requirements. They are the reward for fulfilling these commands; only those who obey them may count upon these benefits, punishment awaits the disobedient. Incidentally, something similar is true of science. Those who disregard its lessons, so it tells us, expose themselves to injury.

The remarkable combination in religion of instruction, consolation and requirements can only be understood if it is subjected to a genetic analysis. This may be approached from the most striking point of the aggregate, from its instruction on the origin of the universe; for why, we may ask, should a cosmogony be a regular component of religious systems? The doctrine is, then, that the universe was created by a being resembling a man, but magnified in every respect, in power, wisdom, and the strength of his passions—an idealized superman. Animals as creators of the universe point to the influence of totemism. It is an interesting fact that this creator is always only a single being, even when there are believed to be many gods. It is interesting, too, that the creator is usually a man, though there is far from being a lack of indications of female deities; and some mythologies actually make the creation begin with a male god getting rid of a female deity,[1] who is degraded into being a monster. Here the most interesting problems of detail open out; but we must hurry on. Our further path is made easy to recognize, for this god-creator is undisguisedly called 'father'. Psycho-analysis infers that he really is the father, with all the magnificence in which he once appeared to the small child. A religious man pictures the creation of the universe just as he pictures his own origin.

This being so, it is easy to explain how it is that consoling assurances and strict ethical demands are combined with a cosmogony. For the same person to whom the child owed his existence, the father (or more correctly, no doubt, the parental agency compounded of the father and mother), also protected and watched over him in his feeble and helpless state, exposed as he was to all the dangers lying in wait in the external world; under his father's protection he felt safe. When a human being has himself grown up, he knows, to be sure, that he is in pos-

---

[1] Freud had considerably more to say about female deities in Essay III, Part I, Section D, of *Moses and Monotheism* (1939a).

41

session of greater strength, but his insight into the perils of life has also grown greater, and he rightly concludes that fundamentally he still remains just as helpless and unprotected as he was in his childhood, that faced by the world he is still a child. Even now, therefore, he cannot do without the protection which he enjoyed as a child. But he has long since recognized, too, that his father is a being of narrowly restricted power, and not equipped with every excellence. He therefore harks back to the mnemic image of the father whom in his childhood he so greatly overvalued. He exalts the image into a deity and makes it into something contemporary and real. The effective strength of this mnemic image and the persistence of his need for protection jointly sustain his belief in God.

The third main item in the religious programme, the ethical demand, also fits into this childhood situation with ease. I may remind you of Kant's famous pronouncement in which he names, in a single breath, the starry heavens and the moral law within us. . . .[1] However strange this juxtaposition may sound—for what have the heavenly bodies to do with the question of whether one human creature loves another or kills him?—it nevertheless touches on a great psychological truth. The same father (or parental agency) which gave the child life and guarded him against its perils, taught him as well what he might do and what he must leave undone, instructed him that he must adapt himself to certain restrictions on his instinctual wishes, and made him understand what regard he was expected to have for his parents and brothers and sisters, if he wanted to become a tolerated and welcome member of the family circle and later on of larger associations. The child is brought up to a knowledge of his social duties by a system of loving rewards and punishments, he is taught that his security in life depends on his parents (and afterwards other people) loving him and on their being able to believe that he loves them. All these relations are afterwards introduced by men unaltered into their religion.

---

[1] In the original edition the present sentence read: 'In a famous pronouncement the philosopher Kant named the existence of the starry heavens and that of the moral law within us as the most powerful witnesses to the greatness of God.' It was changed to the form translated above in *G.S.* (1934)—the earlier quotation of the same passage having no doubt been previously overlooked.

Their parents' prohibitions and demands persist within them as a moral conscience. With the help of this same system of rewards and punishments, God rules the world of men. The amount of protection and happy satisfaction assigned to an individual depends on his fulfilment of the ethical demands; his love of God and his consciousness of being loved by God are the foundations of the security with which he is armed against the dangers of the external world and of his human environment. Finally, in prayer he has assured himself a direct influence on the divine will and with it a share in the divine omnipotence. . . .

This being the prehistory of the religious *Weltanschauung*, let us turn now to what has happened since then and to what is still going on before our eyes. The scientific spirit, strengthened by the observation of natural processes, has begun, in the course of time, to treat religion as a human affair and to submit it to a critical examination. Religion was not able to stand up to this. What first gave rise to suspicion and scepticism were its tales of miracles, for they contradicted everything that had been taught by sober observation and betrayed too clearly the influence of the activity of the human imagination. After this its doctrines explaining the origin of the universe met with rejection, for they gave evidence of an ignorance which bore the stamp of ancient times and to which, thanks to their increased familiarity with the laws of nature, people knew they were superior. . . .

Strengthened by these preliminary exercises, the scientific spirit gained enough courage at last to venture on an examination of the most important and emotionally valuable elements of the religious *Weltanschauung*. People may always have seen, though it was long before they dared to say so openly, that the pronouncements of religion promising men protection and happiness if they would only fulfil certain ethical requirement had also shown themselves unworthy of belief. It seems not to be the case that there is a Power in the universe which watches over the well-being of individuals with parental care and brings all their affairs to a happy ending. On the contrary, the destinies of mankind can be brought into harmony neither with the hypothesis of a Universal Benevolence nor with the partly contradictory one of a Universal Justice. Earthquakes, tidal waves, conflagrations, make no distinction between the virtuous and pious and the scoundrel or unbeliever. Even where what is in question is not inanimate Nature but where an individual's fate depends on his relations to other people, it is by no means the rule that virtue is rewarded and that evil finds its punishment. . . .

The last contribution to the criticism of the religious *Weltanschauung* was effected by psycho-analysis, by showing how religion originated from the helplessness of children and by tracing its contents to the survival into maturity of the wishes and needs of childhood. This did not precisely mean a contradiction of religion, but it was nevertheless a necessary rounding-off of our knowledge about it, and in one respect at least it was a contradiction, for religion itself lays claim to a divine origin. And, to be sure, it is not wrong in this, provided that our interpretation of God is accepted.

In summary, therefore, the judgement of science on the religious *Weltanschauung* is this. While the different religions wrangle with one another as to which of them is in possession of the truth, our view is that the question of the truth of religious beliefs may be left altogether on one side. Religion is an attempt to master the sensory world in which we are situated by means of the wishful world which we have developed within us as a result of biological and psychological necessities. But religion cannot achieve this. Its doctrines bear the imprint of the times in which they arose, the ignorant times of the childhood of humanity. Its consolations deserve no trust. Experience teaches us that the world is no nursery. The ethical demands on which religion seeks to lay stress need, rather, to be given another basis; for they are indispensable to human society and it is dangerous to link obedience to them with religious faith. If we attempt to assign the place of religion in the evolution of mankind, it appears not as a permanent acquisition but as a counterpart to the neurosis which individual civilized men have to go through in their passage from childhood to maturity.[1]

---

[1] The possibility of society suffering from neuroses analogous to individual ones was mentioned by Freud in Chapter VIII of *The Future of an Illusion* (1927*c*), and near the end of *Civilization and its Discontents* (1930*a*). He discussed it at much greater length in Essay III, Part I, Section C of *Moses and Monotheism* (1939*a*). The analogy between religious practices and obsessive actions had been pointed out much earlier (Freud, 1907*b*).

Religion Is an Attempt to Escape Responsibility

JEAN-PAUL SARTRE

Jean-Paul Sartre (1905-1980) was one of the major atheistic existentialist thinkers of the twentieth century. In his view, we live in a godless universe, and this is why values must finally be invented by the individual. There is no transcendent standard for morality to which one can refer, no absolute norm which can provide guidance in moral decisions. The fact that there is no God, in his view, requires us to take responsibility for our own moral decisions; those who cling to the idea of God are simply refusing to accept this responsibility. At the same time, he admits that "even if God did exist, that would change nothing" because we are still left to make our own choices. The idea of God cannot be used to escape the fact that we are "condemned to be free."

Excerpted from Jean-Paul Sartre's *Existentialism and Human Emotions*. New York: Philosophical Library, 1957. Copyright ©1957, Philosophical Library. Reprinted with permission.

QUESTIONS

1. Why does Sartre criticize secular ethics?
2. What does Sartre mean by the idea that "there is no universe other than a human universe"?
3. Why does Sartre state that existentialism "isn't trying to plunge man into despair at all"? Is his view ultimately pessimistic or optimistic about humanity?

■ ■ ■

When we speak of forlornness, a term Heidegger was fond of, we mean only that God does not exist and that we have to face all the consequences of this. The existentialist is strongly opposed to a certain kind of secular ethics which would like to abolish God with the least possible expense. About 1880, some French teachers tried to set up a secular ethics which went something like this: God is a useless and costly hypothesis; we are discarding it; but, meanwhile, in order for there to be an ethics, a society, a civilization, it is essential that certain values be taken seriously and that they be considered as having an *a priori* existence. It must be obligatory, *a priori*, to be honest, not to lie, not to beat your wife, to have children, etc., etc. So we're going to try a little device which will make it possible to show that values exist all the same, inscribed in a heaven of ideas, though otherwise God does not exist. In other words—and this, I believe, is the tendency of everything called reformism in France—nothing will be changed if God does not exist. We shall find ourselves with the same norms of honesty, progress, and humanism, and we shall have made of God an outdated hypothesis which will peacefully die off by itself.

The existentialist, on the contrary, thinks it very distressing that God does not exist, because all possibility of finding values in a heaven of ideas disappears along with Him; there can no longer be an *a priori* Good, since there is no infinite and perfect consciousness to think it. Nowhere is it written that the Good exists, that we must be honest, that we must not lie; because the fact is we are on a plane where there are only men. Dostoievsky said, "If God didn't exist, everything would be possible." That is the very starting point of existentialism. Indeed, everything is permissible if God does not exist, and as a result man is forlorn, because neither within him nor without does he find anything to cling to. He can't start making excuses for himself.

If existence really does precede essence, there is no explaining things away by reference to a fixed and given human nature. In other words, there is no determinism, man is free, man is freedom. On the other hand, if God does not exist, we find no values or commands to turn to which legitimize our conduct. So, in the bright realm of values, we have no excuse behind us, nor justification before us. We are alone, with no excuses.

That is the idea I shall try to convey when I say that man is condemned to be free. Condemned, because he did not create himself, yet, in other respects is free; because, once thrown into the world, he is responsible for everything he does. The existentialist does not believe in the power of passion. He will never agree that a sweeping passion is a ravaging torrent which fatally leads a man to certain acts and is therefore an excuse. He thinks that man is responsible for his passion.

The existentialist does not think that man is going to help himself by finding in the world some omen by which to orient himself. Because he thinks that man will interpret the omen to suit himself. Therefore, he thinks that man, with no support and no aid, is condemned every moment to invent man. . . .

To give you an example which will enable you to understand forlornness better, I shall cite the case of one of my students who came to see me under the following circumstances: his father was on bad terms with his mother, and, moreover, was inclined to be a collaborationist; his older brother had been killed in the German offensive of 1940, and the young man, with somewhat immature but generous feelings, wanted to avenge him. His mother lived alone with him, very much upset by the half-treason of her husband and the death of her older son; the boy was her only consolation.

The boy was faced with the choice of leaving for England and joining the Free French Forces—that is, leaving his mother behind—or remaining with his mother and helping her to carry on. He was fully aware that the woman lived only for him and that his going-off—and perhaps his death—would plunge her into despair. He was also aware that every act that he did for his mother's sake was a sure thing, in the sense that it was helping her to carry on, whereas every effort he made toward going off and fighting was an uncertain move which might run aground and prove completely useless; for example, on his way to England he might, while passing through Spain, be detained indefinitely in a Spanish camp; he might reach England or Algiers and be stuck in an office at a desk job. As a result, he was faced with two very different kinds of action: one, concrete, immediate, but concerning only one individual; the other concerned an incomparably vaster group, a national collectivity, but for that very reason was dubious, and might be interrupted en route. And, at the same time, he was wavering between two kinds of ethics. On the one hand, an ethics of sympathy, of personal devotion; on the other, a broader ethics, but one whose efficacy was more dubious. He had to choose between the two.

Who could help him choose? Christian doctrine? No. Christian doctrine says, "Be charitable, love your neighbor, take the more rugged path, etc., etc." But which is the more rugged path? Whom should he love as a brother? The fighting man or his mother? Which does the greater good, the vague act of fighting in a group, or the concrete one of helping a particular human being to go on living? Who can decide *a priori*? Nobody. No book of ethics can tell him. The Kantian ethics says, "Never treat any person as a means, but as an end." Very well, if I stay with my mother, I'll treat her as an end and not as a means; but by virtue of this very fact, I'm running the risk of treating the people around me who are fighting, as means; and, conversely, if I go to join those who are fighting, I'll be treating them as an end, and, by doing that, I run the risk of treating my mother as a means.

If values are vague, and if they are always too broad for the concrete and specific case that we are considering, the only thing left for us is to trust our instincts. That's what this young man tried to do; and when I saw him, he said, "In the end, feeling is what counts. I ought to choose whichever pushes me in one direction. If I feel that I love my mother enough to sacrifice everything else for her—my desire for vengeance, for action, for adventure—then I'll stay with her. If, on the contrary, I feel that my love for my mother isn't enough, I'll leave."

But how is the value of a feeling determined? What gives his feeling for his mother value? Precisely the fact that he remained with her. I may say that I like so-and-so well enough to sacrifice a certain amount of money for him, but I may say so only if I've done it. I may say "I love my mother well enough to remain with her" if I have remained with her. The only way to determine the value of this affection is, precisely, to perform an act which confirms and defines it. But, since I require this affection to justify my act, I find myself caught in a vicious circle.

On the other hand, Gide has well said that a mock feeling and a true feeling are almost indistinguishable; to decide that I love my mother and will remain with her, or to remain with her by putting on an act, amount somewhat to the same thing. In other words, the feeling is formed by the acts one performs; so, I can not refer to it in order to act upon it. Which means that I can neither seek within myself the true condition which will impel me to act, nor apply to a system of ethics for concepts which will permit me to act. You will say, "At least, he did go to a teacher for advice." But if you seek advice from a priest, for example, you have chosen this priest; you already knew, more or less, just about what advice he was going to give you. In other words, choosing your adviser is involving yourself. The proof of this is that if you are a Christian, you will say, "Consult a priest." But some priests are collaborating, some are just marking time, some are resisting. Which to choose? If the young man chooses a priest who is resisting or collaborating, he has already decided on the kind of advice he's going to get. Therefore, in coming to see me he knew the answer I was going to give him, and I had only one answer to give: "You're free, choose, that is, invent." No general ethics can show you what is to be done; there are no omens in the world. The Catholics will reply, "But there are." Granted—but, in any case, I myself choose the meaning they have. . . .

To say that we invent values means nothing else but this: life has no meaning *a priori*. Before you come alive, life is nothing; it's up to you to give it a meaning, and value is nothing else but the meaning that you choose. In that way, you see, there is a possibility of creating a human community. . . .

Man is constantly outside of himself; in projecting himself, in losing himself outside of himself, he makes for man's existing; and, on the other hand, it is by pursuing transcendent goals that he is able to exist; man, being this state of passing-beyond, and seizing upon things only as they bear upon this passing-beyond, is at the heart, at the center of this passing-beyond. There is no universe other than a human universe, the universe of human subjectivity. This connection between transcendency, as a constituent element of man—not in the sense that God is transcendent, but in the sense of passing beyond—and subjectivity, in the sense that man is not closed in on himself but is always present in a human universe, is what we call existentialism humanism. Humanism, because we remind man that there is no law-maker other than himself, and that in his forlornness he will decide by himself; because we point out that man will fulfill himself as man, not in turning toward himself, but in seeking outside of himself a goal which is just this liberation, just this particular fulfillment.

From these few reflections it is evident that nothing is more unjust than the objections that have been raised against us. Existentialism is nothing else than an attempt to draw all the consequences of a coherent atheistic position. It isn't trying to plunge man into despair at all. But if one calls every attitude of unbelief despair, like the Christians, then the word is not being used in its original sense. Existentialism isn't so atheistic that it wears itself out showing that God doesn't exist. Rather, it declares that even if God did exist, that would change nothing. There you've got our point of view. Not that we believe that God exists, but we think that the problem of His existence is not the issue. In this sense existentialism is optimistic, a doctrine of action, and it is plain dishonesty for Christians to make no distinction between their own despair and ours and then to call us despairing.

Religion Is an Expression of Ultimate Concern

PAUL TILLICH

Paul Tillich (1886-1965) was one of the major Protestant theologians of the first half of the twentieth century. Born in Germany, he lived there until Hitler's rise to power. When the Nazis put into effect their anti-Semitic policies, Tillich was one of the few Christian theologians who spoke out against them. He left Germany and came to the United States, where he spent the rest of his teaching career. He was renowned as a theologian who was able to make connections with diverse disciplines such as psychology and philosophy, as he sought to correlate the questions that arise out of human life with the answers of Christian faith. Central to Tillich's theology was his definition of the core of religion as "ultimate concern." In his view, everyone has an ultimate concern and hence a "religion" or faith, but not all faiths are equally valid or true. The true faith, he maintains, focuses on the true ultimate; any lesser concern is "idolatrous" and hence inadequate as a faith. Tillich thought of Nazism as an idolatrous faith in this sense,

Selected excerpt from pages 1-19 of *The Dynamics of Faith* by Paul Tillich. Copyright ©1957 by Paul Tillich, renewed ©1985 by Hanna Tillich. Reprinted by permission HarperCollins Publishers, Inc.

as it puts its complete confidence in the state. Christianity is the least idolatrous religion, in his view, but he also believes that other religions may express valid responses to the ultimate which we all seek.

QUESTIONS

1. How does an ultimate concern involve both "demand" and "promise," in Tillich's view?
2. Why is an idolatrous faith bound to disappoint one, according to Tillich?
3. Why does Tillich believe that doubt and risk are essential elements of faith?

■ ■ ■

Faith is the state of being ultimately concerned: the dynamics of faith are the dynamics of man's ultimate concern. Man, like every living being, is concerned about many things, above all about those which condition his very existence, such as food and shelter. But man, in contrast to other living beings, has spiritual concerns—cognitive, aesthetic, social, political. Some of them are urgent, often extremely urgent, and each of them as well as the vital concerns can claim ultimacy for a human life or the life of a social group. If it claims ultimacy it demands the total surrender of him who accepts this claim, and it promises total fulfillment even if all other claims have to be subjected to it or rejected in its name. If a national group makes the life and growth of the nation its ultimate concern, it demands that all other concerns, economic well-being, health and life, family, aesthetic and cognitive truth, justice and humanity, be sacrificed. The extreme nationalisms of our century are laboratories for the study of what ultimate concern means in all aspects of human existence, including the smallest concern of one's daily life. Everything is centered in the only god, the nation—a god who certainly proves to be a demon, but who shows clearly the unconditional character of an ultimate concern.

But it is not only the unconditional demand made by that which is one's ultimate concern, it is also the promise of ultimate fulfillment which is accepted in the act of faith. The content of this promise is not necessarily defined. It can be expressed in indefinite symbols or in concrete symbols which cannot be taken literally, like the "greatness" of one's nation in which one participates even if one has died for it, or the conquest of mankind by the "saving race," etc. In each of these cases it is "ultimate fulfillment" that is promised, and it is exclusion from such fulfillment which is threatened if the unconditional demand is not obeyed.

An example—and more than an example—is the faith manifest in the religion of the Old Testament. It also has the character of ultimate concern in demand, threat and promise. The content of this concern is not the nation—although Jewish nationalism has sometimes tried to distort it into that—but the content is the God of justice, who, because he represents justice for everybody and every nation, is called the universal God, the God of the universe. He is the ultimate concern of every pious Jew, and therefore in his name the great commandment is given: "You shall love the Lord your God with all your heart, and with all your soul, and with all your might" (Deut 6:5). This is what ultimate concern means and from these words the term "ultimate concern" is derived. They state unambiguously the character of genuine faith, the demand of total surrender to the subject of ultimate concern. . . .

Another example—almost a counter-example, yet nevertheless equally revealing—is the ultimate concern with "success" and with social standing and economic power. It is the god of many people in the highly competitive Western culture and it does what every ultimate concern must do: it demands unconditional surrender to its laws even if the price is the sacrifice of genuine human relations, personal conviction, and creative *eros*. Its threat is social and economic defeat, and its promise—indefinite as all such promises—the fulfillment of one's being. . . .

The term "ultimate concern" unites the subjective and the objective side of the act of faith—the *fides qua creditur* (the faith through which one believes) and the *fides quae creditur* (the faith which is believed). The first is the classical term for the centered act of the personality, the ultimate concern. The second is the classical term for that toward which this act is directed, the ultimate itself, expressed in symbols of the divine.

This distinction is very important, but not ultimately so, for the one side cannot be without the other. There is no faith without a content toward which it is directed. There is always something meant in the act of faith. And there is no way of having the content of faith except in the act of faith. All speaking about divine matters which is not done in the state of ultimate concern is meaningless. Because that which is meant in the act of faith cannot be approached in any other way than through an act of faith. . . .

This character of faith gives an additional criterion for distinguishing true and false ultimacy. The finite which claims infinity without having it (as, e.g., a nation or success) is not able to transcend the subject-object scheme. It remains an object which the believer looks at as a subject. He can approach it with ordinary knowledge and subject it to ordinary handling. There are, of course, many degrees in the endless realm of false ultimacies. The nation is nearer to true ultimacy than is successes. Nationalistic ecstasy can produce a state in which the subject is almost swallowed by the object. But after a period the subject emerges again, disappointed radically and totally, and by looking at the nation in a skeptical and calculating way does injustice even to its justified claims. The more idolatrous a faith the less it is able to overcome the cleavage between subject and object. For that is the difference between true and idolatrous faith. In true faith the ultimate concern is a concern about the truly ultimate; while in idolatrous faith preliminary, finite realities are elevated to the rank of ultimacy. The inescapable consequence of idolatrous faith is "existential disappointment," a disappointment which penetrates into the very existence of man! This is the dynamics of idolatrous faith: that it is faith, and as such, the centered act of a personality; that the centering point is something which is more or less on the periphery; and that, therefore, the act of faith leads to a loss of the center and to a disruption of the personality. The ecstatic character of even an idolatrous faith can hide this consequence only for a certain time. But finally it breaks into the open. . . .

Faith is certain in so far as it is an experience of the holy. But faith is uncertain in so far as the infinite to which it is related is received by a finite being. This element of uncertainty in faith cannot be removed, it must be accepted. And the element in faith which accepts this is courage. Faith includes an element of immediate awareness which gives certainty and an element of uncertainty. To accept this is courage. In the courageous standing of uncertainty, faith shows most visibly its dynamic character.

If we try to describe the relation of faith and courage, we must use a larger concept of courage than that which is ordinarily used.[1] Courage as an element of faith is the daring self-affirmation of one's own being in spite of the powers of "non-being" which are the heritage of everything finite. Where there is daring and courage there is the possibility of failure. And in every act of faith this possibility is present. The risk must be taken. Whoever makes his nation his ultimate concern needs courage in order to maintain this concern. Only certain is the ultimacy as ultimacy, the infinite passion as infinite passion. This is a reality given to the self with his own nature. It is as immediate and as much beyond doubt as the self is to the self. It *is* the self in its selftranscending quality. But there is not certainty of this kind about the content of our ultimate concern, be it nation, success, a god, or the God of the Bible: They all are contents without immediate awareness. Their acceptance as matters of ultimate concern is a risk and therefore an act of courage. There is a risk if what was considered as a matter of ultimate concern proves to be a matter of preliminary and transitory concern—as, for example, the nation. The risk to faith in one's ultimate concern is indeed the greatest risk man can run. For if it proves to be a failure, the meaning of one's life breaks down; one surrenders oneself, including truth and justice, to something which is not worth it. One has given away one's personal center without having a chance to regain it. The reaction of despair in people who have experienced the breakdown of their national claims is an irrefutable proof of the idolatrous character of their national concern. In the long run this is the inescapable result of an ultimate concern, the subject matter of which is not ultimate. And this is the risk faith must take; this is the risk which is unavoidable if a finite being affirms itself. Ultimate concern is ultimate risk and ultimate courage. It is not risk and needs no courage with respect to ultimacy itself. But it is risk and demands courage if it affirms a concrete concern.

---

[1] Cf. Paul Tillich, *The Courage to Be.* Yale University Press.

And every faith has a concrete element in itself. It is concerned about something or somebody. But this something or this somebody may prove to be not ultimate at all. Then faith is a failure in its concrete expression, although it is not a failure in the experience of the unconditional itself. A god disappears; divinity remains. Faith risks the vanishing of the concrete god in whom it believes. It may well be that with the vanishing of the god the believer breaks down without being able to re-establish his centered self by a new content of his ultimate concern. This risk cannot be taken away from any act of faith. There is only one point which is a matter not of risk but of immediate certainty and herein lies the greatness and the pain of being human; namely, one's standing between one's finitude and one's potential infinity.

All this is sharply expressed in the relation of faith and doubt. If faith is understood as belief that something is true, doubt is incompatible with the act of faith. If faith is understood as being ultimately concerned, doubt is a necessary element in it. It is a consequence of the risk of faith.

Religion Is Defiance of God

KARL BARTH

Karl Barth (1886-1968) was probably even more influential than Tillich as a Protestant theologian. Although Swiss by birth, he also taught in Germany before World War II, and was also critical of the Nazis. When he lost his position in Germany, he returned to Switzerland where he taught for the remainder of his life. His early "dialectical" theology was a conscious attempt to critique the followers of Schleiermacher's liberalism through an insistence on the absolute transcendence of God. Barth claimed that it is not our experience of God but God's Word to us in the Bible which forms the starting point for theology. He abandoned the paradoxical, philosophical form of his dialectical theology when he began to write his *Church Dogmatics* in 1932; at the time of his death, it was still incomplete and comprised thirteen volumes. Barth remained adamant that we should not seek to understand God on any human basis, but must first listen to what God says to us; and so he regarded "religion" as a misguided human attempt to understand God, which must be corrected and displaced by God's revelation. Even the "Christian" reli-

Excerpted from Karl Barth's *Church Dogmatics*, vol 1, part 2, translated by G.T. Thomson and Harold Knight. Edinburgh: T. & T. Clark Ltd., 1956. Reprinted with permission.

gion is false insofar as it seeks to speak for God rather than listening. We can only obtain true knowledge of God through attention to God's revelation, the standard for which Barth believed was only to be found in Christ. For this reason, Barth claims that Christianity can be "true," not because Christianity is a better religion but because it is the bearer of the true revelation.

QUESTIONS

1. Why is religion opposed to revelation, in Barth's view? How does he define each of these terms?
2. In what way is the idea of a "true religion" like that of a "justified [forgiven and accepted] sinner," according to Barth?
3. In what sense would Barth say that Christianity as a religion is "false," and in what sense is it "true"?

■ ■ ■

Revelation is God's self-offering and self-manifestation. Revelation encounters man on the presupposition and in confirmation of the fact that man's attempts to know God from his own standpoint are wholly and entirely futile; not because of any necessity in principle, but because of a practical necessity of fact. In revelation God tells man that He is God, and that as such He is his Lord. In telling him this, revelation tells him something utterly new, something which apart from revelation he does not know and cannot tell either himself or others. . . . We need to renounce all attempts even to try to apprehend this truth. We need to be ready and resolved simply to let the truth be told us and therefore to be apprehended by it. But that is the very thing for which we are not resolved and ready. The man to whom the truth has really come will concede that he was not at all ready and resolved to let it speak to him. The genuine believer will not say that he came to faith from faith, but—from unbelief even though the attitude and activity with which he met revelation and still meets it, is religion. For in faith, man's religion as such is shown by revelation to be resistance to it. From the standpoint of revelation religion is clearly seen to be a human attempt to anticipate what God in His revelation wills to do and does do. It is the attempted replacement of the divine work by a human manufacture. The divine reality offered and manifested to us in revelation is replaced by a concept of God arbitrarily and wilfully evolved by man. . . .

He does not believe. If he did, he would listen; but in religion he talks. If he did, he would accept a gift; but in religion he takes something for himself. If he did, he would let God Himself intercede for God: but in religion he ventures to grasp at God. Because it is a grasping, religion is the contradiction of revelation, the concentrated expression of human unbelief, i.e., an attitude and activity which is directly opposed to faith. It is a feeble but defiant, an arrogant but hopeless, attempt to create something which man could do, but now cannot do, or can do only because and if God Himself creates it for him: the knowledge of the truth, the knowledge of God. We cannot, therefore, interpret the attempt as a harmonious co-operating of man with the revelation of God, as though religion were a kind of outstretched hand which is filled by God in His revelation. Again, we cannot say of the evident religious capacity of man that it is, so to speak, the general form of human knowledge, which acquires its true and proper content in the shape of revelation. On the contrary, we have here an exclusive contradiction. In religion man bolts and bars himself against revelation by providing a substitute, by taking away in advance the very thing which has to be given by God. . . .

True Religion

Religion is never true in itself and as such. The revelation of God denies that any religion is true, i.e., that it is in truth the knowledge and worship of God and the reconciliation of man with God. For as the self-offering and self-manifestation of God, as the work of peace which God Himself has concluded between Himself and man, revelation is the truth beside which there is no other truth, over against which there is only lying and wrong. If by the concept of a "true religion" we mean truth which belongs to religion in itself and as such, it is just as unattainable as a "good man," if by goodness we mean something which man can achieve on his own initiative. No religion is true. It can only become true, i.e., according to that which it purports to be and for which it is upheld. And it can become true only in the way in which man is justified, from without; i.e., not of its own nature and being, but only in virtue of a reckoning and adopting and separating which are foreign to its own nature and being, which are quite inconceivable from its own standpoint, which come to it quite apart from any qualifications or merits. Like justified man, religion is a creature of grace. But grace is the revelation of God. No religion can stand before it as true religion. No man is righteous in its presence. It subjects us all to the judgment of death. But it can also call dead men to life and sinners to repentance. And similarly in the wider sphere where it shows all religion to be false it can also create true religion. The abolishing of religion by revelation need not mean only its negation: the judgment that religion is unbelief. Religion can just as well be exalted in revelation, even though the judgment still stands. It can be upheld by it and concealed in it. It can be justified by it, and—we must at once add—sanctified. Revelation can adopt religion and mark it off as true religion. And it not only can. How do we come to assert that it can, if it has not already done so ? There is a true religion: just as there are justified sinners. If we abide strictly by that analogy—and we are dealing not merely with an analogy, but in a comprehensive sense with the thing itself—we need have no hesitation in saying that the Christian religion is the true religion.

In our discussion of "religion as unbelief" we did not consider the distinction between Christian and non-Christian religion. Our intention was that whatever we said about the other religions affected the Christian similarly. In the framework of that discussion we could not speak in any special way about Christianity. We could not give it any special or assured place in face of that judgment. Therefore the discussion cannot be understood as a preliminary polemic against the non-Christian religions, with a view to the ultimate assertion that the Christian religion is the true religion. If this were the case, our task now would be to prove that, as distinct from the non-Christian religions, the Christian is not guilty of idolatry and self-righteousness, that it is not therefore unbelief but faith, and therefore true religion; or, which comes to the same thing, that it is no religion at all, but as against all religions, including their mystical and atheistical self-criticism, it is in itself the true and holy and as such the unspotted and incontestable form of fellowship between God and man. To enter on this path would be to deny the very thing we have to affirm. . . .

On the contrary, it is our business as Christians to apply this judgment first and most acutely to ourselves: and to others, the non-Christians, only in so far as we recognise ourselves in them, i.e., only as we see in them the truth of this judgment of revelation which concerns us, in the solidarity, therefore, in which, anticipating them in both repentance and hope, we accept this judgment to participate in the promise of revelation. . . .

We must insist, therefore, that at the beginning of a knowledge of the truth of the Christian religion, there stands the recognition that this religion, too, stands under the judgment that religion is unbelief, and that it is not acquitted by any inward worthiness, but only by the grace of God, proclaimed and effectual in His revelation. But concretely, this judgment affects the whole practice of our faith: our Christian conceptions of God and the things of God, our Christian theology, our Christian worship, our forms of Christian fellowship and order, our Christian morals, poetry and art, our attempts to give individual and social form to the Christian life, our Christian strategy and tactics in the interest of our Christian cause, in short our Christianity, to the extent that it is *our* Christianity, the human work which we undertake and adjust to all kinds of near and remote aims and which as such is seen to be on the same level as the human work in other religions. This judgment means that all this Christianity of ours, and all the details of it, are not as such what they ought to be and pretend to be, a work of faith, and therefore of obedience to the divine revelation. What we have here is in its own way—a different way from that of other religions, but no less seriously—unbelief, i.e., opposition to the divine revelation, and therefore active idolatry and self-righteousness. It is the same helplessness and arbitrariness. It is the same self-exaltation of man which means his most profound abasement. But this time it is in place of and in opposition to the self-manifestation and self-offering of God, the reconciliation which God Himself has accomplished, it is in disregard of the divine consolations and admonitions that great and small Babylonian towers are erected, which cannot as such be pleasing to God, since they are definitely not set up to His glory.

CHAPTER

2

What Should One Think About Religions Other than One's Own?

CHAPTER PREFACE

Before considering the beliefs of individual religions, we should ask ourselves how open we are to those beliefs. How can we objectively study the beliefs of others when we have our own ideas and feelings about religion? Can we lay aside our own views to examine other religions from a neutral perspective? Some scholars of religion have tried to use this approach, but an increasing number believe that this is an impossible task. Our own views about religion will affect how we view other religions, whether we like it or not.

At the same time, we can learn to appreciate and understand others' beliefs, even when they differ greatly from our own. We can see the beauty and profundity of other systems of thought, and we can realize that their beliefs offer another way to understand life in this world. But we may still wonder whether their views have as great a claim to truth as our own; can both our religions be true? Are all religions true in some sense, or is there only one religion that has the correct answer to life's questions?

Religion scholars have wrestled with these questions and have generally accepted the idea that there are at least three different approaches one might take to the question of truth in religious traditions other than one's own. *Exclusivists* claim that truth is the exclusive possession of their religion alone: it adequately answers the questions of human existence. *Inclusivists* claim that their religion provides the standard for religious truth, for it answers the questions better than any other religion, but they also allow that other religions may express the same truth, though less adequately. *Pluralists* assert that no religion can claim to provide the standard for truth, as religions are all more or less valid responses to the truth that transcends them all.

These positions give rise to many complex questions. Can one be committed to one's own religion and believe it to be true or the way to salvation, if one is willing to admit that other religions are equally true? Are our beliefs so different that we cannot find a common ground, and so we cannot find truth in other religions? Is religion a matter of simple truth or falsity—like arithmetic or logic, where there is one right answer—or is it a matter of taste—like art, where many responses may be equally valid?

These questions are not easy to answer, and most of the religions of the world are just beginning to grapple with them in an environment of increasing interreligious contact. The student will find here some of the major positions being expressed today on these difficult issues.

Other Religions Are False Paths That Mislead Their Followers

AJITH FERNANDO

Ajith Fernando is national director of Youth for Christ in Sri
Lanka. Although he has spent the better part of his life as a
Christian among non-Christians, he remains convinced that
Christianity is the only true religion and the only way to salvation. He represents a position sometimes known as "exclusivism" because it claims that truth and salvation are found
exclusively in the one Christians call Jesus Christ. This was
perhaps the dominant view of Christians through much of
their history, and today it is still widely supported, especially
by conservative evangelical Christians such as Fernando. He
provides a clear argument for the view that Christians can
and should still claim to know the sole way to salvation, even
in an age of pluralism and interreligious dialogue.

QUESTIONS

1. What does Fernando call "syncretism," and why does he
   reject it?

Excerpted from *The Christian's Attitude Toward World Religions* by Ajith Fernando.
Wheaton, IL: Tyndale House, 1987. Reprinted with permission.

2. What does Fernando mean by "faith"?
3. Why is faith in Christ the only way to salvation, according to Fernando?

■ ■ ■

Though we may accept and learn from certain practices in non-Christian systems, we must reject the systems themselves. We know that Hindu devotion does not lead to salvation, for only faith in Christ does that.

We must disagree with the syncretist who says, "Let us learn from each other and live harmoniously with each other. After all, we are headed in the same direction, even though some of our practices may differ." The biblical Christian says, "We are not headed in the same direction. Some of our practices may be similar. We may learn from each other, but there is a sense in which we cannot live harmoniously with each other. We seek to bring all who are outside of a relationship with Christ into such a relationship, and that necessitates the forsaking of their former religions."

The syncretist says that we are one in the center, though we may differ on some peripheral details. The biblical Christian says that, though we may have some peripheral similarities, we are different in the center. Christianity revolves on a different axis from other religions. The way of Christ leads to life. The Bible teaches that other ways lead to death.

We approach the issue of truth and goodness in other faiths from the basis of our belief in the uniqueness of Christ. If an aspect of a certain religion conforms to the complete revelation in Christ, we affirm it. But if it does not conform to this revelation, we reject it. As Lesslie Newbigin puts it: "Jesus is for the believer the source from whom his understanding of the totality of experience is drawn and therefore the criterion by which other ways of understanding are judged." These are implications of Christ's proclamation that he is "the truth" (John 14:6).

The good points in a religion that have their base in general revelation, as we said, may be used by the Christian evangelist as points of contact and stepping-stones in preaching the gospel. But we need to add that these same good features in a religion can also lead people astray.

The noble ethic of Buddhism, with all its good features,

gives many people the encouragement to try to save themselves. They feel satisfied that they are using their own efforts to win their salvation. But self-effort is the opposite of God's way of salvation, which is by faith. Before one exercises such faith he must first despair of his ability to save himself. The ethic of Buddhism may cause people to trust in their ability to save themselves and so blind them from the way of salvation. So, Satan can use the best in other faiths to lead people away from the truth (2 Corinthians 4:4). . . .

One Way to Salvation

The Bible very clearly teaches that Christ is the only way to salvation. Jesus said, "I am the way and the truth and the life. No one comes to the Father except through me" (John 14:6). Peter told the Jewish leaders, who were very unwilling to accept the supremacy of Christ, "Salvation is found in no one else, for there is no other name under heaven given to men by which we must be saved" (Acts 4:12).

The salvation Christ offers is appropriated through faith in him. So, when the Philippian jailor asked Paul and Silas, 'What must I do to be saved?" they responded, "Believe in the Lord Jesus, and you will be saved" (Acts 16:30, 31). Acts 2:21 and Romans 10:13 summarize this teaching by proclaiming that "Everyone who calls on the name of the Lord will be saved."

But what of those who have never heard? Will they be punished for rejecting a gospel they know nothing about? If so, God would be very unfair. The Bible does not teach that they are lost because they reject the gospel. Rather, it says that people will be judged according to their response to the light they have received. But it also shows that no one lives according to the light he receives, and that no one can be saved without the gospel. . . .

Believing is not merely giving mental assent to what Christ did and then living any way we want. Saving faith has four important steps. First, we must decide to leave behind our past life. Second, we must admit that we cannot help ourselves. Third, we must accept what Christ has done on our behalf. Fourth, we must entrust ourselves to him in this way; we accept his way of life as our way of life. So when he becomes our Savior, he also becomes our Lord.

Why is faith so important for salvation? Faith is the opposite of the basic sin that separates man from God. Man's fall took place when he chose to decide for himself what is good and what is evil. He chose to build his own system of values. So man's basic sin is independence from God. Faith is the opposite of independence from God. When one exercises faith, he rejects his own ways of saving himself and controlling his life and submits to the way God provided for him in Christ Jesus.

Here then is the gospel in a nutshell: God has, in Christ, done all that is necessary for our salvation and we must accept that by faith. . . .

We know beyond a doubt that people need to be converted more than anything else in the world. A young woman in Latin America came up to Stanley Jones at the close of a meeting and said, "You are happy with Christ; now show me how to be happy without Christ." His reply was, "I'm sorry, but I don't know how you can be happy without Christ. Can a railway train be happy without rails, the eye without light, the lungs without air, the heart without love?"

Jones said, "Man is made for conversion. As the duck is made for water, the bird is made for the air, the heart is made for love, the aesthetic nature is made for beauty. When you are converted you find Christ, you find yourself, your Homeland." These are bold claims to make about the gospel. But the nature of the gospel demands such boldness. Through it is communicated man's only hope for salvation—Jesus Christ.

VIEWPOINT

2

Other Religions Are Implicit Forms of Our Own Religion

KARL RAHNER

Karl Rahner (1904-1984) was, by most accounts, the greatest
Roman Catholic theologian of the twentieth century. He had a
significant impact on the theology of the second Vatican
council (1962-1965), which led the Roman Catholic Church to
revise its views on a variety of topics ranging from doctrine
to liturgy. The process of modernizing the Catholic Church—
or "aggiornamento," as Pope John XXIII called it—also included assessing the views the church had held about non-
Christian religions. Rahner's views influenced the council's
statements on the presence of God's grace outside the visible
church, but his own theological works go further in articulat-
ing exactly what he believes this means for Christian doctrine. In his view, non-Christians may find Christ through
their own religions without realizing it, and so are "anonymous Christians." Christ is still the norm for truth in this

Excerpted from Karl Rahner, "Christianity and the Non-Christian Religions." In
Karl Rahner, *Theological Investigations*, vol. 5. Baltimore: Helicon Press, 1966. Ex-
cerpted from Karl Rahner, "Observations on the Problem of the 'Anonymous
Christian.'" In Karl Rahner, *Theological Investigations*, vol. 14. New York: Seabury
Press, 1976. Reprinted by permission of Crossroad Publishing Company.

view, and is the way to salvation, but one need not explicitly confess Christ to be saved. This view is often called "inclusivism," because it allows other religions to share in the truth of one's own religion.

QUESTIONS

1. How does Rahner use the idea that "God desires the salvation of everyone" to argue that other religions can be ways of salvation?
2. Why does Rahner believe that the grace of God must present itself through the religion of a particular culture?
3. Why is it important to treat the non-Christian as one who already partially knows Christ, in Rahner's view?

■ ■ ■

If we wish to be Christians, we must profess belief in the universal and serious salvific purpose of God towards all men which is true even within the post-paradisean phase of salvation dominated by original sin. We know, to be sure, that this proposition of faith does not say anything certain about the *individual* salvation of man understood as something which has in fact been reached. But God desires the salvation of everyone. And this salvation willed by God is the salvation won by Christ, the salvation of supernatural grace which divinizes man, the salvation of the beatific vision. It is a salvation really intended for all those millions upon millions of men who lived perhaps a million years before Christ—and also for those who have lived after Christ—in nations, cultures and epochs of a very wide range which were still completely shut off from the viewpoint of those living in the light of the New Testament. If, on the one hand, we conceive salvation as something specifically *Christian*, if there is no salvation apart from Christ, if according to Catholic teaching the supernatural divinization of man can never be replaced merely by good will on the part of man but is necessary as something itself given in this earthly life; and if, on the other hand, God has really, truly and seriously intended this salvation for all men—then these two aspects cannot be reconciled in any other way than by stating that every human being is really and truly exposed to the influence of divine, supernatural grace which offers an interior union with God and by means of which God communicates himself whether the individual takes up an attitude of acceptance or of refusal towards this grace. It is senseless to suppose cruelly—and without any hope of acceptance by the man of today, in view of the enormous extent of the extra-Christian history of salvation and damnation—that nearly all men living outside the official and public Christianity are so evil and stubborn that the offer of supernatural grace ought not even to be made in fact in most cases, since these individuals have already rendered themselves unworthy of such an offer by previous, subjectively grave offences against the natural moral law. . . .

Furthermore, it must be borne in mind that the individual ought to and must have the possibility in his life of partaking in a genuine saving relationship to God, and this at all times and in all situations of the history of the human race. Otherwise there could be no question of a serious and also actually effective salvific design of God for all men, in all ages and places. In view of the social nature of man and the previously even more radical social solidarity of men, however, it is quite unthinkable that man, being what he is, could actually achieve this relationship to God—which he must have and which if he is to be saved, is and must be made possible for him by God— in an absolutely private interior reality and this outside of the actual religious bodies which offer themselves to him in the environment in which he lives. If man had to be and could always and everywhere be a *homo religiosus* in order to be able to save himself as such, then he was this *homo religiosus* in the concrete religion in which 'people' lived and had to live at that time. He could not escape this religion, however much he may have and did take up a critical and selective attitude towards this religion on individual matters, and however much he may have and did put different stresses in practice on certain things which were at variance with the official theory of this religion. If, however, man can always have a positive, saving relationship to God, and if he always had to have it, then he has always had it within *that* religion which in practice was at his disposal by being a factor in his sphere of existence. . . .

In fact, if every man who comes into the world is pursued by God's grace—and if one of the effects of this grace, even in its supernatural and salvifically elevating form, is to cause changes in consciousness (as is maintained by the better theory in Catholic theology) even though it cannot be simply *as* such a direct object of certain reflection—then it cannot be true that the actually existing religions do not bear any trace of the fact that all men are in some way affected by grace. These traces may be difficult to distinguish even to the enlightened eye of the Christian. But they must be there. And perhaps we may only have looked too superficially and with too little love at the non-Christian religions and so have not really seen them. . . .

Christianity does not simply confront the member of an extra-Christian religion as a mere non-Christian but as someone who can and must already be regarded in this or that respect as an anonymous Christian. It would be wrong to regard the pagan as someone who has not yet been touched in any way by God's grace and truth. If, however, he has experienced the grace of God—if, in certain circumstances, he has already accepted this grace as the ultimate, unfathomable entelechy of his existence by accepting the immeasurableness of his dying existence as opening out into infinity—then he has already been given revelation in a true sense even before he has been affected by missionary preaching from without. For this grace, understood as the *a priori* horizon of all his spiritual acts, accompanies his consciousness subjectively, even though it is not known objectively. And the revelation which comes to him from without is not in such a case the proclamation of something as yet absolutely unknown, in the sense in which one tells a child here in Bavaria, for the first time in school, that there is a continent called Australia. Such a revelation is then the expression in objective concepts of something which this person has already attained or could already have attained in the depth of his rational existence. It is not possible here to prove more exactly that this *fides implicita* is something which dogmatically speaking can occur in a so-called pagan. We can do no more here than to state our thesis and to indicate the direction in which the proof of this thesis might be found. But if it is true that a person who becomes the object of the Church's missionary efforts is or may be already someone on the way towards his salvation, and someone who in certain circumstances finds it, without being reached by the proclamation of the Church's message—and if it is at the same time true that this salvation which reaches him in this way is Christ's salvation since there is no other salvation—then it must be possible to be not only an anonymous theist but also an anonymous Christian. . . .

That man is called an 'anonymous Christian' who on the one hand has *de facto* accepted of his freedom this gracious self-offering on God's part through faith, hope, and love, while on the other he is absolutely not yet a Christian at the social level (through baptism and membership of the Church) or in the sense of having consciously objectified his Christianity to himself in his own mind (by explicit Christian faith resulting from having hearkened to the explicit Christian message). We might therefore put it as follows: the 'anonymous Christian' in our sense of the term is the pagan after the beginning of the Christian mission, who lives in the state of Christ's grace through faith, hope and love, yet who has no explicit knowledge of the fact that his life is orientated in grace-given salvation to Jesus Christ.

Other Religions Are Equally Valid Ways to the Same Truth

JOHN HICK

John Hick is a major contemporary philosopher of religion who has written a great deal about the relationship between Christianity and non-Christian religions. He is regarded as the foremost advocate of a position he calls "pluralism," which avoids making the truths of any religion normative for the others. Unlike Rahner, Hick does not believe that Christianity has any more "truth" than any other major religion, and therefore we should avoid referring to the followers of other religions as "anonymous Christians." The only way to achieve true understanding of other religions is to admit that we all represent ways to the One Reality which brings salvation; no way can claim to be better than any other, because we are equally close to and equally far away from the same Reality which we all seek.

QUESTIONS

1. Why does Hick reject the "dogmatic" view that one religion is more true than another?
2. What is the difference, in Hick's view, between the Real "*an sich*" (in itself) and the Real "as humanly thought and experienced"?
3. Why does Hick believe that all the major religions speak of the same "Reality" and not several different "realities" or gods?

■　■　■

I have argued that it is rational on the part of those who experience religiously to believe and to live on this basis. And I have further argued that, in so believing, they are making an affirmation about the nature of reality which will, if it is substantially true, be developed, corrected and enlarged in the course of future experience. They are thus making genuine assertions and are making them on appropriate and acceptable grounds. If there were only one religious tradition, so that all religious experience and belief had the same intentional object, an epistemology of religion could come to rest at this point. But in fact there are a number of different such traditions and families of traditions witnessing to many different personal deities and non-personal ultimates.

To recall the theistic range first, the history of religions sets before us innumerable gods, differently named and often with different characteristics. A collection of names of Mesopotamian gods made by A. Deinel in 1914 contains 3300 entries (Romer 1969,117–18). In Hesiod's time there were said to be 30000 deities. . . .

What are we to say, from a religious point of view, about all these gods? Do we say that they exist? And what would it be for a named god, say Balder, with his distinctive characteristics, to exist? In any straightforward sense it would at least seem to involve there being a consciousness, answering to this name, in addition to all the millions of human consciousnesses. Are we then to say that for each name in our directory of gods there is an additional consciousness, with the further attributes specified in the description of that particular deity? In most cases this would be theoretically possible since in most cases the gods are explicitly or implicitly finite beings whose powers and spheres of operation are at least approximately known; and many of them could coexist without contradiction. On the other hand the gods of the monotheistic faiths are thought of in each case as the one and only God, so that it is impossible for there to be more than one instantiation of this concept. It is thus not feasible to say that all the named gods, and particularly not all the most important ones, exist—at any rate not in any simple and straightforward sense.

Further, in addition to the witness of theistic religion to this multiplicity of personal deities there are yet other major forms of thought and experience which point to non-personal ultimates: Brahman, the Dharmakaya, Nirvana, Sunyata, the Tao . . . But if the ultimate Reality is the blissful, universal consciousness of Brahman, which at the core of our own being we all are, how can it also be the emptiness, non-being, void of Sunyata? And again, how could it also be the Tao, as the principle of cosmic order, and again, the Dharmakaya or the eternal Buddha-nature? And if it is any of these, how can it be a personal deity? Surely these reported ultimates, personal and non-personal, are mutually exclusive. Must not any final reality either be personal, with the non-personal aspect of divinity being secondary, or be impersonal, with the worship of personal deities representing a lower level of religious consciousness, destined to be left behind in the state of final enlightenment?

The naturalistic response is to see all these systems of belief as factually false although perhaps as expressing the archetypal daydreams of the human mind whereby it has distracted itself from the harsh problems of life. From this point of view the luxuriant variety and the mutual incompatibility of these conceptions of the ultimate, and of the modes of experience which they inform, demonstrates that they are 'such stuff as dreams are made on'. However, it is entirely reasonable for the religious person, experiencing life in relation to the transcendent—whether encountered beyond oneself or in the depths of one's own being—to believe in the reality of that which is thus apparently experienced. Having reached that conclusion one cannot dismiss the realm of religious experience and belief as illusory, even though its internal plurality and diversity must preclude any simple and straightforward account of it.

Nor can we reasonably claim that our own form of religious experience, together with that of the tradition of which we are a part, is veridical whilst the others are not. We can of course claim this; and indeed virtually every religious tradition has done so, regarding alternative forms of religion either as false or as confused and inferior versions of itself. But the kind of rational justification for treating one's own form of religious experience as a cognitive response—though always a complexly conditioned one—to a divine reality must apply equally to the religious experience of others. In acknowledging this we are obeying the intellectual Golden Rule of granting to others a premise on which we rely ourselves. Persons living within other traditions, then, are equally justified in trusting their own distinctive religious experience and in forming their beliefs on the basis of it. For the only reason for treating one's tradition differently from others is the very human, but not very cogent, reason that it is one's own! . . . Let us avoid the implausibly arbitrary dogma that religious experience is all delusory with the single exception of the particular form enjoyed by the one who is speaking.

Having, then, rejected the sceptical view that religious experience is *in toto* delusory, and the dogmatic view that it is all delusory except that of one's own tradition, I propose to explore the third possibility that the great post-axial faiths constitute different ways of experiencing, conceiving and living in relation to an ultimate divine Reality which transcends all our varied visions of it. . . .

We now have to distinguish between the Real *an sich* and the Real as variously experienced-and-thought by different human communities. In each of the great traditions a distinction has been drawn, though with varying degrees of emphasis, between the Real (thought of as God, Brahman, the Dharmakaya . . .) in itself and the Real as manifested within the intellectual and experiential purview of that tradition. . . .

The Taoist scripture, the *Tao Te Ching*, begins by affirming that 'The Tao that can be expressed is not the eternal Tao'. In the West the Jewish thinker Maimonides distinguished between the essence and the manifestations of God and the Kabbalist mystics distinguished between En Soph, the absolute divine reality beyond human description, and the God of the

Bible. In Islam it is proclaimed that Allah transcends human experience and yet is manifested to human awareness: in a haunting Qur'anic phrase, 'The eyes attain Him not, but He attains the eyes'. And among the Sufis, Al Haq, the Real, is the abyss of Godhead underlying the self-revealed Allah. The Christian mystic Meister Eckhart distinguished between the Godhead and God. Again, Paul Tillich has spoken of 'the God above the God of theism'. And Gordon Kaufman has recently distinguished between the 'real God' and the 'available God', the former being an 'utterly unknowable X' and the latter 'essentially a mental or imaginative construction'. Again, Ninian Smart speaks of 'the noumenal Focus of religion which so to say lies beyond the phenomenal Foci of religious experience and practice'. A more traditional Christian form of the distinction is that between God *a se* in God's infinite self-existent being, beyond the grasp of the human mind, and God *pro nobis*, revealed in relation to humankind as creator and redeemer. The infinite divine reality must pass out into sheer mystery beyond the reach of our knowledge and comprehension and is in this limitless transcendence *nirguna*, the ultimate Godhead, the God above the God of theism, the Real *an sich*. . . .

Using this distinction between the Real *an sich* and the Real as humanly thought-and-experienced, I want to explore the pluralistic hypothesis that the great world faiths embody different perceptions and conceptions of, and correspondingly different responses to, the Real from within the major variant ways of being human; and that within each of them the transformation of human existence from self-centredness to Reality-centredness is taking place. These traditions are accordingly to be regarded as alternative soteriological 'spaces' within which, or 'ways' along which, men and women can find salvation/liberation/ultimate fulfilment. . . .

Our various religious languages—Buddhist, Christian, Muslim, Hindu . . . —each refer to a divine phenomenon or configuration of divine phenomena. When we speak of a personal God, with moral attributes and purposes, or when we speak of the non-personal Absolute, Brahman, or of the Dharmakaya, we are speaking of the Real as humanly experienced: that is, as phenomenon. . . .

We cannot say that the Real *an sich* has the characteristics displayed by its manifestations, such as (in the case of the heavenly Father) love and justice or (in the case of Brahman) consciousness and bliss. But it is nevertheless the noumenal ground of these characteristics. In so far as the heavenly Father and Brahman are two authentic manifestations of the Real, the love and justice of the one and the consciousness and bliss of the other are aspects of the Real as manifested within human experience. As the noumenal ground of these and other modes of experience, and yet transcending all of them, the Real is so rich in content that it can only be finitely experienced in the various partial and inadequate ways which the history of religions describes. . . .

Each of the great traditions is oriented to what it regards as the Ultimate as the sole creator or source of the universe, or as that than which no greater can be conceived, or as the final ground or nature of everything. Further, the 'truthfulness' of each tradition is shown by its soteriological effectiveness. But what the traditions severally regard as ultimates are different and therefore cannot all be truly ultimate. They can however be different manifestations of the truly Ultimate within different streams of human thought-and-experience—hence the postulation of the Real *an sich* as the simplest way of accounting for the data. But we then find that if we are going to speak of the Real at all, the exigencies of our language compel us to refer to it in either the singular or the plural. Since there cannot be a plurality of ultimates, we affirm the true ultimacy of the Real by referring to it in the singular. Indian thought meets this problem with the phrase 'The One without a second'. The Real, then, is the ultimate Reality, not one among others; and yet it cannot literally be numbered: it is the unique One without a second.

But if the Real in itself is not and cannot be humanly experienced, why postulate such an unknown and unknowable *Ding an sich*? The answer is that the divine noumenon is a necessary postulate of the pluralistic religious life of humanity. For within each tradition we regard as real the object of our worship or contemplation. If, as I have already argued, it is also proper to regard as real the objects of worship or contemplation within the other traditions, we are led to postulate the Real *an sich* as the presupposition of the veridical character of this range of forms of religious experience. Without this postulate we should be left with a plurality of *personae* and *impersonae* each of which is claimed to be the Ultimate, but no one of which alone can be. We should have either to regard all the reported experiences as illusory or else return to the confessional position in which we affirm the authenticity of our own stream of religious experience whilst dismissing as illusory those occurring within other traditions. But for those to whom neither of these options seems realistic the pluralistic affirmation becomes inevitable, and with it the postulation of the Real *an sich*, which is variously experienced and thought as the range of divine phenomena described by the history of religion.

Other Religions Speak of Different but Equally Valid Truths

JOHN B. COBB JR.

John B. Cobb Jr. has developed a view which differs from the "pluralism" of Hick, as he makes clear in this selection. Through his own extensive involvement in Christian-Buddhist dialogue, he has come to the conclusion that one cannot claim that Christians and Buddhists are speaking of the same "Reality." At the same time, Cobb does not reject the truths of Buddhism, for they may have equal validity with those of Christianity. To truly understand and value other religions, we must learn to hear what they are saying and evaluate it without assuming that it is really the same thing we are saying. In this way, two religions that encounter one another will both be enriched, for they can learn from each other without losing what is distinctive to themselves.

Excerpted from John B. Cobb Jr., "Beyond 'Pluralism.'" In Gavin D'Costa, ed., *Christian Uniqueness Reconsidered: The Myth of a Pluralistic Theology of Religions.* Maryknoll, NY: Orbis Books, 1990. Copyright ©1990 by Orbis Books. Reprinted with permission.

QUESTIONS

1. Why does Cobb reject the notion that there is a common "essence" that all religions share?
2. What is the one norm that governs interreligious dialogue, according to Cobb?
3. How might two seemingly contradictory statements represent different but equally valid "truths," in Cobb's view?

■ ■ ■

I declined to write a paper for the conference that led to the publication of the book *The Myth of Christian Uniqueness*, because I did not share in the consensus that conference was supposed to express and promote. In the minds of the organizers, that consensus was to be around the view that the several major religions are, for practical purposes, equally valid ways of embodying what religion is all about. The uniqueness that is rejected is any claim that Christianity achieves something fundamentally different from other religions. From my point of view, the assumptions underlying these formulations are mistaken and have misled those who have accepted them.

Probably the most basic assumption is that there is an essence of religion. This essence is thought to be both a common characteristic of all "religions" and their central or normative feature. Hence, once it is decided that Buddhism, Confucianism, or Christianity is a religion, one knows what it is all about and how it is to be evaluated. The next step is then the one about which the consensus was to be formed. Given the common essence, let us agree to acknowledge that it is realized and expressed more or less equally well in all the great religions. It is hoped in this way to lay to rest once and for all Christian arrogance and offensive efforts to proselytize. . . .

What strikes the observer of this discussion is that among those who assume that religion has an essence there is no consensus as to what the essence may be. Even individual scholars often change their mind. The variation is still greater when the scholars represent diverse religious traditions. Yet among many of them the assumption that there *is* an essence continues unshaken in the midst of uncertainty as to what that essence is.

I see no a priori reason to assume that religion has an essence or that the great religious traditions are well understood as religions, that is, as traditions for which being religious is the central goal. I certainly see no empirical evidence in favor of this view. I see only scholarly habit and the power of language to mislead. I call for a pluralism that allows each religious tradition to define its own nature and purposes and the role of religious elements within it. . . .

The belief that there is more to truth and wisdom than one's own tradition has thus far attained is the basis for overcoming the alternatives of essentialism and conceptual relativism. It entails belief that while one's own tradition has grasped important aspects of reality, reality in its entirety is always more. This means also that the ultimately true norm for life, and therefore also for religious traditions, lies beyond any extant formulation. As dialogue proceeds, glimpses of aspects of reality heretofore unnoticed are vouchsafed the participants. This is not felt as a threat to the religious traditions from which the participants come but as an opportunity for enrichment and even positive transformation. . . .

For example, in dialogue with Buddhists, Christians can come to appreciate the normative value of the realization of Emptiness, and can expand the way they have thought of the purpose and meaning of life. The norm by which they then judge both Christianity and Buddhism is thereby expanded. Similarly, in dialogue with Christians, Buddhists may come to appreciate the normative value of certain forms of historical consciousness, and the resultant norm by which they judge both Buddhism and Christianity is changed. . . .

So am I affirming Christian uniqueness? Certainly and emphatically so! But I am affirming the uniqueness also of Confucianism, Buddhism, Hinduism, Islam, and Judaism. With the assumption of radical pluralism, nothing else is possible. Further, the uniqueness of each includes a unique superiority, namely, the ability to achieve what by its own historic norms is most important.

The question is whether there are any norms that transcend this diversity, norms that are appropriately applied to all. I have argued that the contemporary situation of pluralism does generate one such norm for those who are committed to dialogue— one that in this situation has relative objectivity. This is the ability of a tradition in faithfulness to its past to be enriched and transformed in its interaction with the other traditions. . . .

I have avoided the issue of conflicting truth claims. This is because I do not find this the most productive approach. Of course, there are such conflicts. There are conflicting views of the natural world, of human nature, and of God. It is not possible that everything that has been said on these topics can correspond with reality, and for this reason many thinkers regard the sorting out of these claims and adjudication among them as crucial for religious thought.

My view is that none of the central claims made by any of the traditions are likely to be literally and exactly correct. Indeed, in many traditions there is an internal emphasis on the difficulty, if not the impossibility, of grasping the truth and expressing its language. Laying out the conflicting doctrines and developing arguments for and against each is a questionable preoccupation. Instead, it is best to listen to the deep, even ultimate, concerns that are being expressed in these diverse statements. Here I am at one with those in opposition to whom this paper is written. They, too, seek to go beyond what is said to something deeper. We differ only in that what they find is something common to all the traditions, whereas I believe that what we find is diverse. My goal is to transform contradictory statements into different but not contradictory ones. My assumption is that what is positively intended by those who have lived, thought, and felt deeply is likely to be true, whereas their formulations are likely to exclude other truths that should not be excluded.

I will illustrate what I mean by the clearly contradictory statements: "God exists" and "No God exists." If we approach these statements with the assumption that the words *God* and *exists* have clear and exact meanings that are identical in the two statements, we have no choice but to say that at least one of them is wrong. But surely we are past this point in our reflections about religious discourse. We have to ask who is speaking and what concerns are being expressed. When a Buddhist says that no God exists, the main point is that there is nothing in reality to which one should be attached. When a Christian says that God exists, the meaning may be that there is that in reality that is worthy of trust and worship. *If* those translations are correct, at least in a particular instance, then it is not impossible that both be correct. Of course, the Buddhist is likely to believe that the Christian is wrong, and the Christian is likely to see no problem with attachment to God. There are then real disagreements between them. But the Buddhist could in principle acknowledge the reality of something worthy of trust and worship without abandoning the central insight that attachment blocks the way to enlightenment. And the Christian could come to see that real trust is not attachment in the Buddhist sense. Both would thereby have learned what is most important to the other without abandoning their central concerns.

Of course, there are many grossly erroneous statements that have been affirmed with great seriousness by adherents of the great religious traditions. It is not true that the world is flat. There is no point in seeking some deeper meaning behind such statements, since we know how they arose from a literalistic reading of certain passages of scripture. There are similar ideas in all the traditions. There are also far more damaging ideas, such as misogynist ones, in most of the religious traditions. These, too, should be condemned as false. But my assumption is that alongside all the errors and distortions that can be found in all our traditions there are insights arising from profound thought and experience that are diverse modes of apprehending diverse aspects of the totality of reality. They are true, and their truth can become more apparent and better formulated as they are positively related to one another.

VIEWPOINT

5

Each Religion Expresses an Important Part of the Truth

RAIMUNDO PANIKKAR

Like Cobb, Raimundo Panikkar rejects any form of religious "pluralism" that would conclude that religions share a common "essence." His own religious and intellectual history is remarkably complex. He was born of a Hindu father and a Roman Catholic mother, and became a Catholic priest who holds doctorates in the sciences, philosophy, and theology. He has written that in his encounter with other religions, "I 'left' as a christian, 'found' myself a hindu and 'return' a buddhist, without having ceased to be a christian." His approach to other religions reflects this complexity, as he argues that we must strive to understand each religion in its own "language" of concepts. We cannot gloss over the differences to conclude that "all shall be one," nor can we ignore what others have to say. Each religion "reflects, corrects, complements, and challenges the other" in the intricate web of interconnections he calls "intrareligious" dialogue.

Excerpted from Raimundo Panikkar, *The Intrareligious Dialogue*. New York: Paulist Press, 1978. Copyright ©1978 by The Missionary Society of St. Paul the Apostle in the State of New York. Excerpted from Raimundo Panikkar, "The Jordan, the Tiber, and the Ganges: Three Kairological Moments of Christic Self-Consciousness." In John Hick and Paul F. Knitter, eds., *The Myth of Christian Uniqueness: Toward a Pluralistic Theology of Religions*. Maryknoll, NY: Orbis Books, 1987. Copyright ©1987 by John Hick and Paul F. Knitter.

QUESTIONS

1. How does Panikkar compare religions to languages, complete with the difficulties of translation? How does this shape the task of dialogue with others?
2. Why is there no "absolute center" to the universe of religions, in Panikkar's view?
3. Why is truth "neither one nor many," according to Panikkar?

■　■　■

Whatever theory we may defend regarding the origin and nature of religion, whether it be a divine gift or a human invention or both, the fact remains that it is at least a human reality and as such coextensive with another also at least human reality called language. . . .

Any religion is complete as any language is also capable of expressing everything that it feels the need to express. Any religion is open to growth and evolution as any language is. Both are capable of expressing or adopting new shades of meaning, of shifting idioms or emphases, refining ways of expression and changing them. When a new need is felt in any religious or linguistic world, there are always means of dealing with that need. Furthermore, although any language is a world in itself, it is not without relations with neighboring languages, borrowing from them and open to mutual influences. And yet each language only takes as much as it can assimilate from a foreign language. Similarly with religions: they influence each other and borrow from one another without losing their identity. As an extreme case a religion, like a language, may disappear entirely. And the reasons also seem very similar—conquest, decadence, emigration, etc.

From the internal point of view of each language and religion, it makes little sense to say that one language is more perfect than another, for you can in your language (as well as in your religion) say all that you feel you need to say. If you would feel the need to say something else or something different, you would say it. If you use only one word for camel and hundreds for the different metals, and another language does just the opposite, it is because you have different patterns of differentiation for camels and metals. It is the same with religions. You may have only one word for wisdom, God, compassion or virtue and another religion scores of them.

The great problem appears when we come to the encounter of languages—and religions. The question here is translation. Religions are equivalent to the same extent that languages are translatable, and they are unique as much as languages are untranslatable. There is the common world of objectifiable objects. They are the objects of empirical or logical verification. This is the realm of terms. Each term is an epistemic sign standing for an empirically or logically verifiable object. The terms 'tree,' 'wine,' 'atom,' 'four,' can be translated into any given language if we have a method of empirically pointing out a visible thing (tree), a physically recognizable substance (wine), a physico-mathematically definable entity (atom) and a logical cipher (four). Each of these cases demands some specific conditions, but we may assume that these conditions can all be empirically or logically verifiable once a certain axiom is accepted. In short, all terms are translatable insofar as a name could easily be invented or adopted even by a language which might lack a particular term ('atom' for instance). Similarly, all religions have a translatable sphere: all refer to the human being, to his well-being, to overcoming the possible obstacles to it and the like. Religious terms—qua terms—are translatable.

The most important part of a language as well as of a religion, however, is not terms but words, i.e., not epistemic signs to orient us in the world of objects, but living symbols to allow us to live in the world of Men and Gods. Now, words are not objectifiable. A word is not totally separable from the meaning we give to it and each of us in fact gives different shades of meaning to the same word. A word reflects a total human experience and cannot be severed from it. A word is not empirically or logically detectable. When we say 'justice,' 'dharma,' 'karunā,' we cannot point to an object, but have to refer to crystallizations of human experiences that vary with people, places, ages, etc. We cannot properly speaking translate words. We can only transplant them along with a certain surrounding context which gives them meaning and offers the horizon over against which they can be understood, i.e., assimilated within another horizon. And even then the transplanted word, if it survives, will soon extend its roots in the soil and acquire new aspects, connotations, etc. Similarly with religions: they are not translatable like terms; only certain transplants are possible under appropriate conditions. There is not an object 'God,' 'justice,' or 'Brahman,' a thing in itself independent of those living words, over against which we may check the correction of the translation. In order to translate them we have to transplant the corresponding world view that makes those words say what they intend to say. . . .

The translator has to speak the 'foreign' language as his own. As long as we speak a language translating from another, we shall never speak fluently or even correctly. Only when we speak that language, only when you 'speak' that religion as your own will you really be able to be a spokesman for it, a genuine translator. And this obviously implies at the same time that you have not forgotten your native tongue, that you are equally capable of expressing yourself in the other linguistic world. . . .

The mention of pluralism by way of conclusion may not be out of place. The aim of the intrareligious dialogue is understanding. It is not to win over the other or to come to a total agreement or a universal religion. The ideal is communication in order to bridge the gulfs of mutual ignorance and misunderstandings between the different cultures of the world, letting them speak and speak out their own insights in their own languages. Some may wish even to reach communion, but this does not imply at all that the aim is a uniform unity or a reduction of all the pluralistic variety of Man into one single religion, system, ideology or tradition. Pluralism stands between unrelated plurality and a monolithic unity. It implies that the human condition in its present reality should not be neglected, let alone despised in favor of an ideal (?) situation of human uniformity. On the contrary, it takes our factual situation as real and affirms that in the actual polarities of our human existence we find our real being. . . .

Either Christians "stick" to their "Christ" and become exclusivistic, or they give up their claims, dilute their beliefs, and become, at best, inclusivistic. These two horns of the dilemma are equally unacceptable. The parallel Copernican revolution consists in shifting the center from linear history to a theanthropocosmic vision, a kind of trinitarian notion, not of the godhead alone, but of reality. The center is neither the earth (our particular religion), nor the sun (God, transcendence, the

Absolute . . .). Rather, each solar system has its own center, and every galaxy turns reciprocally around the other. There is no absolute center. Reality itself is concentric inasmuch as each being (each tradition) is the center of the universe—of its own universe to begin with. The theanthropocosmic insight (which sees the unity between the divine-human-cosmic) suggests a sort of trinitarian dynamism in which all is implied in all (each person represents the community and each tradition reflects, corrects, complements, and challenges the other). . . .

This attitude may be summed up in the following statements:

1. Pluralism does not mean plurality or a reduction of plurality to unity. It is a fact that there is a plurality of religions. It is also a fact that these religions have not been reduced to any sort of unity. Pluralism means something more than sheer acknowledgment of plurality and the mere wishful thinking of unity.

2. Pluralism does not consider unity an indispensable ideal, even if allowance is made for variations within that unity. Pluralism accepts the irreconcilable aspects of religions without being blind to their common aspects. Pluralism is not the eschatological expectation that in the end all shall be one.

3. Pluralism affirms neither that the truth is one nor that it is many. If truth were one, we could not accept the positive tolerance of a pluralistic attitude and would have to consider pluralism a connivance with error. If truth were many, we would fall into a plain contradiction. We said already that pluralism does not stand for plurality—a plurality of truths in this case. Pluralism adopts a nondualistic, advaitic, attitude that defends the pluralism of truth because reality itself is pluralistic—that is, incommensurable with either unity or plurality.

GENERAL INTRODUCTION

The readings in the first two chapters explore some of the methodological questions involved in the study of religion. The remaining three chapters examine some of the beliefs of religious communities that exist around the world. Not all religious communities are represented, and not all of their beliefs are discussed—but these readings represent a sampling of some of the key questions that religions seek to answer and the diversity of their worldviews.

Before exploring the readings, a basic understanding of each religion, including its followers and how it fits into world history, is required.

Judaism has its roots in the religion of ancient Israel, a community that became a nation approximately 3200 years ago. This community recorded its beliefs in the Bible, a group of scriptures that recounts the history of how Israel came to be through the power and guidance of the one true God who chose this people out of all nations as a witness to the world. Though Israel was conquered by foreign invaders of other religions, the religion of the Jews did not come to an end. Israel existed under a series of occupying governments, and when at last all hope of military resistance was crushed by the Roman Empire in the year 135, the religion of Judaism was well on its way to becoming a religion not of a nation but of a people who were dispersed around the globe. Jewish identity and religion survived because of a strong commitment to their God and their scriptures, which their rabbis interpreted in the texts known as the Talmud. Jewish law prescribed how one ought to live as a Jew and so gave meaning to Jewish life throughout history. When the modern state of Israel was founded after World War II, it was the product of this continuing Jewish identity rather than its origin.

Christianity arose in the first century as a Jewish sect that believed that Jesus of Nazareth was the promised Messiah, or Christ, the redeemer of Israel. The early Christians differed from other Jews in their belief that this Messiah had to die the death of a criminal to bring about human redemption. Christians came to believe that their sins were taken away by the death of Jesus suffered on their behalf, that he had risen from the dead, and that he was the Son of God in human form.

91

Through faith in Jesus, they claimed, one can participate in salvation and be assured of a place in the Kingdom of God. Christianity began to welcome non-Jews into its ranks if they agreed to view Jesus as their savior, and soon Christianity was primarily a non-Jewish religion rather than a sect of Judaism. But to this day, Christians share much with Jews—in particular, belief in the one God and acceptance of the Jewish Bible. However, along with the Jewish scriptures (which Christians call the Old Testament), the Christian Bible includes a New Testament, which recounts the history of Jesus' life, death, and resurrection, as well as some other texts from the early church. Christian beliefs about Jesus' special role in the process of salvation remain at the heart of the differences between Jews and Christians.

The religion of Islam also recognizes one God and also believes this God to be the one who was revealed to Jews and Christians. In the seventh century, the prophet Muhammad received revelations from God (later written down as the Quran) commanding him to preach to the Arab peoples about this God and God's laws. Although his message met with initial resistance from many people who disagreed with the views he professed, by the time of his death in the year 632, the Arab world was well on the way to achieving unity as a community of believers who could profess, "There is no God but the one God, and Muhammad is his prophet." These new followers of God ("Allah" in Arabic) gave up many of their former ways, including idolatry (the making of images of a god), polytheism (belief in many gods), the drinking of alcohol, infanticide, and a variety of practices, such as gambling, that were viewed as exploitative of the poor. Muhammad argued that adherence to strict morality is the way to salvation, although God was said also to have great mercy on the repentant sinner (as Jews and Christians also claimed). Islam is probably the most misunderstood major religion in the Western Hemisphere, largely due to conflicts in the Mideast between Muslims and Christians or Jews which have gone on for centuries. For this reason it is especially important to realize that Islam is a religion that professes many of the same values as Judaism and Christianity.

Hinduism is a religion that arose in India about 3000 years ago with the composition of the scriptures known as the Vedas. Most Indians are Hindus, and Hinduism has remained largely an Indian religion—in fact, "Hindu" means "Indian." Hinduism, however, is not primarily an expression of national values, but a complex religion that involves many ways to salvation. Meditation, devotion to various gods and goddesses, and good works all play a role in helping individuals overcome selfishness and realize their unity with the divine nature, or Brahman, in all. Hinduism also professes a belief in reincarnation, that people are reborn over and over as they work toward salvation. Although one can be rewarded for unselfishness with a better "rebirth," the final goal is to escape the process of rebirth and attain unity with the divine Brahman.

Buddhism was developed from the teachings of Siddhārtha Gautama, who was born in India in 563 B.C.E. Although of royal birth, he gave up his kingdom at the age of twenty-nine to wander and seek an understanding of why life is full of suffering. Six years later he obtained "enlightenment," and his new understanding of how to overcome suffering and selfishness became the basis of Buddhism. The "four noble truths" and the "noble eightfold path" of Buddhism spell out a way to salvation that is both similar to and yet different from Hinduism. Gautama believed in rebirth and the idea that good works assist one in moving toward salvation, but his understanding of the goal toward which one should work differed from the traditional Hindu view. One should not seek unity with a divine reality, according to Gautama, as there is no reality that has a permanent substantial nature. To believe that such a reality exists is to be mired in the selfish desire for permanence and immortality, a desire that must be jettisoned along with all selfish desires. Gautama was unconcerned about immortality because he believed that there is no soul to become immortal. Through realizing that there is no eternal soul, one can be free from the suffering caused by selfishness and live as a compassionate and unselfish Buddha, or "enlightened one." In the Buddhist view, Gautama was not a god but a human being who realized the true nature of reality, and anyone else who comes to a similar realization becomes a Buddha as well.

Taoism began in China with the teachings of Lao Tzu, author of the *Tao te Ching*, or *The Way and Its Power*. Little is known about Lao Tzu, and scholars are even uncertain about when he lived—estimates range from the sixth century to the second century B.C.E. His person is less important than his work, a short book that characterizes the Way (Tao) as a mysterious power that is the source and guiding principle behind all reality. The Taoist seeks to live in harmony with the Tao, the natural way of things, by seeking a balance of yin and yang—two forces that are related as complementary opposites associated with, respectively, death and life, winter and summer, cold and heat, and so on. This religion is focused less on extraworldly salvation and more on achieving a harmonious existence in this life through living according to the Tao.

Confucianism arose in China from the teachings of Confucius, who was born in 551 B.C.E. Although he built on earlier Chinese thinkers and claimed not to be an innovator, his teaching helped clarify several ideas that were to become central to Chinese culture. He taught that individuals and societies can find fulfillment through honoring traditional values such as respect for elders, benevolence, honesty, and justice. In this way, one can play a part in the harmonizing of humanity, earth, and heaven. Like the Taoists, Confucius was not especially interested in questions concerning the afterlife or the gods—his attention was focused on this life and the best way to live it. This may make it appear as though Confucianism is merely a system of moral philosophy; but it was the official state religion of the Chinese Empire for over two thousand years, and as such has played a crucial role in providing a meaningful understanding of reality to one of the oldest civilizations in the world.

Sioux religion is an example of nonliterate religious traditions. These religions arose from oral tradition rather than from written scriptures, but that does not mean that their followers reject the written word now. Many Native Americans of the Sioux tribes have written about their experiences and self-understanding in the hope that others will come to understand them, and also because they believe that they have important insights to share—particularly about respect for the natural world and our harmony with it. Their traditions are rich in stories of visions and sacred beings, and it is largely in these that one finds their religious views (rather than in philosophical or doctrinal treatises).

The last three chapters focus on these religions' responses to three basic questions: What Is the Sacred? How Can One Find Meaning? What Lies Beyond Death? Chapter 3 focuses on what each religion believes about gods or goddesses, sacred powers or fundamental principles. Chapter 4 focuses on what lifestyle each religion advocates to find wholeness, purpose, or fulfillment in this life. Chapter 5 explores each religion's beliefs about death or the afterlife. Tremendous diversity exists among these beliefs, but there are also some similarities.

What Is the Sacred?

Chapter Preface

Is there a God? This question is often asked when religious discussions begin, but this question already assumes a certain concept of the sacred that is in keeping with traditions that believe there is one God, probably viewed as a personal creator and redeemer. Even among these monotheistic religions (Judaism, Christianity, and Islam), however, there are significant differences in the conception of God. Other religious traditions believe many gods or spirits live in some transcendent realm beyond this world. Some religious traditions argue that sacred reality is inside each individual and in everything that exists. Still other traditions argue that no sacred reality exists. All of these views and more are expressed in this chapter.

The Sacred Is the God Who Revealed Himself to Israel

EMIL FACKENHEIM

Emil Fackenheim is a major contemporary Jewish thinker who has provided a way for modern Jews to understand how God acts in history. Especially since the Nazi Holocaust during World War II in which six million Jews died, many Jews have asked whether God still acts in history as the Bible indicates, ensuring their survival as God's chosen people. Fackenheim seeks to find meaning in Jewish history by returning to one of its "root experiences"—the salvation of Israel at the Red Sea. Jews have recounted this story to express their faith in the God who miraculously saved them from the Egyptians and so acts concretely in their history. Though some might have viewed the event as a fortunate accident, in Jewish faith it became a testimony to the God who made them His chosen people. As such, this story is still the basis for a belief in a God who does not remain distant but is related to people's daily lives. Fackenheim claims that even when faced with the Holocaust and their apparent abandonment by God, Jews have a duty to endure as the people of this God.

QUESTIONS

1. What does Fackenheim believe to be significant about the fact that the Jewish God is revealed primarily through specific events of history?
2. What are the three key characteristics of a "root experience" of Judaism, in Fackenheim's view?
3. How does the Jew of today gain access to the presence of God at the Red Sea, according to Fackenheim?

■ ■ ■

"The heavens were opened," writes the prophet Ezekiel in his opening chapter, "and I saw visions of God" (Ezek. 1:1). These may be common words in certain types of mystical literature which affirm visions of Divinity freely and easily. In the context of the Hebrew Bible (which shrinks from such visions in awe and terror) they are rare and bold. It is therefore not surprising that the chapter which follows these opening words is full of all-but-unintelligible mysteries. According to rabbinic tradition there is not, with the possible exception of Genesis, chapter 1 (which deals with *Ma'assey Bereshith*—"the Works of the Beginning"), any other chapter in the whole Bible which can match in depth and mysteriousness Ezekiel, chapter 1, which deals with *Ma'assey Merkavah* ("the Works of the Wheel")— nothing less than the nature of Divinity itself. No wonder the rabbis considered it dangerous for all except the most pious and learned to try to fathom the secrets of that chapter.

Yet the same tradition which holds this view also seems deliberately and dramatically to contradict it. In a well-known Midrash it is asserted that what Ezekiel once saw in heaven was far less than what all of Israel once saw on earth. Ezekiel, and indeed all the other prophets, did not see God but only visions and similes of God; they were like men who perceive a king of flesh and blood surrounded by servants of flesh and blood, and who are forced to ask, "which one is the king?" In the sharpest possible contrast, the Israelites at the Red Sea had no need to ask which one was the King: "As soon as they saw Him, they recognized Him, and they all opened their mouths and said, 'This is my God, and I will glorify Him'" (Exod. 15:2). Even the lowliest maidservant at the Red Sea saw what Isaiah, Ezekiel, and all the other prophets never saw.

The Midrash just cited and paraphrased deals with the subject of this discourse—God's presence in history. This subject is dealt with in countless passages in Jewish and Christian literature. The cited Midrash has special significance, however, because it affirms God's presence in history in full awareness of the fact that the affirmation is strange, extraordinary, or even paradoxical. The God of Israel is no mythological deity which mingles freely with men in history. He is beyond man—so infinitely beyond human reach that an opening of the heavens themselves is required if He is to become humanly accessible. Few are the men to whom such an opening was ever granted, and the reports of these few are so obscure as to be unintelligible to nearly all others. So infinitely is the Divine above the human! Nevertheless, the Midrash insists that not messengers, not angels, not intermediaries, but God Himself acts in human history—and He was unmistakably present to a whole people at least once. . . .

We begin with a particular subject—the Jewish faith in God's presence in history. The announced title, however, is a universal one—God's presence in history—and it may appear that this subject calls for concepts of God-in-general, history-in-general, Providence-in-general, and their acceptability to modern-man-in-general. This, however, would be a false start. If God is ever present *in* history, this is not a presence-in-general but rather a presence to particular men in particular situations. To be sure, unless it were that of a mere tribal deity, such a presence must have universal implications. These implications, however, are manifest only in the particular; and they make of the men *to whom* they are manifest, not universalistic philosophers who rise above their situations, but rather witnesses, *in*, *through*, and *because of* their particularity to the nations. Our direct concern is with the destiny of the Jewish faith in the modern world. But inextricably bound up with it is the question of whether, and if so how, it is possible and necessary for the Jew of today to be a witness to the world. Yet for a Jew—today or at any other time—to dissolve the particularity of either his Jewishness or his historical situation into humanity-in-general or history-in-general would not be to rise above a "narrow parochialism" to a "broad universalism." It would be a betrayal of his post.

Root Experiences

It would be incongruous for us to reject, as misleading, any beginning with abstract notions of history-in-general, and yet ourselves begin with Jewish history-in-general. We must rather begin with particular events within the history of the Jewish faith, or, more precisely, with epoch-making events.

Even this term is not yet precise or radical enough. In its millennial career the Jewish faith has passed through many epoch-making events, such as the end of prophecy and the destruction of the first Temple, the Maccabean revolt, the destruction of the second Temple, and the expulsion from Spain. These events each made a new claim upon the Jewish faith and, indeed, would not be epoch-making if it were otherwise. They did not, however, produce a new faith. What occurred instead was a confrontation in which the old faith was tested in the light of contemporary experience. Jewish history abounds with such confrontations between past and present. At least until the rise of the modern world, these have all one common characteristic. The strain of confrontation may often have come near a breaking point, yet present experience, however new, unanticipated, and epoch-making, never destroyed the past faith. Its claims upon the present survived. But—and this is crucial—this past faith had not come from nowhere but had *itself* originated in historical events. These historical events, therefore, are *more* than epoch-making. In the context of Judaism, we shall refer to them as *root experiences*.

What, considered abstractly, are the characteristics of a root experience in Judaism? What are the conditions without which a past event cannot continue to make a present claim—the claim that God is present in history? According to Rabbi Eliezer, the author of the Midrash quoted at the beginning, the maidservants at the Red Sea saw what even Ezekiel did not see. This

THEN MOSES STRETCHED OUT HIS hand over the sea. The
LORD drove the sea back by a strong east wind all night, and
turned the sea into dry land; and the waters were divided. The
Israelites went into the sea on dry ground, the waters forming a
wall for them on their right and on their left. The Egyptians pursued, and went into the sea after them, all of Pharaoh's horses,
chariots, and chariot drivers. At the morning watch the LORD in
the pillar of fire and cloud looked down upon the Egyptian
army, and threw the Egyptian army into panic. He clogged their
chariot wheels so that they turned with difficulty. The Egyptians
said, "Let us flee from the Israelites, for the LORD is fighting for
them against Egypt."

Then the LORD said to Moses, "Stretch out your hand over
the sea, so that the water may come back upon the Egyptians,
upon their chariots and chariot drivers." So Moses stretched out
his hand over the sea, and at dawn the sea returned to its normal depth. As the Egyptians fled before it, the LORD tossed the
Egyptians into the sea. The waters returned and covered the
chariots and the chariot drivers, the entire army of Pharaoh that
had followed them into the sea; not one of them remained. But
the Israelites walked on dry ground through the sea, the waters
forming a wall for them on their right and on their left.

Thus the LORD saved Israel that day from the Egyptians; and
Israel saw the Egyptians dead on the seashore. Israel saw the
great work that the LORD did against the Egyptians. So the people feared the LORD and believed in the LORD and in his servant
Moses.

The Bible, New Revised Standard Version, Exodus 14:21-31

means, on the one hand, that Rabbi Eliezer himself does *not* see
and, on the other hand, that he *knows* that the maidservants
saw, and he does not. If he himself saw, he would not defer to
their vision—his own being superior or equal to theirs and in
any case a present standard by which to measure the past. If he
did not know that they had seen, their past vision would be of
no present relevance and, indeed, would be wholly inaccessible. Only because of this dialectical relation between present
and past can a past experience legislate to the present. *This is the*
first *condition of a root experience in Judaism.*

By itself, however, this condition (as yet far from fully intelligible) is far from sufficient as well. According to our Midrash, this condition would apply to Ezekiel's vision as much as to the maidservants' at the Red Sea. Yet Ezekiel's vision is not a root experience in Judaism. It is the experience of an isolated individual and may legislate to isolated individuals after him—those few to whom the heavens are accessible. At the Red Sea, however, the whole people saw, the lowly maidservants included, and what occurred before their eyes was not an opening of heaven but a transformation of earth—an historic event affecting decisively all future Jewish generations. These future generations, on their part, do not, like the maidservants at the Red Sea, see the presence of God. But to this day they recall twice daily in their prayers the natural-historical event through which that presence was once manifest, and the Passover Seder is wholly dedicated to it. Indeed, according to some rabbis, so profoundly legislating is this past event to future times that it will continue to be remembered even in the Messianic days. *Its public, historical character is the* second *condition of a root experience in Judaism.*

Still missing is a third condition, and this will turn out to be the crucial one. The vision of the maidservants at the Red Sea may be analyzed into two components. First, they experienced impending disaster at the hands of the pursuing Egyptian army and then salvation through the division of the Red Sea; that is, they experienced a natural-historical event. But they also experienced the presence of God. Subsequent generations, on their part, recollect the natural-historical event, but they do not see what the maidservants saw. Both points are not in question in the Midrashic account. What is in question is whether, and if so how, *subsequent generations have access to the vision of the maidservants—to the presence of God.*

If they have no such access, then the event at the Red Sea cannot be a root experience in Judaism. A skeptic would in any case deny that the natural-historical event even happened, or else view it as a mere fortunate coincidence. What matters here is that even a believer would have little cause for remembering it. For the "miracle" remembered would be for him, not a past event of divine Presence, but merely one particular effect of a general—and remote—divine Cause. And, if his concern were with the general divine Cause, no particular effect would stand out in importance; and, if it were with particular effects, it should be with *present* effects, not with the dimly remembered past. In connection with a discussion of the religious relevance of history, Hegel somewhere wryly quotes a proverb to the effect that with the passage of time the past loses its truth. If later generations of Jewish believers have no access whatever to the vision of the maidservants, this proverb would be applicable to the event at the Red Sea.

Such proverbs cease to apply, however, if the past vision of the maidservants is somehow still presently accessible; for in that case a divine Presence, manifest in and through the past natural-historical event, could not fail to legislate to future generations. (This is true at least if, as the Midrash states, the Divinity manifest is not a finite, tribal deity but the universal "Creator of the World." The past presence of such a God can continue to legislate even in the Messianic days.) *This accessibility of past to present is the* third *and* final *characteristic of a root experience in Judaism.*

This characteristic is clearly if implicitly asserted by Jewish tradition. Thus the pious Jew remembering the Exodus and the salvation at the Red Sea does not call to mind events now dead and gone. He reenacts these events *as a present reality*: only thus is he assured that the past saving God saves still, and that He will finally bring ultimate salvation. We have already stressed that Rabbi Eliezer knows that the maidservants saw the divine Presence at the Red Sea; we must now add that *he could not have this knowledge unless he had somehow himself access to their vision. . . .*

How then is Rabbi Eliezer (and the pious Jew during the Passover Seder) related to the maidservants at the Red Sea? *In reenacting the natural-historical event, he reenacts the abiding astonishment as well, and makes it his own.* Hence the "sole Power" present then is present still. Hence memory turns into faith and hope. Hence the event at the Red Sea is recalled now and will continue to be recalled even in the Messianic days. Thus the reenacted past legislates to present and future. Thus, in Judaism, it is a root experience.

VIEWPOINT

2

The Sacred Is the Triune God Revealed in Christ

KARL BARTH

Karl Barth was perhaps the first major twentieth-century Christian theologian to make the doctrine of the Trinity central to his theology. The doctrine—that there is one God manifested in the three persons of Father, Son, and Holy Spirit—had always distinguished Christian views from those of other monotheists (believers in one God, such as Jews and Muslims). However, in the eighteenth and nineteenth centuries many Christian theologians began to emphasize the unity of God rather than God's "tri-unity," which they considered an outdated notion. Barth returned to an emphasis on the Trinity, arguing that it is crucial to Christian thought and the belief in the full divinity of Jesus Christ. The Christian concept of God is unlike any human notion of God, he argues, because it involves not a distant supreme deity but a God who is related to us in grace and love. Since Barth made this case, many theologians have returned to an emphasis on this central doctrine of the Christian faith.

Excerpted from Karl Barth, *Dogmatics in Outline*, translated by G.T. Thomson. New York: Harper & Row, 1959. Reprinted by permission of SCM Press, London.

QUESTIONS

1. How does the history related in the Bible express the Christian idea of God, in Barth's view?
2. What does Barth mean by asserting that "the highness of God consists in His descending"?
3. How does each person of the Trinity express in a different way the "one work of God," according to Barth?

■ ■ ■

We must be clear that when we are speaking of God in the sense of Christian faith, He who is called God is not to be regarded as a continuation and enrichment of the concepts and ideas which usually constitute religious thought in general about God. In the sense of Christian faith, God is not to be found in the series of gods. He is not to be found in the pantheon of human piety and religious inventive skill. So it is not that there is in humanity something like a universal natural disposition, a general concept of the divine, which at some particular point involves the thing which we Christians call God and as such believe in and confess; so that Christian faith would be one among many, an instance within a general rule. A Christian Father once rightly said that *Deus non est in genere*, 'God is not a particular instance within a class'. When we Christians speak of 'God', we may and must be clear that this word signifies *a priori* the fundamentally Other, the fundamental deliverance from that whole world of man's seeking, conjecturing, illusion, imagining and speculating. It is not that on the long road of human seeking and longing for the divine a definite stopping-place has in the end been reached in the form of the Christian Confession. The God of the Christian Confession is, in distinction from all gods, not a found or invented God or one at last and at the end discovered by man; He is not a fulfillment, perhaps the last, supreme and best fulfillment, of what man was in course of seeking and finding. But we Christians speak of Him who completely takes the place of everything that elsewhere is usually called 'God', and therefore suppresses and excludes it all, and claims to be alone the truth. . . .

Let us attempt to describe more closely, in a few concrete sketches, what I have been outlining. I said that God is He who, according to Holy Scripture, exists, lives and acts, and makes Himself known. By this definition something fundamentally different is taking place from what would happen, if I should try and set before you conceptually arranged ideas of an infinite, supreme Being. In such a case I would be speculating. But I am not inviting you to speculate. I maintain that this is a radically wrong road which can never lead to God, but to a reality called so only in a false sense. God is He who is to be found in the book of the Old and New Testaments, which speaks of Him. . . .

Holy Scripture describes a work, and first the work of Creation. Alongside Himself God puts something else, something different from Himself—namely, the creature, without having need of it, in the power of His Almightiness, in His holy, overflowing love. Secondly, a covenant is set up between God and one of His creatures, between God and man. Once more an inconceivable fact: why precisely between God and *man*, of whom from the beginning it is narrated that he is unthankful to God, that he is a sinner? In spite of this sin, sovereignly overlooking it, reserving for Himself its amendment, God surrenders Himself. He lends Himself to become the God of a tiny, despised people in Asia Minor, Israel. He lends Himself to become a member of this people, a little child, and then to die. And thirdly—but the whole thing is one—there is the work of redemption, the unveiling of the purpose of God's free love for man and the world, the annihilation of all that would hinder this purpose; there is the revelation and the manifestation of the new heaven and the new earth. All this is a way, under the sign of the name of Jesus Christ, the man Jesus Christ, in whom God Himself has become visible and active on earth, who is at once the goal of the history of the nation Israel, and the beginning and starting-point of the Church, and at the same time the revelation of the redemption, of the completion, of the whole. The whole work of God lives and moves in this one Person. He who says God in the sense of Holy Scripture will necessarily have to say Jesus Christ over and over again.

This work of creation, of the covenant and of redemption is the reality in which God exists, lives and acts and makes Himself known. From this work we must make no abstractions, if we would know God's nature and existence. Here, in this work, God is the Person who expounds Himself, and is

PHILIP SAID TO HIM, "LORD, show us the Father, and we will be satisfied." Jesus said to him, "Have I been with you all this time, Philip, and you still do not know me? Whoever has seen me has seen the Father. How can you say, 'Show us the Father'? Do you not believe that I am in the Father and the Father is in me? The words that I say to you I do not speak on my own; but the Father who dwells in me does his works. Believe me that I am in the Father and the Father is in me; but if you do not, then believe me because of the works themselves. . . .

"If you love me, you will keep my commandments. And I will ask the Father, and he will give you another Advocate, to be with you forever. This is the Spirit of truth, whom the world cannot receive, because it neither sees him nor knows him. You know him, because he abides with you, and he will be in you. . . .

"I have said these things to you while I am still with you. But the Advocate, the Holy Spirit, whom the Father will send in my name, will teach you everything, and remind you of all that I have said to you."

John 14:8-11, 15-17, 25-26

thus the subject of this work. It is the work of God's free love. We may venture to describe the reality which the work expounds, the nature and the essence of God, by these two concepts of freedom and love. But we must be careful, lest we tumble back again out of the concrete into the abstract, out of history into the realm of ideas. I would not say that God is freedom or that God is love—even though the second pronouncement is a biblical one. We do not know what love is and we do not know what freedom is; but *God* is love and *God* is freedom. What freedom is and what love is, we have to learn from Him. As predicate to this subject it may be said that He is the God of free love. In His work of creation, covenant and redemption, He proves Himself to be this God. It is there that we experience what love is, this desire of the other for his own sake, so that the one is no longer alone, but completely together with the other. This is love, this is God's *free* love. God is not lonely, not even without the world. He does not need the other and nevertheless He loves. This love cannot be understood apart from the majesty of His freedom. It is God's love, that He, the Father, loves the Son, who Himself is God. What in His work becomes visible is an uncovering of this mystery of His inner Being, where all is freedom and all is love.

And now perhaps the title of this lecture, 'God in the highest', becomes comprehensible. By being the Father, the Son and the Holy Ghost in His work in Jesus Christ, God is in the highest. He whose nature and essence consist, whose existence is proved, in His descending into the depths, He the Merciful, who gives Himself up for His creature to the utter depths of the existence of His creature—He is God in the highest. Not in spite of this, not in remarkable paradoxical opposition, but the highness of God consists in His thus descending. This is His exalted nature, this His free love. Anyone who wants to look up to some other height has not understood the utter otherness in God, he would still be in the tracks of the heathen, who look for God in an endlessness. But He is utterly other than we think our gods. It is He who calls Abraham and who led that wretched nation through the desert, who never swerves through the centuries-long disloyalty and disobedience of this nation, who causes Himself to be born in the stable at Bethlehem as a little child and who dies on Golgotha. He is the glorious Lord, He is divine. Do you understand what monotheism in Christian faith means? God knows, not the foolish delight in the number 'one'. It has nothing to do with the number 'one', but with this subject in His sheer uniqueness and otherness over against all others, different from all the ridiculous deities whom man invents. Once we have realised this, we can only laugh, and there is a laugh running through the Bible at these figures. Once the true God has been seen, the gods collapse into dust, and He remains the only One. 'I am the Lord thy God . . . thou shalt have no other gods before Me.' This 'thou shalt not' has the force of 'thou canst not'. He who calls himself god alongside Him becomes the mere shadow of man's extravagant longing, which has its ill results. And the Second Commandment also becomes quite clear then: 'Thou shalt not make unto thee any image nor any sort of likeness. Thou shalt not bow down to them nor worship them.' That too is not a sign of Israelite ways of thinking and there is no philosophical concept of invisibility in the background. But God has Himself done everything in order to present Himself. How should man make an image of Him after He has presented His likeness

Himself? A well-intentioned business, this entire 'spectacle' of Christian art, well-intentioned but impotent, since God Himself has made His own image. Once a man has understood 'God in the highest', it becomes impossible for him to want any imagery in thought, or any other kind of imagery. . . .

The One God is by nature and in eternity the Father, the source of His Son and, in union with Him, the source of the Holy Spirit. In virtue of this way of being of His He is by grace the Father of all men, whom He calls in time, in His Son and through His Spirit, to be His children.

The One God, God in the highest, the Only God, is the Father. In pronouncing this word, in saying Father along with the first article of the Confession, we are straightway bound to look ahead to the second, He is the Son, and to the third, He is the Holy Spirit. It is the one God, of whom the three articles of the Confession speak. These are not three Gods, a God split and separated in Himself. The Trinity does not speak of three Gods, but of the Trinity—that is how the Christian Church has always understood it and could find it in no other form in Scripture—that speaks once again, and with all the more emphasis, of the one, single God. This is no sort of theoretical business. But everything depends on the fact that the content of the three articles cannot be separated from each other, that in all that is said in these three articles about God the Creator and God in His action in Jesus Christ and in His operation as the Holy Spirit, it is not a matter of three divine departments, with a 'Director' for each. What is involved is the *one* work of the *One* God, but the one work that is moved within itself. For God in whom we Christians may believe is not a dead God, and He is not a lonely God. But since He is the only God, He is in Himself, in His divine Majesty in the highest, One, and yet not alone, and so His work in which He meets us and in which we may know Him, is in itself a living work, moved within itself; He is, in Himself by nature and in eternity, and for us in time, *the One in three ways of being.* The language of the early Church states that God is in three persons. In the way in which the early Church understood the concept of person, this concept is unassailable. For in Latin and in Greek usage person meant exactly what I have just been describing as 'way of being'. But when we speak to-day of person, involuntarily and almost irresistibly the idea arises of something rather like the way in which we men are persons. And actually this idea is as ill-suited as possible to describe what God the Father, the Son and the Holy Spirit is. Calvin once mockingly suggested that we should not imagine the triune God as all the artists have depicted Him, three manikins or *marmousets*. That is not the Trinity. But when the Christian Church speaks of the triune God, it means that God is not just in one way, but that He is the Father and the Son and the Holy Spirit. Three times the One and the Same, threefold, but above all triune, He, the Father, the Son and the Holy Spirit, in Himself and in the highest and in His revelation.

So above all we have to state that when God the 'Father' is called 'our Father', we are thereby saying something about God that is valid, that is true, and true, moreover, in the deepest depths of His nature, true unto all eternity. He is the Father. And exactly the same holds for the Son and for the Holy Spirit. Thus God's name of Father is not merely a surname which we men attach to God; so that the meaning would be that 'man thinks he knows something like fatherhood, like man's relationship to his father in the flesh, and now he transfers this relationship to God: the presupposition being that His nature is ultimately something quite different and has nothing to do with what we term fatherhood. That God is the Father holds true in view of His revelation, in view of us. But in Himself, by nature and in eternity, we do not know what He is. But He issues forth from this mystery of His and is then, and in this way, the Father for us.' But that is inadequate to describe the content with which in fact we are concerned here. When Holy Scripture and along with it the Confession of the Church calls God the Father, its meaning is that God is first of all Father. He is Father in Himself, by nature and in eternity, and then, following on that, for us as well, His creatures. It is therefore not that there is first of all human fatherhood and then a so-called divine Fatherhood, but just the reverse: true and proper fatherhood resides in God, and from this Fatherhood of God what we know as fatherhood among us men is derived. The divine Fatherhood is the primal source of all natural fatherhood. As is said in Ephesians, every fatherhood in heaven and on earth is of Him. We are thinking the truth, the first and proper truth, when we see God the Father in the ultimate, when we recognise Him as the Father, and may be called His children.

God the Father—in these words we are speaking of God's way of being, as the source and origin of another divine way of being, of a second one which is distinct from the first and which is yet *His* way of being and so is identical with Him in His divinity. God is God in such a way that He is the Father, the Father of His Son, that he establishes Himself and through His own agency is God a second time. Established by Himself, not created by Himself—the Son is not created. But this relationship of Father and Son does not yet exhaust the reality, the nature of God. It is not that this establishing and being established of God threatens the unity of God. It is the Father and the Son *together*, who clinch the unity of God a third time in the Holy Spirit. . . . Not *although* God is Father and Son, but *because* God is Father and Son, unity exists. So God, as He who establishes Himself, who exists through Himself, as God in His deity, is in Himself different and yet in Himself alike. And for that very reason He is not lonely in Himself. He does not need the world. All richness of life, all fullness of action and community exists in Himself, since He is the Triune. He is movement and He is rest. Hence it can be plain to us that all that He is on our behalf—that He is the Creator, that He has given us Himself in Jesus Christ and that He has united us to Himself in the Holy Spirit—is His free grace, the overflow of His fullness. Not owed to us, but overflowing mercy! It is His will that what He is for Himself should be not only for Himself; but He wills to be for us also the One He is in eternity. We have of ourselves no grip on this truth, that God in the power of His eternal Fatherhood—of free grace, not because it is His *métier*—wills to be also our Father. Because He is what He is, His work also can only be His Fatherly work. That God becomes the Creator of another, which in distinction from the Son is different from Him, that He wills to be present for this other, means nothing else than that He gives us a share in Himself. 'We become partakers of the divine nature' (2 Pet. I. 4). We say no more and no less when we call God our Father. We may now call Him that which He names Himself in His Son. Man as such is not God's child, but God's creature. . . .

This creature man is, so far as the eye reaches, in rebellion against God, is godless and nevertheless God's child. It is

God's free work, His condescension and mercy, that we may be His children. We are that, we are because He is the Father and because He makes us so. We are His children *in His Son and through the Holy Spirit*, not on the ground of a direct relationship between us and God, but on the ground of the fact that God of Himself lets us participate in His nature, in His life and essence. It is God's good will and resolve that His relationship to us should be comprehended in His being, in His begetting of the Son; that we may be called His children in Him, in the Son through the Holy Spirit, . . . which unites the Father and the Son. Our calling is meant to be comprehended in this way of God's being as the Holy Spirit, and that, once more, is God's eternal decree. *You* are meant; for you it holds good and is to your good, what God is and does in His Son. And what is true in God's nature becomes true in time. So no more and no less than a repetition of the divine life, a repetition which we do not bring about and which we cannot take from ourselves, but which it is God's will to allow in the creaturely realm—that is, outside the Godhead. Glory to God in the highest! That is the first thing we utter, when we call God our Father. And 'peace on earth', because He is not the Father apart from the Son, and because both exist for us 'among men of good will'.

VIEWPOINT

3

The Sacred Is Allah, the One True God

MOHAMMAD ZIA ULLAH

Many people in the Western world believe that Muslims worship a god named "Allah" who is distinct from the Christian God or the Jewish God. In fact, "Allah" simply means "God" in Arabic, and it is a central claim of Islam that there is only one God and wherever that one God is worshiped, the true God is worshiped. It does not matter what one calls this God; what is important is that one recognize that there is only one, and that this God is the all-powerful and all-merciful creator and lawgiver who rules over and guides the universe at all times. In the following viewpoint Mohammad Zia Ullah defends this Muslim view with quotations from the Quran and points out another central Muslim belief—that the existence of this God is obvious to all who look at the world, and that it is only the perversity of humans that causes us to deny this obvious fact. He also details the characteristics of God and the idea that we should worship God alone. To Muslims, the greatest sin is "shirk," to worship a created object instead of the true God who transcends all images. But if we turn to the

Excerpted from Mohammad Zia Ullah, *Islamic Concept of God*. London: Kegan Paul International, 1984. Reprinted with permission.

true God, Ullah claims, we will find a powerful and loving Lord who protects us from adversity, forgives our sins, and guides the universe to its ultimate fulfillment.

QUESTIONS

1. How does Ullah refute what he calls the modern, materialistic denial of God?
2. Why should we worship only the one God, according to Ullah?
3. What characteristics of God does Ullah detail?

■ ■ ■

The basic values of modern civilization are purely materialistic. Its widespread evil influences permeate everywhere. As a result all religious truths are denied and religion is held in ridicule. The central point in religious faith is the being and person of God. But God is dismissed as an invention of the human mind. Man, it is said, invented gods and goddesses during the days of his infancy and ignorance. Thus, conception of God is an extension of the same infantile attitude of mind and amounts to no more than saying after Copernicus that the sun moves round the earth. But the truth is that belief in God is one of the natural dispositions of man. It is not a question requiring any subtlety of logical argumentation. Says God in the Holy Quran.

And in the earth are Signs for those who have *certainty* of faith. And also in your own selves. Will you not then see? (51:21, 22)

There is evidence galore only if man would occasionally withdraw into solitude and contemplate with an unprejudiced mind. Did he come to birth of himself? Is he his own Creator? Who will say 'Yes' to such questions? So much will be obvious to anyone who consults his own conscience. No, his conscience will say. Then, if man is not his own creator, the Creator has to be someone else, outside of him. Could it be his parents? No, again. For, what is true of one man is true *ipso facto* of his parents. Man, in short, is himself proof of the existence of God. . . .

All our little movements throughout our life are witness sure of the existence of the God of might and power, the God eternal. Just as the millstone of the water-mill is proof of the running stream of water. So is my life—and every movement of my life—proof of the existence and power of God. The water-mill will not run without a running stream. Nor will life pulsate in me without the eternal and powerful Lord of Life.

Similarly the Quran bears witness to the sacred covenant between mankind and its creator:

> And when thy Lord brings forth from Adam's children—out of their loins—their offspring and makes them witnesses against their own selves by saying: Am I not your Lord? they say, 'Yes, we do bear witness' (7:173).

To a sane person, this covenant is undeniable evidence of the existence of the great Creator. Planted in man's nature is the vital seed of the Almighty's love and avowal of His existence. The seed needs life—giving sustenance to flourish and flower, and, unless denied this sustenance by a polluted environment, it remains a constant and continuous guide to the Lord, and the nature of man ever keeps proclaiming, irresistibly, at all times and all places, 'Yes, yes, we are witness to Thy creation.'. . .

Alas the terrifying stresses of modern materialism have buried the sacred seed of the Almighty's love and avowal of His existence deep beneath a heavy weight of moral decay. But without these corrupting materialistic influences the existence of the Supreme Being remains the great, the ever-present and eternal truth. Compared to this truth nothing else could be more true, more real. Everything else but He would be as naught. Because everything would then be a manifestation, a sign, or a proof of Him. We know sunshine and we know shade. But could there be sunlight without the sun or shade without the tree? . . .

All religions have taught about Him. It is Him they have urged men to know and to love. It is He Who has been the centre of their teaching, their message. True, they have taught in the main two kinds of duties, duties we owe to God and duties we owe to fellow men. But these duties have one great end in view, and that is God.

Duties we owe to God are prescribed, so that we can get

nearer and nearer to Him. Duties we owe to fellow men have the same end in view. For, when we serve our fellow men we please our God and get closer to Him. In a sense, creatures of God are God's children. If we show love and affection to children—lift one to our lap and give a sweet to another—will it not please their parents? Will they not wish to show love and affection to you? So it is with God.

But for the moment we are not concerned so much with our duties to men. Therefore, we will deal rather with the duties we owe to God. And dealing with this subject every religion including Islam has laid special stress on two points.

Firstly, that in our faith we should associate no-one else with Him.

Secondly, we must love God more than anyone else.

IT IS GOD WHO CAUSETH

The seed-grain
And the date-stone
To split and sprout.
He causeth the living
To issue from the dead,
And He is the One
To cause the dead
To issue from the living.
That is God : then how
Are ye deluded
Away from the truth?

He it is that cleaveth
The day-break (from the dark) :
He makes the night
For rest and tranquillity,
And the sun and moon
For the reckoning (of time) :
Such is the judgment
And ordering of (Him),
The Exalted in Power,
The Omniscient.

Quran, Surah 6.95-96

It is a pity that with the passage of time Muslims also, like the followers of other religions, have mixed other things with the truth about God. Worship of tombs, of dead or hereditary saints goes on side by side with indifference to this our primary duty—to love God. Dividing our belief in one God with belief in other gods is prohibited because greater deviation from the true and straight path there could not be. This is disloyalty to God, *Shirk* in Islamic parlance. For one who has yet to find the object of true belief, the question of getting close to God does not arise. *Shirk* (associating other deities with the one God) is also self-degrading. Man has been created to subjugate, to use and to rule other things. Could he bow in obeisance to these things? It is unthinkable. . . .

Now let us ponder. The perfections worthy of God, perfections attributable to the divine being, are all to be found in Him. Only He possesses the most perfect attributes, only He is free from defects, weaknesses. He is one and the only one. He has no equal, no partner. He is all-powerful. He is beneficent; that is, He confers and endows without any deserts. He gives without our asking or deserving. He is merciful. That is, He rewards our deeds fully. He is the Lord of all worlds. That is, He is the nourisher, the developer, the guarantor of progress. He raises the imperfect to perfection. Ultimate rewards and punishment are in His hands. Everything in this world, this universe, owes its existence and excellence to Him. He is unique, He is not begotten, but He creates everything. He is self-subsistent, but everything subsists because of Him. If He withdraws His sustaining hand, everything will come to naught. Death or decay or decline is not for Him. Everything without Him is subject to death and destruction. He is above want or need. But all things have wants and needs. He provides food and nourishment for everyone, everything, but Himself is above the need of food or drink. He is the supreme ruler. His rule is over everything, He Himself is free from all limitations, all constraints. He is all-hearing, all-seeing. Nothing is hidden from Him. Past, present or future are the same for Him. No-one can interfere in His plans, His wishes or wills. But not a leaf can move without His will. He is above the limitations of time and space. He is the originator, the source and spring of the entire universe. He is all-wise, all-free in His actions and dealings, His power knows no limits, His knowledge no gaps.

His mercy encompasses everything. His forgiveness has precedence over His wrath. His magnanimity knows no bounds, His mercy no limits. He forgives without cause, without atonement. His mercy is all-embracing, ultimate, basic. Yet He is master, mighty, and punishes when He should. He would not treat loyal and disloyal servants alike. If He did so, it would be a sign of weakness. He manifests Himself with a new glory every day, every moment. The most truly magnanimous is He. Others give in the hope of reward hereafter, or to be praised here in this world. And they only give out of what the Lord has given them. If the Lord had not given *them*, they would have had nothing to give. They give out of what the Lord has trusted them with. He provides for peace, protects us from all afflictions, guards us against mishaps. He is dominant over all, the One Who compensates us for our losses. He turns to us with mercy ever and ever. His greatness is unique. He shields us from the consequences of our mistakes, our sins. He resolves for us our difficulties. Honour and disgrace are in His hands, He is the One Who raises us in public esteem and pulls us down if He so wills. He is the true judge and real justice comes only from Him. His eye is on every small detail. His is the true appreciation. Glory and greatness belong only to him. He is the watcher of us all, the protector, the helper. He is the One Who listens to the prayers of men, the One Who accepts their prayers and their good deeds. He is most loving, most worthy. His attributes are ever with Him. He is the most manifest, the most hidden, the very first, the very last. He is the dispenser of forgiveness and He is the forgiver. Everything we have is His gift. He is most tolerant, most patient, even with those who are ungrateful or unmannerly. He is the One Who turns to men with mercy, and again and again. He is the possessor of all the good names. The Holy Prophet counted ninety-nine of them. But it would be wrong to think the ninety-nine names are the only names He has. This inadequate expression of His greatness and majesty is all that is possible for us earth-bound creatures of limited capacity and knowledge. His wonderful and glorious attributes surpass all description and understanding.

Understanding and reasoning,
and imagining besides,

may do their utmost;
but beyond, ever beyond,
remains the core—the essence—of His Being.

Now you are the judge. A being, a person, of such attributes, who would say He is not entitled to our love and our worship? Shall we not give our full devotion, the devotion of our heart and soul to such a being? Is there another one deserving of our love in a like manner?

The Sacred Is the One True Reality of Brahman

SWAMI NIKHILANANDA

Swami Nikhilananda has written extensively about Hinduism in English and so helped bring a knowledge of this ancient religion to Western readers. Here he tries to explain the basic Hindu concept of "Brahman," the sacred reality that is the basis of all existence. Although Brahman can be spoken about in its "conditioned" aspect as a personal god one worships, this is only the way in which our minds seek to express this inexpressible reality. Brahman in itself—the absolute or "unconditioned" Brahman—is the "Being" which is presupposed in all beings, so we can never perceive Brahman except in the form of other beings. Brahman is the real within all of us, the same as the soul or inner true self (what Hindus call "atman") within human consciousness. It is the substance of all things and all people, and so can be seen everywhere—even though it is never seen in its pure unconditioned state. It

Excerpted from *Hinduism: Its Meaning for the Liberation of the Spirit* by Swami Nikhilananda, as published by the Ramakrishna Vivekananda Center, ©1958 by Swami Nikhilananda; originally published by Harper & Bros. as part of the World Perspectives series. Reprinted by permission of the Ramakrishna Vivekananda Center, New York.

is the universe as well as the mind by which we perceive the universe. In fact, there is only Brahman; no other reality exists but this One Reality. Hence the Sacred is not a God who is fundamentally different from us, ultimately; rather, what we call God and World are in fact the same reality. In rejecting the illusion of duality, one comes to see that all things are the one Brahman.

QUESTIONS

1. In what sense can Brahman be said to be infinite and yet "smaller than a mustard seed," according to Nikhilananda?
2. How is the "existence" of Brahman both like and unlike our own existence, in Nikhilananda's view?
3. Why does Nikhilananda believe that the nature of Brahman can be called "bliss" and "knowledge"?

■　■　■

As early as Vedic times, the Indo-Aryan thinkers investigated the nature of reality from two levels of experience, one of which may be called the absolute, acosmic, or transcendental level and the other the relative, cosmic, or phenomenal level. At the phenomenal level one perceives the universe of diversity and is aware of one's own individual ego, whereas at the transcendental level all differences merge into an inexplicable non-dual consciousness. Both of these levels of experience are real from their respective standpoints, though what is perceived at one level may be negated at the other.

In the Vedas, reality experienced at the transcendental level is called Brahman. This term denotes a non-dual pure consciousness which pervades the universe and yet remains outside it. Brahman is described as the first principle; from it all things are derived, by it all are supported, and into it all finally disappear. In Brahman alone the apparent differences of the phenomenal world are unified. According to the non-dualistic Vedanta philosophy, Brahman is identical with the self of man, known as atman.

Etymologically, the word *Brahman* denotes an entity whose greatness, powers, or expansion no one can measure. The word *atman* signifies the consciousness in man which experiences gross objects during the waking state, subtle objects during the dream state, and the bliss arising from absence of the duality of subject and object in dreamless sleep.

Let us try to understand the nature of Brahman in both its aspects: transcendental and phenomenal. The Upanishads speak of the transcendental Brahman as devoid of qualifying attributes and indicative marks, and of the phenomenal Brahman as endowed with them. The attributeless Brahman is called the supreme or unconditioned Brahman, and the other the inferior or conditioned Brahman. The supreme Brahman, or pure being, is described by a negative method in such striking passages as: "Not this, not this," or "Where there is duality, as it were, one sees another, but when only the self is all this, how should one see another?" The conditioned Brahman, on the other hand, has been described by such positive statements as: "Whose body is spirit, whose form is light, whose thoughts are true, whose nature is like akasa, from whom all works, all desires, all odours proceed." The Upanishads generally designate the conditioned Brahman by the masculine *He* and the unconditioned Brahman by the neuter *it*.

There is no real conflict between the two Brahmans; for Brahman is one and without a second, and can be regarded either from the phenomenal or from the transcendental point of view. When the sense-perceived world is regarded as real, Brahman is spoken of as its omnipotent and omniscient Creator, Preserver, and Destroyer. But when the world is not perceived to exist, as for instance in a deep meditation, then one experiences Brahman as the unconditioned Absolute; the idea of a Creator, omnipotent and omniscient, becomes irrelevant. One worships the conditioned Brahman in the ordinary state of consciousness; but one loses one's individuality in the experience of the unconditioned Brahman. The transcendental Brahman appears as the cause of the universe in association with maya, and becomes known as the conditioned Brahman or Brahman with attributes, or by such other epithets as the Lord and the Personal God.

Let us consider the unconditioned Brahman. Indescribable in words, it is indicated by the Vedas as that "from which all speech, together with the mind, turns away, unable to reach it." Ramakrishna has said that all the scriptures and all the state-

> **"THESE RIVERS, MY DEAR, FLOW,** the eastern toward the east, the western toward the west. They go just from the ocean to the ocean. They become the ocean itself. As there they know not 'I am this one,' 'I am that one'—even so, indeed, my dear, all creatures here, though they have come forth from Being, know not 'We have come forth from Being.' Whatever they are in this world, whether tiger, or lion, or wolf, or boar, or worm, or fly, or gnat, or mosquito, that they become.
>
> "That which is the finest essence—this whole world has that as its self. That is Reality. That is *Atman*. That art though, Svetaketu. . . ."
>
> **Chandogya Upanishad, VI.X.1-3**
> quoted in A *Source Book in Indian Philosophy*, 1957.

ments of holy men have been polluted, as it were, like food that has come in contact with the tongue; Brahman alone remains unpolluted, because it has never come in contact with any tongue. He used to say, further, that he had to come down three levels, so to speak, from the experience of non-duality before he could utter the word *Om*, a holy symbol of Brahman. Experienced as silence, the attributeless Brahman is described as "not that which is conscious of the external (objective) world, nor that which is conscious of the internal (subjective) world, nor that which is conscious of both, nor that which is a mass of sentiency, nor that which is simple consciousness, nor that which is insentient. It is unperceived [by any sense-organ], unrelated [to anything], incomprehensible [to the mind], uninferable, unthinkable, indescribable."

Sometimes the Upanishads ascribe to the unconditioned Brahman irreconcilable attributes in order to deny to it all empirical predicates and indicate that it is totally other than anything we know: "That non-dual Brahman, though never stirring, is swifter than the mind. Though sitting still it travels far; though lying down it goes everywhere." "It is subtler than an atom and greater than the great." The opposing predicates in these passages are ascribed to Brahman in such a manner that they cancel each other, leaving to the mind the idea of an indefinable pure consciousness free of all attributes. Though nothing definite can be predicated of Brahman, yet the search for it is not futile. The Upanishads repeatedly say that its realization is the supreme purpose of life, because it bestows immortality. When Brahman is known all is known.

The unconditioned Brahman is free from the limiting adjuncts of space, time, and causation. In describing Brahman as infinitely great and infinitely small, the Upanishads only point out that it is absolutely spaceless. It is "one and infinite: infinite in the east, infinite in the south, infinite in the west, infinite in the north, above and below and everywhere infinite. The east and the other directions do not exist for it—no athwart, no beneath, no above. The supreme Brahman is not to be fixed; it is unlimited, unborn, not to be reasoned about, not to be conceived." "It is my self within the heart, smaller than a corn of rice, smaller than a corn of barley, smaller than a mustard seed, smaller than a canary seed or the kernel of a canary seed. It is my self within the heart, greater than the earth, greater than the sky, greater than heaven, greater than all these worlds."

The timelessness of the unconditioned Brahman is indicated by the statement that it is free from the limitations of past, present, and future. Sometimes it is described as eternal, without beginning or end; sometimes as momentary, involving no time at all. Brahman is "what they say was, is, and will be." It is that "at whose feet, rolling on, the year with its days passes by." "It is like a flash of lightning; it is like a wink of the eye."

Brahman is independent of causation. The law of cause and effect operates only in the realm of becoming, or manifestation, and cannot affect pure being. Brahman, according to the Vedas, is not born; it does not die. But from the level of relative experience Brahman is described as the cause of the universe.

Brahman is unknown and unknowable. To be known, a thing must be made an object. Brahman, as pure consciousness, is the eternal subject, and therefore cannot be made an object of knowledge. "You cannot see that which is the seer of seeing; you cannot hear that which is the hearer of hearing; you cannot think of that which is the thinker of thought; you cannot know that which is the knower of knowing." Brahman is unknowable for still another reason: it is infinite. What is the infinite? "Where one sees nothing else, hears nothing else, understands nothing else—that is the infinite. Where one sees something else, hears something else, understands something else—that is the finite. The infinite is immortal; the finite, mortal."

Hindu philosophers often describe the unconditioned Brahman as Satchidananda, existence-knowledge-bliss pure and absolute. Existence, knowledge, and bliss are not attributes of reality; they are its very stuff. Pure existence is the same as pure knowledge and pure bliss. The word *existence* indicates that Brahman is not non-existence; the phenomenal universe, which is perceived to exist, cannot have been produced from nothing. But Brahman does not exist as an empirical object—like a pot or a tree, for instance—but as absolute existence, without which material objects would not be perceived to exist. Just as a mirage could not be seen without the desert, which is its unrelated substratum, so also the universe could not be seen if Brahman did not exist as its substratum. When the process of negation is carried on, step by step, there always remains a residuum of existence which cannot be negated. No object, illusory or otherwise, could exist without the foundation of an immutable existence—and that existence is Brahman. Therefore the term *existence*, as applied to Brahman, is to be understood as the negation of both empirical reality and its correlative, unreality. Whether the universe is seen or not seen, Brahman remains as the witness-consciousness. Brahman is often described as the "reality of reality," that is to say, the reality of the tangible world whose empirical reality is accepted.

Brahman is knowledge or intelligence. The identity of Brahman and atman, or the self, has been expressed in the well-known Vedic formula "that thou art." The very conception of atman in the Upanishads implies that it is the knowing subject within us. It is the inner consciousness and the real agent of perception, the senses being mere instruments. Perception, which is a conscious act, is impossible without the presence of a sentient principle, which is atman. "He who says: 'Let me smell this'—he is atman; the nose is the instrument of smelling. He who says: 'Let me utter this'—he is atman; the tongue is the instrument of speaking. He who says: 'Let me hear this'—he is atman; the ear is the instrument of hearing. He who says: 'Let me think this'—he is atman; the mind is his divine eye." "Into him, as eye, all forms are gathered; by the eye he reaches all forms. Into him, as ear, all sounds are gathered; by the ear he reaches all sounds." Because Brahman is identical with atman, Brahman is consciousness, knowledge, light. It is self-luminous and needs no other light to illumine itself. "It is the light of lights; it is that which they know who know the self." All material objects, such as trees, rivers, houses, and forests, are illumined by the sun. But the light that illumines the sun is the light of Brahman. "The sun does not shine there, nor the moon and the stars, nor these lightnings, not to speak of this fire. When he shines everything shines after him; by his light everything is lighted." "The universe is guided by knowledge, it is grounded in knowledge, it is governed by knowledge; knowledge is its foundation. Knowledge is Brahman."

Brahman is bliss because it is knowledge. No real bliss is possible without knowledge. Needless to say, the bliss of Brahman is utterly different from the happiness that a man experiences from agreeable sense-objects; it is characterized by absence of the subject-object relationship. Worldly happiness is but an infinitesimal part of the bliss of Brahman. Again, Brahman is bliss because of the absence of duality in it; friction, fear, jealousy, secretiveness, and the other evils which plague a man's daily life arise from consciousness of duality. Brahman as bliss pervades all objects; that is why there is attraction between husband and wife, parents and children, creature and creature, God and man. Furthermore, Brahman is bliss because it is infinite. There is no real and enduring joy in the finite. The bliss of Brahman cannot be measured by any relative standard, human or other. Through the performance of religious rites and the fulfillment of moral obligations one may experience, after death, different measures of happiness in ascending degrees in the different heavenly worlds. But if a person is completely free from desire and possesses the knowledge of Brahman, he can attain here, before death, the measureless bliss of Brahman.

To summarize what has been said about the unconditioned Brahman, or pure being: Brahman is the negation of all attributes and relations. It is beyond time, space, and causality. Though it is spaceless, without it space could not be conceived; though it is timeless, without it time could not be conceived; though it is causeless, without it the universe, bound by the law of cause and effect, could not be conceived to exist. Only if one admits the reality of pure being as the unchanging ground of creation can one understand proximity in space, succession in time, and interdependence in the chain of cause and effect. Without the unchanging white screen, one cannot relate in time and space the disjoined pictures on a cinema film. Brahman is not a philosophical abstraction, but is more intimately known than any sense-object. It is Brahman that, as the inner consciousness, makes the perception of sense-objects possible. Brahman is the intangible reality that unifies all the discrete objects in the phenomenal universe, making it appear a cosmos and not a chaos. In the Vedas, Brahman is compared to a dike that keeps diverse objects asunder and prevents their clashing together, or again, to a bridge that connects the visible world with the invisible.

From the transcendental standpoint, there exists, therefore, no universe which is other than Brahman. Since Brahman is free from causality, the question of creation does not arise. Nothing is ever produced. Where, on account of ignorance, a man sees names and forms, substance and attributes, causal and other relationships, the knower of reality sees only pure being. To the illumined, nature itself is pure being. Duality being mere illusion, unconditioned pure being is the sole reality.

The Sacred Is Complete Emptiness

DAISETZ T. SUZUKI

Zen is a branch of Mahayana ("The Greater Vehicle") Buddhism that is practiced in the Far East, especially in Japan. Through his translations of Zen texts and his own explications of them, Daisetz T. Suzuki (1870-1966) did more than anyone else to bring an understanding of Zen Buddhism to the West. The Zen tradition expresses its insights in a unique way, which may seem to reject Buddhism altogether—hence many scholars argue that it is a distinct religion. But the followers of Zen believe that they understand the true nature of the Buddha's message, as he transmitted a "wordless wisdom" to his chosen disciples who have passed it on through time to them. Beginning with the Buddha's conviction that there is no permanent nature within anything, not even ourselves, and hence no "self" to be saved, Zen Buddhism developed the notion that everything is "empty" (shunya) and so there is nothing to cling to—not even the Buddha's teaching, or the notion of "emptiness" itself. Understood in this way, the goal of Buddhism is to realize there is no goal, nothing to be done or said. To strive for release from reincarnation to achieve the goal of "nirvana" or extinction of the self is to still

Excerpted from Daisetz T. Suzuki, *An Introduction to Zen Buddhism*. London: Rider, 1949. Reprinted by permission of the Random Century Group Ltd., London.

be attached to this goal, and hence clinging to something. One must give up all attachment, even (paradoxically) attachment to the goal of non-attachment.

Because Zen Buddhists have refused to attach themselves to any doctrine or any particular understanding of reality, many view Zen as advocating "nihilism," a complete rejection of all beliefs and meaning. Suzuki argues that although it may seem this way, in fact Zen speaks in negative terms to bring out a deeper positive fact. Zen affirms reality and does not negate it, because it leads the disciple to affirm experience directly for what it is. All attachments are discarded, and only the pure experience of being remains. In this way, the belief that everything is "empty" leads to a deeper understanding of life in the world. Zen Buddhists would almost certainly reject the way we have expressed their philosophy, that "the sacred is complete emptiness," because there is no sacred reality to be grasped—but one can at least say that in Zen, to understand the emptiness of all is to understand the true nature of reality, and in this sense, the final truth about what we call the "sacred" as well.

QUESTIONS

1. How does a slap in the face show that Zen is not nihilistic, according to Suzuki?
2. What does Zen reject, and what does it affirm, in Suzuki's view?
3. In what sense is "absolute purity of mind" above both purity and non-purity, according to Zen?

■ ■ ■

In the history of Zen, Enō, traditionally considered the sixth patriarch of the Zen sect in China, cuts a most important figure. In fact, he is the founder of Zen as distinguished from the other Buddhist sects then existing in China. The standard set up by him as the true expression of Zen faith is this stanza:

The Bodhi (True Wisdom) is not like the tree;
The mirror bright is nowhere shining:

As there is nothing from the first,
Where does the dust itself collect?

This was written in answer to a stanza composed by another
Zen monk who claimed to have understood the faith in its purity. His lines run thus:

This body is the Bodhi-tree;
The soul is like a mirror bright;
Take heed to keep it always clean,
And let no dust collect upon it.

They were both the disciples of the fifth patriarch, Gunin,
and he thought that Enō rightly comprehended the spirit of
Zen, and, therefore, was worthy of wearing his mantle and carrying his bowl as his true successor in Zen. This recognition by
the master of the signification of the first stanza by Enō stamps
it as the orthodox expression of Zen faith. As it seems to
breathe the spirit of nothingness, many people regard Zen as
advocating nihilism. The purpose of this viewpoint is to refute
this.

It is true that there are many passages in Zen literature
which may be construed as conveying a nihilistic doctrine, for
example, the theory of *śūnyatā* (emptiness). . . .

To a certain extent, superficially at least, this view is justi-
fiable. For instance, read the following:

"I come here to seek the truth of Buddhism," a disciple
asked a master.

"Why do you seek such a thing here?" answered the master. "Why do you wander about, neglecting your own precious
treasure at home? I have nothing to give you, and what truth
of Buddhism do you desire to find in my monastery? There is
nothing, absolutely nothing.". . .

A Japanese Zen master who flourished several hundred
years ago used to say to his disciples who would implore him
to instruct them in the way to escape the fetters of birth-and-
death, "There is no birth-and-death."

Bodhidharma, the first patriarch of the Zen sect in China,
was asked by Wu, the first Emperor (reigned A.D. 502–549) of
the Liang dynasty, as to the ultimate and holiest principle of
Buddhism. The sage is reported to have answered, "Vast empti-

ness and nothing holy in it."

These are passages taken at random from the vast store of Zen literature, and they seemed to be permeated with the ideas of emptiness (śūnyatā), nothingness (nāsti), tranquillity (śānti), no-thought (acintā), and other similar notions, all of which we may regard as nihilistic or as advocating negative quietism.

A quotation from the Prajñāpāramitā-hridaya-sūtra may prove to be more astounding than any of the above passages. In fact, all the sutras belonging to this prajñā class of Mahayana literature are imbued thoroughly with the idea of śūnyatā, and those who are not familiar with this way of thinking will be taken aback and may not know how to express their judgment. This sutra, considered to be the most concise and most comprehensive of all the prajñā sutras, is daily recited at the Zen monastery; in fact it is the first thing the monks recite in the morning as well as before each meal.

"Thus, Śāriputra, all things have the character of emptiness, they have no beginning, no end, they are faultless and not faultless, they are not perfect and not imperfect. Therefore, O Śāriputra, here in this emptiness there is no form, no perception, no name, no concepts, no knowledge. No eye, no ear, no nose, no tongue, no body, no mind. No form, no sound, no smell, no taste, no touch, no objects. . . . There is no knowledge, no ignorance, no destruction of ignorance. . . . There is no decay nor death; there are no four truths, viz., there is no pain, no origin of pain, no stoppage of pain, and no path to the stoppage of pain. There is no knowledge of Nirvana, no obtaining of it, no not-obtaining of it. Therefore, O Śāriputra, as there is no obtaining of Nirvana, a man who has approached the Prajñāpāramitā of the Bodhisattvas, dwells unimpeded in consciousness. When the impediments of consciousness are annihilated, then he becomes free of all fear, is beyond the reach of change, enjoying final Nirvana."

Going through all these quotations, it may be thought that the critics are justified in charging Zen with advocating a philosophy of pure negation, but nothing is so far from Zen as this criticism would imply. For Zen always aims at grasping the central fact of life, which can never be brought to the dissecting table of the intellect. To grasp this central fact of life, Zen is forced to propose a series of negations. Mere negation, however, is not the spirit of Zen, but as we are so accustomed to the

ALL THINGS CONDITIONED ARE INSTABLE, impermanent,
Fragile in essence, as an unbaked pot,
Like something borrowed, or a city founded on sand,
They last a short while only.
They are inevitably destroyed,
Like plaster washed off in the rains,
Like the sandy bank of a river—
They are conditioned, and their true nature is frail.
They are like the flame of a lamp,
Which rises suddenly and as soon goes out.
They have no power of endurance, like the wind
Or like foam, unsubstantial, essentially feeble.
They have no inner power, being essentially empty,
Like the stem of a plantain, if one thinks clearly,
Like conjuring tricks deluding the mind,
Or a fist closed on nothing to tease a child. . . .
All things conditioned are conditioned by ignorance,
And on final analysis they do not exist,
For they and the conditioning ignorance alike are Emptiness
In their essential nature, without power of action. . . .
The mystic knows the beginning and end
Of consciousness, its production and passing away—
He knows that it came from nowhere and returns to nowhere,
And is empty [of reality], like a conjuring trick.

From *Lalitavistara*, 13.175-77
quoted in *The Buddhist Tradition*, 1969.

dualistic way of thinking, this intellectual error must be cut at its root. Naturally Zen would proclaim, "Not this, not that, not anything." But we may insist upon asking Zen what it is that is left after all these denials, and the master will perhaps on such an occasion give us a slap in the face, exclaiming, "You fool, what is this?" Some may take this as only an excuse to get away from the dilemma, or as having no more meaning than a practical example of ill-breeding. But when the spirit of Zen is grasped in its purity, it will be seen what a real thing that slap is. For here is no negation, no affirmation, but a plain fact, a pure experience, the very foundation of our being and thought. All the quietness and emptiness one might desire in the midst of most active mentation lie therein. Do not be carried away by anything outward or conventional. Zen must be seized with bare hands, with no gloves on.

Zen is forced to resort to negation because of our innate ignorance (*avidyā*), which tenaciously clings to the mind as wet clothes do to the body. "Ignorance" is all well as far as it goes, but it must not go out of its proper sphere. "Ignorance" is another name for logical dualism. White is snow and black is the raven. But these belong to the world and its ignorant way of talking. If we want to get to the very truth of things, we must see them from the point where this world has not yet been created, where the consciousness of this and that has not yet been awakened and where the mind is absorbed in its own identity, that is, in its serenity and emptiness. This is a world of negations but leading to a higher or absolute affirmation—an affirmation in the midst of negations. Snow is not white, the raven is not black, yet each in itself is white or black. This is where our everyday language fails to convey the exact meaning as conceived by Zen.

Apparently Zen negates; but it is always holding up before us something which indeed lies right before our own eyes; and if we do not take it up, it is our own fault. Most people, whose mental vision is darkened by the clouds of ignorance, pass it by and refuse to look at it. To them Zen is, indeed, nihilism just because they do not see it. . . .

Hakuin, the founder of modern Japanese Zen, while still a young monk eagerly bent on the mastery of Zen, had an interview with the venerable Shōju. Hakuin thought that he fully comprehended Zen and was proud of his attainment, and this interview with Shōju was in fact intended to be a demonstration of his own high understanding. Shōju asked him how much he knew of Zen. Hakuin answered disgustingly: "If there is anything I can lay my hand on, I will get it all out of me." So saying, he acted as if he were going to vomit.

Shōju took firm hold of Hakuin's nose and said, "What is this? Have I not after all touched it?"

Let our readers ponder with Hakuin over this interview and find out for themselves what is that something which is so realistically demonstrated by Shōju.

Zen is not all negation, leaving the mind all blank as if it were pure nothing; for that would be intellectual suicide. There is in Zen something self-assertive, which, however, being free and absolute, knows no limitations and refuses to be handled in abstraction. Zen is a live fact, it is not like an inorganic rock or like an empty space. To come into contact with this living fact, nay, to take hold of it in every phase of life, is the aim of all Zen discipline.

Nansen was once asked by Hyakujō, one of his brother monks, if there was anything he dared not talk about to others. The master answered, "Yes."

Whereupon the monk continued, "What then is this something you do not talk about?"

The master's reply was, "It is neither mind, nor Buddha, nor matter."

This looks to be the doctrine of absolute emptiness, but even here again we observe a glimpse of something showing itself through the negation. Observe the further dialogue that took place between the two. The monk said

"If so, you have already talked about it."

"I cannot do any better. What would you say?"

"I am not a great enlightened one," answered Hyakujō.

The master said: "Well, I have already said too much about it."

This state of inner consciousness, about which we cannot make any logical statement, must be realized before we can have any intelligent talk on Zen. Words are only an index to this state; through them we are enabled to get into its signification, but do not look to words for absolute guidance. Try to see first of all in what mental state the Zen masters are so acting. They are not carrying on all those seeming absurdities, or, as some might say, those silly trivialities, just to suit their capricious moods. They have a certain firm basis of truth obtained from a deep personal experience. There is in all their seemingly crazy performances a systematic demonstration of the most vital truth. When seen from this truth, even the moving of the whole universe is of no more account than the flying of a mosquito or the waving of a fan. The thing is to see one spirit working throughout all these, which is an absolute affirmation, with not a particle of nihilism in it.

A monk asked Jōshū, "What would you say when I come to you with nothing?"

Jōshū said: "Fling it down to the ground."

Protested the monk, "I said that I had nothing, what shall I let go?"

"If so, carry it away," was the retort of Jōshū.

Jōshū has thus plainly exposed the fruitlessness of a nihilistic philosophy. To reach the goal of Zen, even the idea of "having nothing" ought to be done away with. Buddha reveals himself when he is no more asserted; that is, for Buddha's sake Buddha is to be given up. This is the only way to come to the realization of the truth of Zen. So long as one is talking of nothingness or of the absolute, one is far away from Zen, and ever receding from Zen. Even the foothold of *sūnyatā* must be kicked off. The only way to get saved is to throw oneself right down into a bottomless abyss. And this is, indeed, no easy task.

"No Buddhas," it is boldly asserted by Engo, "have ever appeared on earth; nor is there anything that is to be given out as a holy doctrine. Bodhidharma, the first patriarch of Zen, has never come east, nor has he ever transmitted any secret doctrine through the mind; only people of the world, not understanding what all this means, seek the truth outside of themselves. What a pity that the thing they are so earnestly looking for is being trodden under their own feet. This is not to be grasped by the wisdom of all the sages. However, we see the thing and yet it is not seen; we hear it and yet it is not heard; we talk about it and yet it is not talked about; we know it and yet it is not known. Let me ask, How does it so happen?"

Is this an interrogation as it apparently is? Or, in fact, is it an affirmative statement describing a certain definite attitude of mind?

Therefore, when Zen denies, it is not necessarily a denial in the logical sense. The same can be said of an affirmation. The idea is that the ultimate fact of experience must not be enslaved by any artificial or schematic laws of thought, nor by any antithesis of "yes" and "no," nor by any cut-and-dried formulas of epistemology. Evidently Zen commits absurdities and irrationalities all the time; but this only apparently. No wonder it fails to escape the natural consequences—misunderstandings, wrong interpretations, and ridicules which are often malicious. The charge of nihilism is only one of these.

When Vimalakīrti asked Mañjuśrī what was the doctrine of non-duality as realized by a Bodhisattva, Mañjuśrī replied: "As I understand it, the doctrine is realized when one looks upon all things as beyond every form of expression and demonstration and as transcending knowledge and argument. This is my comprehension; may I ask what is your understanding?" Vimalakīrti, thus demanded, remained altogether silent. The mystic response, that is, the closing of the lips seems to be the only way one can get out of the difficulties in which Zen often finds itself involved, when it is pressed hard for a statement. Therefore, Engo, commenting on the above, has this to say:

"I say, 'yes,' and there is nothing about which this affirmation is made; I say, 'no,' and there is nothing about which this is made. I stand above 'yes' and 'no,' I forget what is gained and what is lost. There is just a state of absolute purity, a state of stark nakedness.". . .

A monk asked: "According to Vimalakīrti, one who wishes for the Pure Land ought to have his mind purified; but what is the purified mind?" Answered the Zen master: "When the mind is absolutely pure, you have a purified mind, and a mind is said to be absolutely pure when it is above purity and impurity. You want to know how this is to be realized? Have your mind thoroughly void in all conditions, then you will have purity. But when this is attained, do not harbor any thought of it, or you get non-purity. Again, when this state of non-purity is attained, do not harbor any thought of it, and you are free of non-purity. This is absolute purity." Now, absolute purity is absolute affirmation, as it is above purity and non-purity and at the same time unifies them in a higher form of synthesis. There is no negation in this, nor any contradiction. What Zen aims at is to realize this form of unification in one's everyday life of actualities, and not to treat life as a sort of metaphysical exercise. In this light all Zen "questions and answers" are to be considered. There are no quibblings, no playing at words, no sophistry; Zen is the most serious concern in the world.

The Sacred Is Tao, the Natural Way of Things

JOHN BLOFELD ON THE BAMBOO PIN RECLUSE

As Taoists are devoted to living in harmony with the "Natural Way," they are often more interested in quiet contemplation than in writing books explaining their ideas to others. To hear their views, one sometimes needs an intermediary like John Blofeld to visit Taoists and record their philosophy. Blofeld spent many years visiting monasteries in China and Tibet and has recorded his observations and conversations in numerous books. This selection pertains to his visit to the Moon Terrace Hermitage in China, a retreat founded by contemplative Taoist mystics who seek the Tao in quiet isolation from modern society. Blofeld conversed here with one such mystic who called himself the "Bamboo Pin Recluse" (Taoists sometimes take names such as this which are associated with nature to illustrate their harmony with it). He explains his own understanding of the Tao as the "void," the origin of the universe which has countless forms. One can encounter this Tao through tranquil stillness and a combination of contemplation and observation. This enables one to accept all that occurs as an expression of the ever-changing Way which governs all things.

Excerpted from John Blofeld, *Beyond the Gods: Buddhist and Taoist Mysticism*. London: George Allen & Unwin, 1974. Reprinted by permission of Unwin Hyman Ltd.

QUESTIONS

1. Why should one alternate contemplation on the pure Tao with observation of nature, according to the Bamboo Pin Recluse?
2. How does the Bamboo Pin Recluse believe one should seek to perceive the void and its forms?
3. Why is the Bamboo Pin Recluse unconcerned about immortality?

■ ■ ■

That evening, wanting to think over all the things of which Dark Valley had spoken, I strolled out to a rocky perch overlooking the noisy, foaming torrent to watch the sunset. A shower of rain had deepened the colour of the rocks and scattered jewels upon the foliage. A sharp breeze blew from the west. The setting sun cast its light upon massed banks of cloud, dyeing them with glorious tints—coral, crimson and gold. The rushing water, blue mountains and majestic clouds and the beauties of the 'hidden garden' combined to stimulate awareness of the workings of the mysterious Tao, mother of everlasting change. The rapid transformations of the clouds were a reminder that the seemingly eternal mountains were, however slowly, undergoing transformations no less stupendous. Clearly the founders of the hermitage had not erred in choosing to contemplate the Tao in this magic spot where nature's unending dance was presented in such dramatic form. Here the world of corrupt officials, money-grubbing merchants and gun-toting policemen seemed as far off as another planet. Living a few years in this place and using one's eyes, one might stumble upon the innermost secrets of those bearded sages without so much as leafing through their ancient books.

Driven back to the hermitage by darkness and a sudden freshening of the breeze, I heard from somewhere the music of an evening rite. To the accompaniment of gong and cymbals, two voices were uplifted in a strangely haunting air, melancholy and yet evocative of sweetness and tranquillity. Chilled by my vigil on the rocky perch, at evening rice I drank gratefully of the mulled, herb-scented wine which was the nearest thing to a luxury in the daily lives of those abstemious men.

Presently I caught the eye of the Bamboo Pin Recluse and, addressing him as Your Immortality, a Taoist term indicative of great respect, asked if I might visit him after the meal. Hitherto, not a little intimidated by his air of remoteness from human concerns, I had scarcely exchanged words with him, so his eyes betrayed a flicker of surprise as he answered courteously: 'By all means. We shall drink tea from the plants that now grow wild on the southern slope of this mountain. One of the pleasures of visiting out-of-the-way places in this part of the country is tasting the local teas, infused, of course, with local water. Taken away and brewed elsewhere, they never taste as good.'

His cell was much like the others. At first sight, the tea-things he brought out looked coarse and rustic, but the loving

---

THERE WAS SOMETHING UNDIFFERENTIATED AND yet complete,
Which existed before heaven and earth.
Soundless and formless, it depends on nothing and does not change.
It operates everywhere and is free from danger.
It may be considered the mother of the universe.
I do not know its name; I call it Tao.
If forced to give it a name, I shall call it Great.
Now being great means functioning everywhere.
Functioning everywhere means far-reaching.
Being far-reaching means returning to the original point.
Therefore Tao is great.
Heaven is great.
Earth is great.
And the king is also great.
There are four great things in the universe, and the king is one of them.
Man models himself after Earth.
Earth models itself after Heaven.
Heaven models itself after Tao.
And Tao models itself after Nature.

Lao Tzu, *Tao te Ching*, Chapter 25
quoted in A *Source Book in Chinese Philosophy*, 1963.

---

way he handled them suggested they were old and in some sense precious. The rough glaze ended in an irregular line far from the base, as though thick honey had been poured onto unglazed earthenware from above. The tea itself was honey-coloured, slightly bitter but with a strange and attractive fragrance. Since it would have been discourteous to come straight to the subject of my visit, I found the tea-things a pleasant subject for conversation. The tea-pot, I learnt, though generally similar in appearance to the cups, was unworthy of notice, whereas the cups were a family heirloom, not only very old but replicas of a form so ancient that the world's first tea-drinkers might be presumed to have used cups much like them.

'I am fond of them', remarked my host, 'because they symbolise what Laotzû calls the uncarved block—a man or object in its natural state, moulded by the Tao, unsophisticated, holy. They are, as you see, close to being "uncouth", a word sometimes used of our great sages. We modern Taoists—I mean those during the last thousand years or so—are, to my mind, over-ceremonious and too fond of tradition for its own sake, whereas the sages of old were, to quote from the Tao Tê Ching, "as simple as babes", their manners "as artless as the uncarved block". It also says: "Ceremonious behaviour betokens lack of loyalty and good faith".'

Presently an opportunity arose to beg him to expound something within my comprehension of the mysteries of the Tao.

'Mysteries?' he answered, laughing. 'Viewed properly, every detail of life, of nature, is a mystery as profound as any you can name, so how should our doctrine be especially mysterious? Let me tell you what we do here in our community—*not do* might be a better term for it, since a distinguishing characteristic of Taoists is refraining from all calculated action, responding only to the needs of the moment. The essence of our belief is summed up in a few sentences from the Tao Tê Ching: "The universe had its beginning in what is called the mother of the universe. Know the mother, that you may know the child. Know the child, that you may return to and hold fast to the mother; then, as long as life lasts, nothing can harm you". The mother is the formless Tao; the child is the Tao of a myriad transformations. Or, as Laotzû puts it: "Voidness is the name for that in which the universe had its origin; actuality is the name for the mother of the myriad objects. Therefore, empty your minds to view the secret source; and observe actuality in order to view its manifestations. These two arise together, though separate in name. Both are mysterious—mystery upon mystery! Such is the gateway of all secrets !"

'I shall explain. Voidness and the actuality one sees all around are simultaneously one and the same. Therefore, to know the undifferentiated source of the myriad objects comprising actuality, one must sometimes empty the mind of thought and sometimes contemplate the world of form. Neither has meaning apart from the other. To fix the mind always upon emptiness would be to become like wood or stone. To keep it always upon the form realm would be to behave like a simpleton who mistakes dreams for reality. We are not philosophers lost in speculation. Bandying metaphysical arguments is not our way. Direct perception takes the place of concepts. Now we rest in the mother, the pure undifferentiated Tao; now, in the child, observing the rhythms of the seasons, the objects of nature, the flux of change in which our lives are passed. Learning to dwell above duality, we perceive no contradiction between the void which is also form and the form which is also void. Thus we come to know things as they really are—void, yet capable of taking countless forms; possessing form, yet intrinsically void. Secure in this knowledge, we view gain and loss, meetings and partings, the rise and fall of circumstance, life and death with cheerful equanimity. What then can harm us? If the omens point to one's living another twenty or thirty years, well and good; if death must be faced tomorrow or today, well and good. But it is useless to know this from hearsay or from a book as one knows that in Kiangsi province there are twenty-seven different species of dragonfly. You must open the inner chamber of your mind and experience it there as you experience the sun's heat or water's wetness by *direct perception*!

'How then to set about this? First, by paring away wants and superficialities of every kind as so much useless baggage; and also by following a simple régime free from poisons to mind and body, that you may enjoy unending health, energy and mental clarity. Anxiety, covetousness, irritation recede as wants grow fewer and energy increases; thus the first taste of tranquillity is won. In tranquillity, the mind perceives its inner stillness; contemplate that stillness that you may attain perception of the all-pervading void. Yet, since voidness is not truth if the non-void is excluded, alternate the hours you spend in inward contemplation with hours spent in observation of the myriad processes and forms, noting how each comes into being, waxes, wanes, decays and passes on. Neither withdrawing the mind from things, nor content to accept them as they appear to eye, ear and touch, come to know them as they are. Alternating periods of meditation with gardening or with culling herbs and studying their healing properties is a way we favour. Landscape painting is another, since it involves a union of without and within. The painter observes mountains, oceans, trees, rocks until he has gained such an all-embracing knowledge of their nature that, unless his hand wants skill, he can scarcely err in portraying them; yet he does not seek to reproduce what he sees, but conjures other formations forth from the voidness of the mind, while taking care that they are true to nature. Those unskilled in painting often contemplate rocks or trees with another purpose, that of causing the mind to enter its object and intuitively sense its thusness. Once intuition dawns, the sight of bees at work among the flowers will produce the taste of honey as surely as if it lay upon the tongue.'

The Bamboo Pin Recluse gazed at me thoughtfully as if to gauge how much I had understood.

'How I envy you!' I said. 'It is lovely to live in this place, free from all desire for fame and power and wealth and happily content with simple things. And what a boon to be so imperturbable that the imminence of death and the prospect of continuing this idyllic life for many years to come are equally welcome! But what comes after death? The body, I know, decays; its juices nourish the grass on which other creatures feed and so on in a perpetual cycle. Is there also spirit? Do you aim, like certain other Taoists, at achieving immortality?'

'Why aim?' he laughed. 'What would be the use of that? If there is a spirit apart from the body, it will undergo cycles of change just like flesh and blood and everything else, whether one *aims* at that or not. If there is no spirit, what good would aiming do? Faced by this unresolved enigma, as in all other circumstances, it is best to reflect that things always take their natural course whether one likes it or not. Having aims does not affect them one way or the other. Besides, since nothing within the realm of form remains without change even for a moment, what is the difference between mortality and immortality? The juices rising from your grave to feed the grasses will no longer be *yours*; why should any spiritual residue you may have be otherwise? Suppose you have a spirit destined to exist for aeons, since it can never cease changing, for how long will it be *your* spirit? Believe me, dear guest from the Western Ocean region, nothing is gained by speculation. Things are always as they are. Learning to accept whatever comes is the only gateway to tranquillity.'

VIEWPOINT

7

The Sacred Is Heaven, the Basis for Self-Realization

TU WEI-MING

Tu Wei-Ming is a leading scholar of Confucianism who believes that this religion is an important spiritual resource to
the world of today. In his view, the self is always involved in a
process of creative self-transformation through its interrela-
tionship with realms outside itself. The individual is part of a
family; the family is part of a larger society or nation; nations
are part of the world community. Furthermore, humanity is
related to the wider sphere of nature, and the natural world is
related to the transcendent realm of Heaven. All these realms
are interconnected, and it is Heaven which provides the basis
for their harmony and transformation. In Confucian thought,
Heaven is not a place or an afterlife but an ideal realm which
is the source of creativity and meaning in this life. Largely for
this reason, Confucian philosophers do not say a great deal
about the heavenly or transcendent realm except insofar as it
is viewed as the motivating force behind our moral endeavors
and the ideal which we seek to actualize in our lives. Tu Wei-
Ming stands in the tradition of those who speak of Heaven in
this way, and eloquently represents the Confucian position as
one which remains relevant to our global community.

Excerpted from Tu Wei-Ming, "Confucianism." In Arvind Sharma, ed., *Our
Religions*. Copyright ©1993 by HarperCollins Publishers, Inc. Reprinted by
permission of HarperCollins Publishers, Inc.

1. How does Tu Wei-Ming describe the Confucian integration of self, community, nature, and Heaven?
2. Why does the self require a community to be fulfilled, according to Tu Wei-Ming?
3. How is the "Way of Heaven" related to daily life, in Tu Wei-Ming's view?

■ ■ ■

Are we isolated individuals, or do we live as a center of interpersonal relationships? Is moral self-knowledge necessary for personal growth? Can any society prosper or endure without developing a basic sense of duty and responsibility among its members? Should our pluralistic society deliberately cultivate shared values and a common ground of human understanding? As we become acutely aware of our earth's vulnerability and increasingly wary of our own fate as an "endangered species," what are the critical spiritual questions we must ask?

The fundamental concern of the Confucian tradition is learning to be human. The focus is not on the human in contrast with nature or with Heaven but the human that seeks harmony with nature and mutuality with Heaven. Indeed, learning to be human, in the Confucian perspective, entails a broadening and deepening process that acknowledges the interconnectedness of all the modalities of existence defining the human condition. Through an ever-expanding network of relationships encompassing the family, community, nation, world, and beyond, the Confucian seeks to realize humanity in its all-embracing fullness. This process of inclusion helps deepen our self-knowledge at the same time through a ceaseless effort to make our body healthy, our mind-and-heart alert, our soul pure, and our spirit brilliant. Self-cultivation is an end in itself and its primary purpose is self-realization.

A defining characteristic of Confucian humanism is faith in the creative transformation of our human condition as a communal act and as a dialogical response to Heaven. This involves the integration of four dimensions of humanity: self, community, nature, and Heaven. An exploration of Confucian spiritu-

> **"THE WAY OF THE SUPERIOR** man functions everywhere and
> yet is hidden. Men and women of simple intelligence can share
> its knowledge; and yet in its utmost reaches, there is something
> which even the sage does not now. Men and women of simple
> intelligence can put it into practice; and yet in its utmost
> reaches there is something which even the sage is not able to
> put into practice. Great as heaven and earth are, men still find
> something in them with which to be dissatisfied. Thus with [the
> Way of] the superior man, if one speaks of its greatness, noth-
> ing in the world can contain it, and if one speaks of its small-
> ness, nothing in the world can split it. The Book of Odes says, 'The
> hawk flies up to heaven; the fishes leap in the deep.' This means
> that [the Way] is clearly seen above and below. The Way of the
> superior man has its simple beginnings in the relation between
> man and woman, but in its utmost reaches, it is clearly seen in
> heaven and on earth."
>
> **The Doctrine of the Mean Chapter 12**
> quoted in A Source Book in Chinese Philosophy, 1963.

ality must take the following into consideration: the self as creative transformation; the community as a necessary vehicle for
human flourishing; nature as the proper home for our form of
life; and Heaven as the source of ultimate self-realization.

Self as Creative Transformation

Confucius made it explicit that learning is for the sake of the self
rather than for the sake of others. On the surface, this seems to
imply a sense of individuality fundamentally different from the
conventional view of the primacy of the group in Confucian
ethics. However, the Confucian insistence on learning for the
sake of the self is predicated on the conviction that self-
cultivation is an end in itself rather than a means to an end.
Those who are committed to the cultivation of their personal
life for its own sake can create inner resources for self-realization unimaginable to those who view self-cultivation merely as
a tool for external goals such as social advancement and political success. Although we are obligated to assume social respon-

sibility and participate in political affairs, it is self-cultivation, as the root, securely grounding us in our lifeworld that enables us to participate in society and politics as independent moral agents rather than pawns in a game of power relationships. If we do not take self-realization seriously, we may easily allow ourselves to be defined by power and wealth totally external to our inner resources and our personal sense of worth.

For the Confucians, a personal sense of worth is vitally important, because their commitment to improving the world from within compels them to take the status quo as the point of departure for their spiritual journey. If they do not subscribe to the thesis that learning is primarily for self-improvement, the demand for social service will undermine the integrity of self-cultivation as a noble end in itself. Therefore, learning as character-building is for the sake of self-realization. The self so conceived is an open system involved in continuous transformation; it is never a static structure. The idea of the self as a discrete entity, isolated from the world, is diametrically opposed to the Confucian self as an open, dynamic, and transformative process.

The Confucian self, rooted in personal worth, seeks to generate its inner resources for self-transformation. Self-transformation, the result of self-cultivation, signifies a process of self-realization. However, since the idea of selfhood devoid of communication with the outside world is alien to the Confucian tradition, Confucian self-transformation does not take the form of searching exclusively for one's own inner spirituality. Rather, in the Confucian perspective, authentic self-transformation involves tapping spiritual resources from the cumulative symbolic tradition (culture), the sympathetic resonance of society, the vital energy of nature, and the creative power of Heaven.

Community as a Necessary Vehicle for Human Flourishing

A distinctive feature of the Confucian spiritual orientation is the view that the human community is an integral part of our quest for self-realization. The idea of cutting loose from our primordial ties—ethnicity, gender, language, land, and other intractable realities of life—as a precondition for our salvation is not even a rejected possibility in the Confucian tradition. Confucians are profoundly aware that we are embedded in this world and that our spiritual journey must begin at home here and now. Although the sense of embeddedness may impose a structural limitation on the range of possibility we can realistically envision in our spiritual self-transformation, it does not inhibit us from shaping the form of life most appropriate to our human condition. The Confucian proposal that we begin our spiritual journey at home is based on the strong belief that our self, far from being an isolated individuality, is experientially and practically a center of relationships. As a center of relationships, it constantly enters into communication with a variety of human beings. The significance of the other for our self-cultivation is evident, because we rarely cultivate ourselves in isolation. It is through constant human interaction that we gradually learn to appreciate our selfhood as a transformative process. Indeed, our feelings, thoughts, and ideas are not necessarily our private properties. While they are intensely personal, they need not be private; they are often better thought of as shareable public goods. The willingness to share empowers us to generate a dynamic process of interchange, first with members of our family and, then, with our neighborhood community, and beyond.

This broadening process is central to the Confucian project of self-cultivation. As the opening statement of the Confucian classic, the *Great Learning*, states:

> The ancients who wished to illuminate "brilliant virtue" all under Heaven first governed their states. Wishing to govern their states, they first regulated their families. Wishing to regulate their families, they first cultivated their personal lives. Wishing to cultivate their personal lives, they first rectified their hearts and minds. Wishing to rectify their hearts and minds, they first authenticated their intentions. Wishing to authenticate their intentions, they first refined their knowledge. The refinement of knowledge lay in the study of things. For only when things are studied is knowledge refined; only when knowledge is refined are intentions authentic; only when intentions are authentic are hearts and minds rectified; only when hearts and minds are rectified are personal lives cultivated; only when personal lives are cultivated are families regulated; only when families are regulated are states governed; only when states are governed is there peace all under

Heaven. Therefore, from the Son of Heaven to the common people, all, without exception, must take self-cultivation as the root.

This statement suggests not only a broadening but also a deepening process. The way that the community is "embodied" in our self-transformation implies a continuous interplay between an inclusive process and a penetrating awareness. The assumption is that the more we broaden ourselves to involve others, the more we are capable of deepening our self-awareness; our persistence in deepening our self-awareness is the basis for our fruitful interaction with an ever-expanding network of human-relatedness.

Nature as Home

The Confucian ideal of human flourishing is, strictly speaking, not anthropological and is certainly not anthropocentric. Men, or rather human beings, are not the measure of all things. Such an idea strikes the Confucians as parochial. The proper measure for humanity is cosmological as well as anthropological; indeed it is "anthropocosmic." In the order of things, nature provides not only sustenance for life but also an inspiration for sustainable life. Implicit in the course of nature—the alternations of day and night and the changes of the four seasons—is a lesson in the enduring pattern of transformation: regularity, balance, and harmony.

Human civilization through time has endured natural calamities such as floods and hurricanes, but, despite the hardships of survival, the Confucians find nature a hospitable environment for our existence. They feel fortunate to have been blessed with "Heaven's timeliness and Earth's efficaciousness" and with the "wind and water," essentially wholesome for good health. Nature is revered for its generosity and its grandeur. Its awe-inspiring presence enables us to appreciate the fecundity and sanctity of our "home":

The sky before us is only this bright, shining mass; but when viewed in its unlimited extent, the sun, moon, stars, and constellations are suspended in it and all things are covered by it. The earth before us is but a handful of soil; but in its breadth and

depth, it sustains mountains like Hua and Yüeh without feeling
their weight, contains the rivers and seas without letting them
leak away, and sustains all things. The mountain before us is but
a fistful of straw; but in all the vastness of its size, grass and trees
grow upon it, birds and beasts dwell on it, and stores of precious
things [minerals] are discovered in it. The water before us is but
a spoonful of liquid, but in all its unfathomable depth, the mon-
sters, dragons, fishes, and turtles are produced in them, and
wealth becomes abundant because of it.

This sense of nature as home empowers the Confucians to
find ultimate meaning in ordinary human existence, to cultivate
a regularized, balanced, and harmonious life-style, and to regard what many other religions refer to as "secular" as "sacred."

Heaven as the Source of Ultimate Self-Transformation

Although radical transcendence, such as conceptualizing God
as the "wholly other," is absent in Confucian symbolism,
Heaven as a source for moral creativity, meaning of life, and ultimate self-transformation features prominently throughout
the Confucian tradition. In this sense, all major Confucian
thinkers are profoundly religious. Their ways of being religious are significantly different from those in organized religions such as Christianity, Buddhism, or Islam, but their reverence for life, commitment to work, and dedication to ultimate
self-transformation are based on a calling comparable in intensity of feeling and seriousness of purpose to any of the great
world religions.

The Confucian calling presupposes that Heaven is omniscient and omnipresent, if not omnipotent. What we do here
and now as human beings has implications for ourselves, for
our human community, for nature, and for Heaven. We need
not appropriate the Way of Heaven by departing from where
we are here and now, but since the Way of Heaven is right here,
near at hand, and inseparable from our ordinary daily existence, what we do in the confines of our home is not only an-
thropologically but also cosmologically significant. If we properly nurture our human way, we will never be estranged from

the Way of Heaven. Indeed, as we learn to appreciate the richness of ordinary daily existence, we understand that the great mystery of life is inherent in our common experience of living, as if the secret code of the Way of Heaven is embedded in the human way.

However, our internal organic connectedness with the transcendent through our own personal experience makes us aware of our inadequacy as well as strength because we are charged with the awesome responsibility of realizing Heaven's Way through our humble human endeavors. The deepest meaning of humanity lies in its authentic manifestation as the guardian of nature and the cocreator of the cosmos:

> Only those who are absolutely sincere can fully develop their nature. If they can fully develop their nature, they can fully develop the nature of others. If they can fully develop the nature of others, they can then fully develop the nature of things. If they can fully develop the nature of things, they can then assist in the transforming and nourishing process of Heaven and Earth. If they can assist in the transforming and nourishing process of Heaven and Earth, they can thus form a trinity with Heaven and Earth.

It is humanly possible to assist in the transforming and nourishing process of Heaven and Earth; it is authentically human to form a trinity with Heaven and Earth; and it is our categorical imperative to respond to Heaven's calling to serve as the guardian of nature and the cocreator of the cosmos.

VIEWPOINT

8

The Sacred Is in All Things

JOHN (FIRE) LAME DEER, INTERVIEWED BY RICHARD ERDOES

In this book, Richard Erdoes recorded the words of the Sioux holy man Lame Deer, who was also called John Fire Lame Deer, who spoke about his life and his people, as well as about his religious beliefs. He explained how everything is holy to the Sioux people, because everything is "wakan" or sacred. The Great Spirit, "Wakan Tanka," is in numbers, names, stones, plants, animals, people, and the gods. Although these are individual spirits, they are also all the same spirit; Lame Deer compares this idea to the Christian notion of the Trinity. Almost anything can be sacred and be a symbol of the Great Spirit. This attitude has led the Sioux to recognize the sacrality of nature in a way that many Westerners have come to admire.

QUESTIONS

1. How can even a pot of stew symbolize the sacred, according to Lame Deer?

Excerpted from John (Fire) Lame Deer and Richard Erdoes, *Lame Deer: Seeker of Visions.* Copyright ©1972 by John (Fire) Lame Deer and Richard Erdoes. Reprinted by permission of Simon & Schuster, Inc.

2. Why is the number *four* a symbol of the sacred, in Lame Deer's understanding? What are some of the important "fours" in Sioux religion?
3. How does Lame Deer contrast the Sioux attitude toward symbols with the white man's attitude toward symbols?

■ ■ ■

What do you see here, my friend? Just an ordinary old cooking pot, black with soot and full of dents.

It is standing on the fire on top of that old wood stove, and the water bubbles and moves the lid as the white steam rises to the ceiling. Inside the pot is boiling water, chunks of meat with bone and fat, plenty of potatoes.

It doesn't seem to have a message, that old pot, and I guess you don't give it a thought. Except the soup smells good and reminds you that you are hungry. Maybe you are worried that this is dog stew. Well, don't worry. It's just beef—no fat puppy for a special ceremony. It's just an ordinary, everyday meal.

But I'm an Indian. I think about ordinary, common things like this pot. The bubbling water comes from the rain cloud. It represents the sky. The fire comes from the sun which warms us all—men, animals, trees. The meat stands for the four-legged creatures, our animal brothers, who gave of themselves so that we should live. The steam is living breath. It was water; now it goes up to the sky, becomes a cloud again. These things are sacred. Looking at that pot full of good soup, I am thinking how, in this simple manner, Wakan Tanka takes care of me. We Sioux spend a lot of time thinking about everyday things, which in our mind are mixed up with the spiritual. We see in the world around us many symbols that teach us the meaning of life. We have a saying that the white man sees so little, he must see with only one eye. We see a lot that you no longer notice. You could notice if you wanted to, but you are usually too busy. We Indians live in a world of symbols and images where the spiritual and the commonplace are one. To you symbols are just words, spoken or written in a book. To us they are part of nature, part of ourselves—the earth, the sun, the wind and the rain, stones, trees, animals, even little insects like ants and grasshoppers. We try to understand them not with the head but with the heart, and we need no more than a hint to give us the meaning.

What to you seems commonplace to us appears wondrous through symbolism. This is funny, because we don't even have a word for symbolism, yet we are all wrapped up in it. You have the word, but that is all. . . .

Every day in my life I see symbols in the shape of certain roots or branches. I read messages in the stones. I pay special attention to them, because I am a Yuwipi man and that is my work. But I am not the only one. Many Indians do this.

Inyan—the rocks—are holy. Every man needs a stone to help him. There are two kinds of pebbles that make good medicine. One is white like ice. The other is like ordinary stone, but it makes you pick it up and recognize it by its special shape. You ask stones for aid to find things which are lost or missing. Stones can give warning of an enemy, of approaching misfortune. The winds are symbolized by a raven and a small black stone the size of an egg. . . .

A stone fits right into our world of symbols. It is round and endless. Its power is endless too. All round things are kin to each other, like *wagmuha*—the gourd, the holy rattle—which has 405 little stones inside it, pebbles collected from anthills.

Nothing is so small and unimportant but it has a spirit

I WILL FIRST MAKE AN offering and send a voice to the Spirit of the World, that it may help me to be true. See, I fill this sacred pipe with the bark of the red willow; but before we smoke it, you must see how it is made and what it means. These four ribbons hanging here on the stem are the four quarters of the universe. The black one is for the west where the thunder beings live to send us rain; the white one for the north, whence comes the great white cleansing wind; the red one for the east, whence springs the light and where the morning star lives to give men wisdom; the yellow for the south, whence come the summer and the power to grow.

But these four spirits are only one Spirit after all, and this eagle feather here is for that One, which is like a father, and also it is for the thoughts of men that should rise high as eagles do. Is not the sky a father and the earth a mother, and are not all living things with feet or wings or roots their children?

From *Black Elk Speaks*, 1972.

given to it by Waken Tanka. Tunkan is what you might call a stone god, but he is also part of the Great Spirit. The gods are separate beings, but they are all united in Waken Tanka. It is hard to understand—something like the Holy Trinity. You can't explain it except by going back to the "circles within circles" idea, the spirit splitting itself up into stones, trees, tiny insects even, making them all *wakan* by his ever-presence. And in turn all these myriad of things which makes up the universe flowing back to their source, united in the one Grandfather Spirit.

Tunkan—the stone god—is the oldest spirit, we think, because he is the hardest. He stands for creation, you know, like the male part. Hard, upright, piercing—like the lance and arrowheads fashioned from it in the old days.

Inyan Wasicun Waken—the Holy White Stone Man—that's what we call Moses. He appeals to us. He goes up all alone to the top of his mountain like an Indian, to have his vision, be all alone with his God, who talks to him through fire, bushes and rocks. Moses, coming back from the hill carrying stone tablets with things scratched on them—he would have made a good Indian medicine man.

Tunkan, the stone spirit; Wakinyan, the thunder spirit; Takuskanska, the moving spirit; Unktehi, the water spirit—they are all *wakan*: mysterious, wonderful, incomprehensible, holy. They are all part of the Great Mystery. These are our four great supernaturals, which brings us to yet another form of symbolism—the magic of numbers which we share with many other peoples.

Four is the number that is most *wakan*, most sacred. Four stands for Tatuye Topa—the four quarters of the earth. One of its chief symbols is Umane. . . . It represents the unused earth force. By this I mean that the Great Spirit pours a great, unimaginable amount of force into all things—pebbles, ants, leaves, whirlwinds—whatever you will. Still there is so much force left over that's not used up, that is in his gift to bestow, that has to be used wisely and in moderation if we are given some of it.

This force is symbolized by the Umane. In the old days men used to have an Umane altar made of raised earth in their tipis on certain special occasions. It was so *wakan* you couldn't touch it or even hold your hand over it.

Even today we still set up altars—mounds of earth decorated with tobacco ties and flags—for our Yuwipi ceremonies.

Four, the sacred number, also stands for the four winds, whose symbol is the cross.

The Great Mystery Medicine Bag contained four times four things. Unktehi, the water spirit, created the earth and the human beings in it. Everything has its beginning in the water. Unktehi gave us this Bag of Mysteries. In it the down of the swan stood for all the fowls, a tuft of buffalo hair symbolized the four-legged animals, grass stood for all the herbs, bark and roots for the trees. The bundle contained four kinds of skins from the birds, four kinds of fur from the animals, four kinds of plants, four kinds of rocks and stones.

Four things make the universe: earth, air, water, fire.

We Sioux speak of the four virtues a man should possess: bravery, generosity, endurance, wisdom. For a woman these are bravery, generosity, truthfulness and the bearing of children.

We Sioux do everything by fours: We take four puffs when we smoke the peace pipe. Those of us who believe in the Native American Church take four times four spoons of peyote during a night of prayer. We pour water four times over the hot rocks in the sweat lodge. For four nights we seek a vision during a *hanblechia*. Men abstain for four days and nights from the company of women before an important ceremony. The women in their turn stay away from the men's camp for four days when they are *isnati*—menstruating—or after giving birth. . . .

Words, too, are symbols and convey great powers, especially names. Not Charles, Dick and George. There's not much power in those. But Red Cloud, Black Elk, Whirlwind, Two Moons, Lame Deer—these names have a relationship to the Great Spirit. Each Indian name has a story behind it, a vision, a quest for dreams. We receive great gifts from the source of a name; it links us to nature, to the animal nations. It gives power. You can lean on a name, get strength from it. It is a special name for you and you alone—not a Dick, George, Charles kind of thing. . . .

To a white man symbols are just that: pleasant things to speculate about, to toy with in your mind. To us they are much, much more. Life to us is a symbol to be lived. Here you see me spread some red earth on the floor. I flatten it with my palm and smoothen it with an eagle feather. Now I make a circle in it with my finger, a circle that has no end. The figure of a man is part of this circle. It is me. It is also a spirit. Out of its head come four horns. They stand for the four winds. They are forked at the end, split into a good and a bad part. This bad part of the fork could be used to kill somebody. If you look again at that circle without end you can see that it also forms a half moon. With my thumb I make twenty-four marks around the circle. This represents the twenty-four new medicine men who I was told I would have to ordain. Eighteen I have ordained already. A wise old woman once told me that I would die after I had ordained the last one. So you can see that I am in no hurry to do this. Study my earth picture well. It is a spiritual design a man has to think about.

The twenty-four marks also represent the four directions of the universe, four dots each for the north, the east, the west, the south, the sky above and the earth below. I point my peace pipe toward all these directions. Now we are one with the universe, with all the living things, a link in the circle which has no end. It means we were here long before the first white man came, we are here now, we will still be here at the end of time—Indian Time. We will live! Now let us smoke. *He-hetchetu* [It is certainly true].

How Can One Find Meaning in Life?

Chapter Preface

All religions promote a particular method of defining and adhering to a meaningful life, the way one ought to think and live in order to find purpose and satisfaction. Each religion explores the idea that in the face of insurmountable problems like death, suffering, and human evil, individuals must still lead a fulfilling life. The selections in this chapter explore this topic from the perspectives of eight religious traditions. Each religion explores the meaning of life through various topics—obedience to divine law, faith in a redeemer, an experience of enlightenment or spiritual unity—and the many methods used to pursue these ideals. While readers will find much diversity in the views presented, they will also find similarities.

Meaning Is Found in Following God's Commandments Given in Torah

JOSEPH SOLOVEITCHIK

Rabbi Joseph Soloveitchik is probably the greatest twentieth-century exponent of traditional Jewish orthodoxy based in the observance of God's commandments to Israel revealed in the first five books of the Bible (the Torah). In the Orthodox view, to follow these commandments—to live a life of "Halakhah"—is to honor and praise God in all aspects of one's life. It is also, as Soloveitchik argues, a way of "sanctifying" or making holy our lives on this earth. Salvation does not consist of escape from the world, but redemption of the world by making it a holy place. It is in this sense that he contrasts "halakhic man" with the usual type of "religious man" (*homo religiosus*): whereas the latter seeks God, in Judaism, it is God who seeks out humans and the world to redeem them. The way to this redemption, Soloveitchik contends, is found in the complex way of life prescribed by

Excerpted from Joseph Soloveitchik, *Halakhic Man*, translated by Lawrence Kaplan. Philadelphia: Jewish Publication Society of America, 1983. Reprinted with permission.

Halakhah which determines times and rules governing worship, eating, sexual activity, and every other aspect of our everyday lives. Halakhah offers an ideal world which exists apart from or prior to (a priori) the world of our experiences, and so sets a standard much like a mathematical ideal. Although it may never exist in "reality," it is a beautiful construct with which the Jew seeks to harmonize his life and the life of the cosmos.

QUESTIONS

1. What are some of the ways in which "Halakhic man" differs from *homo religiosus*, in Soloveitchik's estimation?
2. What are some of the aspects of life with which Halakhah is concerned?
3. How does Soloveitchik describe the relation between this world and Halakhah, for example, on the Day of Atonement?

■ ■ ■

Halakhic man differs in his world view from the universal *homo religiosus*. He resembles in various ways cognitive man, yet, he differs in many respects from him as well.

Halakhic man's approach to reality is, at the outset, devoid of any element of transcendence. Indeed, his entire attitude to the world stands out by virtue of its originality and uniqueness. All of the frames of reference constructed by the philosophers and psychologists of religion for explaining the varieties of religious experience cannot accommodate halakhic man as far as his reaction to empirical reality is concerned. Halakhic man studies reality not because he is motivated by plain curiosity the way theoretical man is; nor is he driven to explore the world by any fear of being or anxiety of nonbeing. Nor, for that matter, does halakhic man orient himself to the world in terms of a nebulous feeling of absolute dependence, or yearnings for the redemption of man, or visions of a great, revealed ethical ideal. Halakhic man orients himself to reality through a priori images of the world which he bears in the deep recesses of his personality. . . .

In order to overcome the mystery in existence, he constructs an ideal, ordered, and fixed world, one that is perfectly clear and lucid; he fashions an a priori, ideal creation with which he is greatly pleased. This creation does not cause him any anxiety. It does not attempt to elude him; it can not conceal itself from him. He knows it full well and delights in the knowledge. Whenever he wishes to orient himself to reality and to superimpose his a priori ideal system upon the realm of concrete empirical existence, he comes with his teaching in hand—his a priori teaching. He has no wish to passively cognize reality as it is in itself. Rather, first he creates the ideal a priori image, the ideal structure, and then compares it with the real world. His approach to reality consists solely in establishing the correspondence in effect between his ideal, a priori creation and concrete reality. More, even when the theoretician with his a priori system gets involved in the technological, utilitarian aspects of science, there, too, his sole aim is to reveal the parallelism that prevails between the ideal series and the concrete series. And having achieved this aim he has fulfilled his task. For he is concerned not with the concrete, qualitative phenomena themselves but only with the relationship that prevails between them and his a priori, ideal constructs.

This latter approach is that of mathematics and the mathematical, natural sciences, the crowning achievement of civilization. It is both a priori and ideal—i.e., to know means to construct an ideal, lawful, unified system whose necessity flows from its very nature, a system that does not require, as far as its validity and truth are concerned, precise parallelism with the correlative realm of concrete, qualitative phenomena. On the contrary, all that we have is an approximate accord. The concrete empirical triangle is not exactly identical with the ideal triangle of geometry, and the same holds true for all other mathematical constructs. There exists an ideal world and a concrete one, and between the two only an approximate parallelism prevails. In truth, not only from a theoretical, ideal perspective does mathematics pay no attention to concrete correlatives, but even from a utilitarian standpoint the mathematical approach has no desire to apprehend the concrete world per se but seeks only to establish a relationship of parallelism and analogy.

When halakhic man approaches reality, he comes with his Torah, given to him from Sinai, in hand. He orients himself to the world by means of fixed statutes and firm principles. An en-

> **SEE, I HAVE SET BEFORE** you today life and prosperity, death and adversity. If you obey the commandments of the LORD your God that I am commanding you today, by loving the LORD your God, walking in his ways, and observing his commandments, decrees, and ordinances, then you shall live and become numerous, and the LORD your God will bless you in the land that you are entering to possess. But if your heart turns away and you do not hear, but are led astray to bow down to other gods and serve them, I declare to you today that you shall perish; you shall not live long in the land that you are crossing the Jordan to enter and possess. I call heaven and earth to witness against you today that I have set before you life and death, blessings and curses. Choose life so that you and your descendants may live, loving the LORD your God, obeying him, and holding fast to him; for that means life to you and length of days, so that you may live in the land that the LORD swore to give to your ancestors, to Abraham, to Isaac, and to Jacob.
>
> **Deuteronomy 30:15-20**

tire corpus of precepts and laws guides him along the path leading to existence. Halakhic man, well furnished with rules, judgments, and fundamental principles, draws near the world with an a priori relation. His approach begins with an ideal creation and concludes with a real one. To whom may he be compared? To a mathematician who fashions an ideal world and then uses it for the purpose of establishing a relationship between it and the real world, as was explained above. The essence of the Halakhah, which was received from God, consists in creating an ideal world and cognizing the relationship between that ideal world and our concrete environment in all its visible manifestations and underlying structures. There is no phenomenon, entity, or object in this concrete world which the a priori Halakhah does not approach with its ideal standard. . . .

When halakhic man looks to the western horizon and sees the fading rays of the setting sun or to the eastern horizon and sees the first light of dawn and the glowing rays of the rising sun, he knows that this sunset or sunrise imposes upon him anew obligations and commandments. Dawn and sunrise obligate him to fulfill those commandments that are performed during the day: the recitation of the morning *Shema*, *tzitzit*, *tefillin*, the morning prayer, *etrog*, *shofar*, *Hallel*, and the like. They make the time fit for the carrying out of certain halakhic practices: Temple service, acceptance of testimony, conversion, *halitzah*, etc., etc. Sunset imposes upon him those obligations and commandments that are performed during the night: the recitation of the evening *Shema*, *matzah*, the counting of the *omer*, etc. The sunset on Sabbath and holiday eves sanctifies the day: the profane and the holy are dependent upon a natural cosmic phenomenon—the sun sinking below the horizon. It is not anything transcendent that creates holiness but rather the visible reality—the regular cycle of the natural order. Halakhic man examines the sunrise and sunset, the dawn and the appearance of the stars; he gazes into the horizon—Is the upper horizon pale and the same as the lower?—and looks at the sun's shadows—Has afternoon already arrived? When he goes out on a clear, moonlit night (until the deficiency of the moon is replenished) he makes a blessing upon it. He knows that it is the moon that determines the times of the months and thus of all the Jewish seasons and festivals, and this determination must rely upon astronomical calculations. . . .

Halakhic man explores every nook and cranny of physical-biological existence. He determines the character of all of the animal functions of man—eating, sex, and all the bodily necessities—by means of halakhic principles and standards: the bulk of an olive (*ke-zayit*), the bulk of a date (*ke-kotevet*), the time required to eat a half-loaf meal (*kedai akhilat peras*), the time required to drink a quarter log (*revi'it*), eating in a normal or nonnormal manner, the beginning of intercourse, the conclusion of intercourse, normal intercourse and unnatural intercourse, etc., etc. Halakhah concerns itself with the normal as well as abnormal functioning of the organism, with the total biological functioning of the organism: the laws of menstruation, the man or woman suffering from a discharge, the mode of determining the onset of menstruation, virginal blood, pregnancy, the various stages in the birth process, the various physical signs that make animals or birds fit or unfit for consumption, etc., etc.

There is no real phenomenon to which halakhic man does not possess a fixed relationship from the outset and a clear, definitive, a priori orientation. He is interested in sociological creations: the state, society, and the relationship of individuals within a communal context. The Halakhah encompasses laws of business, torts, neighbors, plaintiff and defendant, creditor and debtor, partners, agents, workers, artisans, bailees, etc. Family life—marriage, divorce, *halitzah*, *sotah*, conjugal refusal (*mi'un*), the respective rights, obligations, and duties of a husband and a wife—is clarified and elucidated by it. War, the high court, courts and the penalties they impose—all are just a few of the multitude of halakhic subjects. The halakhist is involved with psychological problems—for example, sanity and insanity, the possibility or impossibility of a happy marriage, *miggo* [i.e., the principle that a party's plea gains credibility when a more advantageous plea is available], and assumptions as to the intention behind a specific act (*umdana*), the presumption that a particular individual is a liar or a sinner, the discretion of the judges, etc., etc. "The measure thereof is longer than the earth and broader than the sea" (Job 11:9).

Halakhah has a fixed a priori relationship to the whole of reality in all of its fine and detailed particulars. Halakhic man orients himself to the entire cosmos and tries to understand it by utilizing an ideal world which he bears in his halakhic consciousness. All halakhic concepts are a priori, and it is through them that halakhic man looks at the world. As we said above, his world view is similar to that of the mathematician: a priori and ideal. Both the mathematician and the halakhist gaze at the concrete world from an a priori, ideal standpoint and use a priori categories and concepts which determine from the outset their relationship to the qualitative phenomena they encounter. Both examine empirical reality from the vantage point of an ideal reality. There is one question which they raise: Does this real phenomenon correspond to their ideal construction?

And when many halakhic concepts do not correspond with the phenomena of the real world, halakhic man is not at all distressed. His deepest desire is not the realization of the Halakhah but rather the ideal construction which was given to him from Sinai, and this ideal construction exists forever. . . .

The ideal of halakhic man is the redemption of the world not via a higher world but via the world itself, via the adaptation of empirical reality to the ideal patterns of Halakhah. If a Jew lives in accordance with the Halakhah (and a life in accordance with the Halakhah means, first, the comprehension of the Halakhah per se and, second, comparing the ideal Halakhah and the real world—the act of realization of the Halakhah), then he shall find redemption. A lowly world is elevated through the Halakhah to the level of a divine world.

If a Jew cognizes, for example, the Sabbath laws and the precepts concerning the sanctity of the day in all their particulars, if he comprehends, via a profound study and understanding that penetrates to the very depths, the basic principles of Torah law that take on form and color within the tractate Shabbat, then he will perceive the sunset of a Sabbath eve not only as a natural cosmic phenomenon but as an unsurpassably awe-inspiring, sacred, and exalted vision—an eternal sanctity that is reflected in the setting of the sun. I remember how once, on the Day of Atonement, I went outside into the synagogue courtyard with my father [R. Moses Soloveitchik], just before the *Ne'ilah* service. It had been a fresh, clear day, one of the fine, almost delicate days of summer's end, filled with sunshine and light. Evening was fast approaching, and an exquisite autumn sun was sinking in the west, beyond the trees of the cemetery, into a sea of purple and gold. R. Moses, a halakhic man par excellence, turned to me and said: "This sunset differs from ordinary sunsets for with it forgiveness is bestowed upon us for our sins" (the end of the day atones). The Day of Atonement and the forgiveness of sins merged and blended here with the splendor and beauty of the world and with the hidden lawfulness of the order of creation and the whole was transformed into one living, holy, cosmic phenomenon.

When the righteous sit in the world to come, where there is neither eating nor drinking, with their crowns on their heads, and enjoy the radiance of the divine presence [cf. Berakhot 17a; Maimonides, *Laws of Repentance* 8:2], they occupy themselves with the study of the Torah, which treats of bodily life in our lowly world. "Now they were disputing in the heavenly academy thus: If the bright spot [of the leper] preceded the white hair, he is defiled; if the reverse, he is clean. If [the order is] in doubt, the Holy One, blessed be He, ruled he is clean; while the entire heavenly academy ruled he is defiled." "When Moses ascended on high, he found the Holy One, blessed be He, studying the pericope of [the red] cow and saying: My son Eliezer says: A heifer [whose neck is to be broken must not be more than] a year old, and a [red] cow [neither more nor less than] two years old." The Creator of worlds, revealed and unrevealed, the heavenly hosts, the souls of the righteous all grapple with halakhic problems that are bound up with the empirical world—the red cow, the heifer whose neck is to be broken, leprosy, and similar issues. They do not concern themselves with transcendence, with questions that are above space and time, but with the problems of earthly life in all its details and particulars. And when the sages stated, "The day consists of twelve hours; during the first three hours the Holy One, blessed be He, sits and occupies Himself with the Torah, etc.," they referred to the Torah, which was given to us—the Torah, which deals with civil law, forbidden foods, forbidden sexual relations, marriage and divorce, *hametz* and *matzah*, *shofar*, *lulav*, *sukkah*, and all other similar commandments.

The universal *homo religiosus* proclaims: The lower yearns for the higher. But halakhic man, with his unique mode of understanding, declares: The higher longs and pines for the lower.

Meaning Is Found Through Faith in Christ as the Redeemer

JÜRGEN MOLTMANN

Jürgen Moltmann is a contemporary Protestant theologian who seeks to make Christian thought relevant to the often complex and ambiguous lives people lead today. In particular, he often relates the content of Christian doctrine to a commitment to political responsibility, arguing that faith leads one into the world rather than away from it. In this selection, taken from the third volume of his systematic theology, he deals with the significance of Jesus' death and resurrection and how faith in the redeeming power of those events can transform one's life. He interprets the biblical letters of the apostle Paul, which speak of how we are "justified" by our faith, as meaning that God creates justice for us, overcoming the power of sin and death. In fact, it is not only we who are justified—the justification of God ("theodicy") also occurs when God shows that the divine nature is just and merciful. Saved by this good news ("gospel") of God's forgiveness and grace, we are empowered to fight against injustice wherever it exists.

Excerpted from *The Way of Jesus Christ: Christology in Messianic Dimensions* by Jürgen Moltmann. English translation ©1990 by Margaret Kohl. Reprinted by permission of HarperCollins Publishers, Inc.

QUESTIONS

1. What goals are achieved by the death of Jesus, in Molt-mann's view?
2. What does it mean to be saved by faith rather than "works of the law," according to Moltmann?
3. Why does Moltmann believe that this justifying faith leads Christians to fight injustice?

■ ■ ■

We shall first of all ask quite simply: *why did Christ die? Why did Christ rise again? What future* is hidden in his death and his resurrection, and when will this hidden future be revealed? When we examine the answers which emerge from the experiences of Christian faith, we discover that the question 'why?' is a difficult one. It relativizes all the answers supplied by experience and perception, moving them into the eschatologically open dimension. To think eschatologically means thinking something through to the end. But what is the end of the history of Christ's suffering and his resurrection? The answers offered are these:

1. *Christ 'was put to death for our trespasses and raised for our justification'* (Rom. 4.25). The meaning and purpose of his suffering is our liberation from the power of sin and the burden of our guilt. The meaning and purpose of his resurrection from the dead is our free life in the righteousness of God. Forgiveness of sins and new life in the righteousness of God: this is the experience of faith. And in this experience Christ is there 'for us'. But for what are people justified? What is the meaning of justifying faith?

We come to the next answer to the question about the meaning of the history of Christ.

2. *'Christ died and lived again, that he might be Lord both of the dead and of the living'* (Rom. 14.9). If justifying faith is the purpose of the history of Christ which is proclaimed and experienced first of all, then the meaning of justifying faith is the redeeming lordship of Christ over the dead and the living. In community with him, those who are separated by death again find their community with one another. The dead Christ became the brother of the dead. The risen Christ gathers the liv-

170

ing and the dead into his community of love because this is community in a common hope. He is head of the new humanity, and the future of those who belong to the present *and* those who belong to the past.

3. *'For Christ must reign until he has put all his enemies under his feet. The last enemy to be destroyed is death ... so that God may be all in all'* (I Cor. 15.25f., 28). The fellowship of Christ with the dead and the living is not a goal in itself. It is a fellowship on the way to the raising of all the dead to eternal life, and to the annihilation of death in the new creation of all things. Only then will 'all tears be wiped away' and perfect joy unite all created beings with God and with one another. So if the meaning of justifying faith is community with Christ, then the meaning of the community in Christ of the dead and the living is the new creation in which death will be no more.

4. *'Therefore God has highly exalted him and bestowed on him the name which is above every name . . . that every tongue should confess that Jesus Christ is Lord, to the glory of God the Father'* (Phil. 2.9, 11). Even the universal salvation of the new creation is not yet in itself the goal but serves the justification of God—that is, the glorifying of God, the Father of Jesus Christ. All created beings find their bliss in participation in his glory. But God only arrives at his rest in the sabbath of his new creation. Only then will the theodicy trial—which is also a theodicy process—be finished. Only then will all created beings be able to say: 'True and just, Lord, are all thy judgments' (Rev. 16.7). The final goal of the history of Christ therefore lies in the healing of all created beings for the glory of God the Father. The goal is soteriological, yet it is at the same time doxological through and through. The bliss of the new creation finds expression in the eternal song of praise.

All these horizons of purpose and meaning emerge from the history of Christ. The first goal is justifying faith. The second goal is lordship over the dead and the living. The third goal is the conquest of death, and new creation. The fourth goal is the glorification of God through a redeemed world. The immediate goal is the justification of human beings, but the supervening goal is the justification of God, while the common goal is to be found in the reciprocal justification of God and human beings, and in their shared life in justice and righteousness. Righteousness creates lasting peace. Justification is not a unique event, pin-pointed to a certain moment in time. It is a process which begins in the individual heart through faith, and leads to the just new world. This process begins with the forgiveness of sins and ends with the wiping away of all tears. Here Luther's question about the gracious God is answered, and Job's question about God's justice is kept open until it finds its reply. With God's raising of the Christ murdered on the cross, a universal theodicy trial* begins which can only be completed eschatologically with the resurrection of all the dead and the annihilation of death's power—which is to say through the new creation of all things. Then the pain of the theodicy question will be transformed into the universal cosmic doxology. Because this is the ultimate goal, this doxology is already anticipated here and now in faith and in fellowship, in consolation and in hope. It is anticipated as a 'song of the Lord in a strange land'.

Justifying Faith

The true perception of Christ necessarily leads the perceiving person to justifying faith. It cannot remain purely theoretical knowledge (*notitia*), but leads on, beyond that, to existential involvement (*fiducia*). Only justifying faith corresponds to the Christ crucified 'for us', for it is only through justifying faith that the liberating power of Christ's resurrection is experienced. That is why christology and the doctrine of justification are inextricably bound up with one another theologically. This was the insight of the Reformers, and in arriving at it they were going back to Paul himself.

Paul developed his christology in the conflict between the law of God and the gospel of Christ, with the help of the idea of dialectical conversion. Here he of course understood the law as the power in whose name he himself had persecuted the Christians. Christ died the accursed death on the cross, con-

---

* The German word *Prozess* means both trial (in the legal sense) and process, and this double aspect should be borne in mind. The theodicy *trial* is still open as an on-going *process*, and will be completed only when all the tears are wiped away.

demned in the name of God's law. If he has been raised by God and 'justified', then he redeems from the curse of the law those who are his (Gal. 3.13). If Christ met his earthly end through the law, then the law ends eschatologically through his resurrection. If the crucified Christ was counted among the sinners and 'made sin', then the risen Christ liberates from the power of sin. That is why the gospel in which the crucified Christ is present by virtue of his resurrection becomes the power of God for the salvation of everyone who believes. It brings the new justifying divine righteousness 'without the works of the law'. The gospel of Christ fulfils and surmounts in itself the divine Torah, ushering in the messianic era for Jews and Gentiles. 'The just shall live' was the promise of the Torah. But the law itself was the condition of this justice and righteousness. 'He who through faith is righteous shall live' (Rom. 1.17) is the assurance of the gospel of Christ. The power of the life-giving Spirit of God is now immanent in the gospel of Christ's resurrection. Consequently, this gospel now mediates the Spirit of the resurrection and of the new creation of all things, anticipating in believers the victory of life over death by liberating them from the power of sin. God is just because he makes the unjust just and creates justice for those who suffer under injustice.

> **BUT NOW, APART FROM LAW,** the righteousness of God has been disclosed, and is attested by the law and the prophets, the righteousness of God through faith in Jesus Christ for all who believe. For there is no distinction, since all have sinned and fall short of the glory of God; they are now justified by his grace as a gift, through the redemption that is in Christ Jesus, whom God put forward as a sacrifice of atonement by his blood, effective through faith. He did this to show his righteousness, because in his divine forbearance he had passed over the sins previously committed; it was to prove at the present time that he himself is righteous and that he justifies the one who has faith in Jesus.
>
> Then what becomes of boasting? It is excluded. By what law? By that of works? No, but by the law of faith. For we hold that a person is justified by faith apart from works prescribed by the law.
>
> **Romans 3:21-28**

Paul understood the righteousness of God as God's creative acts in and for those who are threatened by absolute death because they have come under 'the power of sin', which is contrary to God. We understand by 'sin' the condition in which a person closes himself off from the source of life, from God. A closing of the self like this comes about when the purposes for which human beings are by nature destined are not discovered or not fulfilled, because of hybris, or depression, or 'the God complex', or because of a refusal to accept what human existence is about. This leads to the self-destruction of the regenerating energies of life, and thus to death. The self-deification of human beings is the beginning of their self-destruction, and the destruction also of the world in which they live. This death has to be understood as absolute death, because it is not identical with the natural life process. 'Sin' in this sense means missing the mark of being, and has to be used in the singular. It is a happening in the created being as a whole, and it precedes morality, although it is the source of the acts and kinds of behaviour which in a moral sense can be recognized as infringing the laws of life—that is, sins in the plural. Because every created being belongs to a social context shared with other beings, 'sin' always destroys life in the social sense too. We talk about the trans-personal 'power of sin' because sin involves the inescapable structural processes of destruction over which Paul cries out when he acknowledges for himself personally: 'I do not do the good I want, but the evil I do not want is what I do' (Rom. 7.19). Today everyone can see these processes at work in the developments for which he shares responsibility and at the same time helplessly deplores. Ordered systems which once ministered to life are toppling over into their very opposite, so that they now work for death.

The gospel has its own time. Its kairos is 'this present time' in which 'the wrath of God', as Paul puts it, 'is revealed . . . against all ungodliness and wickedness of men' (Rom. 1.18). People are becoming beset by this end-time tribulation because universal death is descending on their godless injustice—since injustice has this death as its inescapable consequence. Time is running out. The end of time is approaching. Against the apocalyptic horizon where men and women sink into the nothingness which they are preparing for themselves and nature, the gospel of Christ brings the saving power of God into the world. It saves because it justifies. It is the power of rebirth from the life-giving Spirit and the beginning of the new creation. Here we may think too of the apocalyptic tribulation of all creation in 'the sufferings of this present time' (Rom. 8.18). Through *the forgiveness of sins* the gospel breaks through the compulsive acts of sinners which are the enemies of life, cutting sinners loose from sin, and creating the possibility of 'conversion', a turn to life. Through *the justification of sinners*, the gospel brings men and women who are closed in upon themselves into the open love of God. Through *rebirth from the Spirit*, it brings people who have been subject to death into touch with the eternal source of life, setting them in the closer framework of the rebirth of human community and against the wider horizon of the rebirth of the cosmos.

The universal meaning of the gospel of Christ for Jews and Gentiles is founded on the character of God's justifying righteousness, which is prevenient and has no preconditions. Because justification has no preconditions but is given only out of grace, there are no longer any privileges for the one, and no longer any disparagement of the other. The gospel of Christ saves and justifies 'sinners', and therefore turns to all human beings in what they are *not* and in what they do *not* have (Rom. 3.23), whatever differences there may be in the things they are and have.

The Lutheran theology of the Reformation period based justifying faith solely on the suffering and death of Christ 'for us'. But this was one-sided. They perceived the *pro nobis* in Christ's cross, but not in his resurrection. They therefore understood the justification of the sinner too narrowly as 'the forgiveness of sins', but not as new life in righteousness. The meaning of Christ's resurrection was reduced to this saving significance of his death on the cross. But according to Paul, Christ was raised 'for our justification' (Rom. 4.25) and so that we might be saved (Rom. 5.10). Christ's resurrection has an added value and a surplus of promise over Christ's death: Christ 'died, yes, was raised from the dead . . .' (Rom. 8.34). This surplus of Christ's resurrection over his death is manifested in the surplus of grace compared with the mere cancellation of sin: 'Where sin increased, grace *abounded all the more*' (Rom. 5.20). If while we were enemies we were 'reconciled' with God through his death, '*how much more* shall we be saved by his life' (Rom. 5.10). So justifying grace is not merely a making-present of the Christ crucified 'for us'; it is even more a making-present of the risen and coming Christ. Faith is Easter jubilation, and the forgiveness of all guilt springs from this joy, as the Orthodox liturgy proclaims: 'The day of resurrection! Let us be light on this feast. And let us embrace one another. Brethren, let us speak to those who hate us. For the resurrection's sake will we forgive one another everything, and so let us cry: Christ is risen from the dead. . . .'

What happened to the dead Christ in his resurrection to eternal life happens to us in a corresponding way in the justification of sinners: 'In illo resurrectio, ita in nobis vera justificatio.' Because the raising of Christ shows this added value and surplus over against his death, the justification of sinners initiates a process of exuberant intensification: justification—sanctification—glorification (Rom. 8.30). Justifying faith is not yet the goal and end of Christ's history. For every individual believer it is no more than the beginning of a way that leads to the new creation of the world and to the justification of God. That is why those who are justified by faith are the people who 'hunger and thirst' for righteousness and justice (Matt. 5.6) and 'are persecuted for righteousness' sake' (Matt. 5.10). It is they who weep over this world which Albert Camus describes as the place 'where children suffer and die'. That is why they wait for the future in which 'all tears will be wiped away' (Isa. 25.8; Rev. 7.17; 21.4). The person whom God has justified protests against the injustice in this world. The person in whose heart God has put peace can no longer come to terms with the discord in the world, but will resist it and hope for 'peace on earth'. Injustice and suffering acquire a meaning only to the degree in which we refuse to accept them. Faith and hope for the righteousness and justice of God are the spur to keep us from surrendering to them, and to make us fight injustice and suffering wherever and however we can.

Meaning Is Found Through Following the Law of Allah

SEYYED HOSSEIN NASR

Seyyed Hossein Nasr is an Iranian Muslim philosopher who taught at Tehran University until 1979 and has since taught Islamic studies in the United States. He has written several books on the relationship between Islam and the modern world in which he argues that Islam should not sacrifice its traditional ideals to accommodate itself to "modernism." In this selection, he points out that Western civilization, with its Christian basis, resists the notion that the Divine Law can be spelled out in any detail. In contrast, the Muslim *Sharī'ah* (Interpretations of the Divine Law) has been developed in considerable detail by the *fuqahā'*, or legal experts. To Muslims, God's Law is based on the *Sunnah* of the prophet Muhammad, comprised of the Quran (revealed to him by God) and the Hadiths (reports of Muhammad's own opinions). A society that is based on the *Sharī'ah*, according to Nasr, is one that has chosen to base itself on God's will rather than on human custom, which is constantly in flux. Muslim society aims to live in accord with "the Divine Norm which alone gives meaning to human life."

Reprinted from *Islamic Life and Thought* by Seyyed Hossein Nasr by permission of the State University of New York Press. Copyright © by George Allen & Unwin (Publishers) Ltd., 1981.

QUESTIONS

1. Why does Nasr believe that interpretation of the Law should not be based on "keeping up with the times"?
2. How did the "false idol" of progress lead to the modern tendency to believe immutability is bad, according to Nasr?
3. How does Muslim Law deal with changing situations, and how does this contrast with the modernist attitude toward change?

■　■　■

It must be made clear that in discussing Muslim personal law, we are dealing with the *Sharī'ah* and not simply man-made laws. Thus, the emphasis is more on religion than on law, as these two terms are used in European languages today. Every discussion of Islamic Law involves the most basic religious beliefs and attitudes of Muslims. This is because in Islam the Divine Will manifests itself concretely as specific law, and not abstractly as more or less general moral injunctions. Christianity teaches that God asks man to be charitable or humble as the teachings of Christ clearly indicate. However, one is not told how in a concrete sense one should apply these virtues, so that the general religious teaching remains on an abstract level unaffected by changes in the concrete laws which govern human society. That is why Europeans, as well as modernised Muslims who are more at home in Western culture than in their own, cannot understand the insistence of traditional Muslims on preserving the letter of the Divine Law.

It could be said quite justifiably that the modern West is not the product of Christianity. Yet even those who oppose Christianity in the modern world cannot eradicate *ad hoc* two thousand years of a heritage which they carry in their souls in spite of themselves. This heritage manifests itself clearly when such a question as Muslim personal law is approached. Here, the attitude of secularists and Christians, and also many modernised Muslims, is the same. All is based on the general attitude taken towards law in Western civilisation derived mostly from the particular nature of Christianity as a 'way of love' without a Divine Law.

What must be taken into account is the profound difference between the Semitic and more particularly Islamic conception of law on the one hand and the modern one on the other. The Semitic conception, shared by Judaism and Islam, sees law as the embodiment of the Divine Will, as a transcendent reality which is eternal and immutable, as a model by which the perfections and shortcomings of human society and the conduct of the individual are judged, as the guide through which man gains salvation and, by rejecting it, courts damnation and destruction. It is like the Law of Manu of Hinduism and the *dharma* which each human being must follow in order to gain felicity. To discuss law in Islam is therefore as essential to the Islamic religion as the discussion of theology is to Christianity. To discuss, much less change, Islamic Law cannot be done by anyone except those competent in the *Sharī'ah*, no more than Christian theology could be discussed and doctrines of the Christian church altered by any other than those vested with authority in such matters. It would be as unthinkable from the Islamic point of view to change Muslim personal law through any simply elected legislative body as it would be to change doctrines of the Christian church through a similar body of laymen. It is only because the similarity of the role of theology in Christianity to the Divine Law in Islam is not understood that the validity of such an analogy is not accepted by so many people today.

Let us now examine how the *Sharī'ah* is related to the world in which we live. To many people, reality is exhausted by the physico-psychological world which surrounds us and what does not conform to this world is considered to be unreal. Islamic doctrine, like all other traditional metaphysics, is based on the belief that reality is comprised of multiple states of existence (*marātib al-wujūd*) of which the physical world is the lowest and furthest removed from the Divine Origin of all reality. Therefore the *Sharī'ah*, being an eternal truth belonging to a higher order of existence, is by no means abrogated if it does not conform to the particular conditions of a certain point in space or moment in time. Rather, it is the world which must conform to the Divine Law. The Law loses nothing if it is not followed by men. Conversely man and his world lose everything by not conforming to the Divine Will of which the *Sharī'ah* is the concrete embodiment.

These days we are often told that we must keep up with

179

the times. Rarely does one ask what have the 'times' to keep up with. For men who have lost the vision of a reality which transcends time, who are caught completely in the mesh of time and space and who have been affected by the historicism prevalent in modern European philosophy, it is difficult to imagine the validity of a truth that does not conform to their immediate external environment. Islam, however, is based on the principle that truth transcends history and time. Divine Law is an objective transcendent reality, by which man and his actions are judged, not vice versa. What are called the 'times' today are to a large extent a set of problems and difficulties created by man's ignorance of his own real nature and his stubborn determination to 'live by bread alone'. To attempt to shape the Divine Law to the 'times' is therefore no less than spiritual suicide because it removes the very criteria by which the real value of human life and action can be objectively judged and thus surrenders man to the most infernal impulses of his lower nature. To say the least, the very manner of approaching the problem of Islamic Law and religion in general by trying to make them conform to the 'times' is to misunderstand the whole perspective and spirit of Islam.

Islam has always considered the positive aspect of the intellect ('aql) and man's ability to reach the cardinal doctrine of Islam, that is to say the doctrine of Unity (tawḥīd), through his 'aql. In fact, the Quran often describes those who have gone astray from religion as those who cannot 'intellect' (lā ya'qilūn). But this is no licence for rationalism and an ad hoc treatment of the Sharī'ah as judged by human reason, because man can reach tawḥīd through his own 'aql only under the condition that this 'aql is in a wholesome state (salīm). And it is precisely the Sharī'ah whose practice removes the obstacles in the soul which prevent the correct functioning of the intellect and obscure its vision. It is the Sharī'ah that guarantees the wholesomeness of the intellect so that to change the Sharī'ah through the judgement of human reason with the excuse that the Quran has ordered man to use his intellectual faculties, is no more than sheer sophistry and a chimerical manner of leading simple souls astray.

We may ask why the question of changing Muslim personal law has been posed at all in so many parts of the Islamic world. Having briefly outlined the nature of Islamic Law, we

> **SERVE GOD, AND JOIN NOT**
> Any partners with Him ;
> And do good—
> To parents, kinsfolk,
> Orphans, those in need,
> Neighbours who are near,
> Neighbours who are strangers,
> The Companion by your side,
> The way-farer (ye meet),
> And what your right hands possess.
>
> **Quran, Surah 4.36**

must now turn to two elements which deserve to be analysed: one the question of change and the other personal law. In traditional Muslim sources, there is no term to denote personal law, because theoretically the *Sharī'ah* covers all human life, both personal and social. If such a term has come into recent usage and has even found its way into contemporary Islamic Law (the adjective *shakhṣiyyah* being usually used for personal), it is because even during the Umayyad period the *Sharī'ah* was in practice not applied fully in certain realms such as that of general taxation. Also, many political dealings of Muslim rulers remained outside its injunctions. That is why the so-called reforms carried out by many Muslim states in their attempt to introduce certain European codes, such as the *Tanẓīmāt* of the Ottomans, did not profoundly affect the structure of Islamic society. What has remained intact through the ages has been that aspect of the *Sharī'ah* which concerns directly the human person, such as marriage, divorce and inheritance. These are thus labelled as personal law. This domain has been the refuge and stronghold that has enabled Islamic society to remain Islamic in spite of the various forms of political institution that have ruled over it in past centuries. Therefore what is under discussion is the last refuge of the legal aspect of the *Sharī'ah* in Islamic society as a whole.

As for the question of change involved in the subject matter of this essay, it lies in that complex set of factors which characterise modernism in general, in the West as well as in the East. First of all, through the spread of belief in that false idol of eighteenth- and nineteenth-century European philosophy, namely progress, many in the East unconsciously equate change with progress. And, since they have surrendered their intelligence to the dictum of historicism, they evaluate all things in the light of change and becoming rather than with regard to their immutable aspect. They thus equate the immutability of the Truth with solidification and petrifaction. Secondly, the structure of Western civilisation, even before modern times, was such as to view law only in its mutable aspect. This trait has been inherited by modernism, which is naturally a product of Western civilisation. . . .

That is the basic reason why Westerners cannot usually understand the meaning of the *Sharī'ah* and Westernised Muslims approach the problems of Islamic Law in the modern world from the point of view so prevalent today.

To this misunderstanding must be added the psychological factors which are the result of centuries of pressure imposed by the West on all Oriental civilisations. In the minds of many Muslims, there is a sense of inferiority *vis-à-vis* the West, which forces them to be its blind followers and to regard their own tradition either with disdain or at best with an attitude of apologetic acceptance. In that state of mind, they usually try to change those aspects of their religion and law which do not conform to today's fashions and which, to cover one's intellectual and spiritual weakness, is called 'keeping up with the times'.

For example, let us take the question of polygamy, which is far from limited to Islam (we remember that Charlemagne had many wives). Many modernised Muslims feel embarrassed by this feature of the *Sharī'ah* for no other reason than that Christianity eventually banned it and that in the West today it is forbidden. The arguments against it are not so much logical as sentimental and carry mainly the weight and prestige of the modern West with them. All the arguments given, based on the fact that polygamy is the only way of preventing many social ills of today, have no effect on those for whom the fashion of the day has replaced the *Sunnah* of the Holy Prophet. . . .

Of course we do not propose that Muslims should remain oblivious of the world around them. This is neither desirable nor possible. No Islamic state can avoid owning trains and planes, but Muslims can avoid hanging surrealistic paintings on their walls. By this is meant that there are certain conditions in twentieth-century life which the Muslim world cannot alter and with which it must live while others can be avoided. The whole difference lies in the attitude towards the modern world. One can regard a situation as one in which it is difficult to practise the *Sharī'ah* fully, not because the *Sharī'ah* itself is imperfect, but because the conditions in which we live have fallen short of those immutable principles which of necessity ultimately govern all things. One can still follow and practise Islamic Law in such conditions by following the teachings of Islam itself, for the Prophet even allowed prayers to be said on horseback in time of war.

Or one can, as is so common today, take the world as the sole reality and judge the validity of the *Sharī'ah* according to its degree of conformity to this world. This attitude is totally un-Islamic and is like putting the cart before the horse. Such an attitude makes the world and man's imperfect judgements informing it take the place of God. Such an attitude commits the sin which theologically is the gravest of all in Islam, namely *shirk* or 'polytheism'.

Islam is a way of peace based on the establishment of equilibrium between all human tendencies and needs, which must of necessity serve as a basis for all man's spiritual strivings. The *Sharī'ah* is the maker and preserver of this equilibrium and the personal laws play a particularly significant role in keeping this human order and equilibrium. Were this equilibrium to be destroyed, both inner and outward peace, which everyone seeks today but rarely finds, would disappear. All 'reforms' and changes—especially in matters of personal law—proposed today should aim to preserve and build rather than destroy this equilibrium whose chief symbol in Islam is the square Ka'bah. The question of changing Islamic personal law should be approached with the spirit of belief in the *Sharī'ah*, thereby attempting to apply and preserve it to the extent possible in the modern world, and to build the life of Muslim society according to it. It should not be approached with a firm belief in all 'values' and norms prevalent in the West today according to which one should seek to change Islamic Law. These practices and 'values' which seem permanent today are as impermanent as the most impermanent aspect of human nature upon which they are based.

If the question of changes in Islamic Law is approached by

the Muslim intelligentsia in the spirit thus proposed, it will be seen in a completely different light. The rift between the Western-educated classes and the rest of the Muslim community will pass and everyone will realise the real significance of the *Sharī'ah* as the basis of stability in human life. They will also learn that, although to concern oneself with matters pertaining to Islam is the duty of every Muslim, applying the *Sharī'ah* in detail to newly created situations is a question of *fiqh* that should be dealt with by the *fuqahā'*. If one understands the real nature of the *Sharī'ah*, one would think no more of passing on a sick person to someone who is not a physician than to turn over matters concerning Muslim personal laws to one who is not a specialist in the *Sharī'ah*, that is to say a *faqīh* or *'ālim* who specialises in *fiqh*. Otherwise, in both cases, the patient, whether he be an individual or a society, faces the danger of a graver malady and even death.

In conclusion, it may be added that the blind following of Western ideas in matters concerned with law, as in so many other domains, will never solve any basic problem of Islamic society. It is a form of *taqlīd* or blind following much more dangerous than the traditional type of *taqlīd* which has always been decried by Muslim sages over the ages. Only by accepting the validity of the *Sharī'ah* and especially of the personal laws promulgated by it and by relying upon these laws can Islamic society face the problems of the modern world. And only through the *Sharī'ah* can meaningful change be brought about. In fact the value of any change can only he gauged *vis-à-vis* a permanent truth. If we were to lose the *Sharī'ah*, we would lose that very thing for whose subsistence we are trying to 'reform' our present society. In such a case, our reformations would only become deformations. Thus we would only let loose forces which would disrupt the very basis of our society and open doors which would enable individual whims and fancies to exert themselves over the Divine Norm which alone gives meaning to human life.

Meaning Is Found Through Realizing Oneness with All Reality

SRI AUROBINDO

Sri Aurobindo (Aurobindo Ghose, 1872-1950) was a mystical Hindu philosopher who believed in a spiritual transformation of humanity as the culmination of a cosmic process of evolution. In common with traditional Hindu mysticism, Sri Aurobindo believed that all things must finally realize their unity in a single divine nature which he calls "the Absolute." He also held that the physical world is not to be rejected, but viewed as a stage in the process of cosmic transformation which leads to the development of "Spirit" and its expression in the world. One who can experience this will obtain "the intimate consciousness of one-being, of one self in all beings."

QUESTIONS

1. Why does Sri Aurobindo believe that the spiritual aspect of reality is distinct from both physical and mental life?

Excerpted from Sri Aurobindo, *The Future Evolution of Man,* by kind permission of Sri Aurobindo Ashram Trust, ©1963 Sri Aurobindo Ashram.

2. In what sense is spiritual knowledge something which involves "silence," in Sri Aurobindo's view?
3. Why does Sri Aurobindo argue that spiritual knowledge will help one to overcome selfishness?

■ ■ ■

Spirituality is something else than intellectuality; its appearance is the sign that a Power greater than mind is striving to emerge in its turn.

It is quite true that to a surface view life seems only an operation of Matter, mind an activity of life, and it might seem to follow that what we call the soul or spirit is only a power of mentality, soul a fine form of mind, spirituality a high activity of the embodied mental being. But this is a superficial view of things due to the thought's concentrating on the appearance and process and not looking at what lies behind the process. One might as well on the same lines have concluded that electricity is only a product or operation of water and cloud matter, because it is in such a field that lightning emerges; but a deeper inquiry has shown that both cloud and water have, on the contrary, the energy of electricity as their foundation, their constituent power or energy-substance: that which seems to be a result is—in its reality, though not in its form—the origin; the effect is in the essence pre-existent to the apparent cause, the principle of the emergent activity precedent to its present field of action. So it is throughout evolutionary Nature; Matter could not have become animate if the principle of life had not been there constituting Matter and emerging as a phenomenon of life-in-matter; life-in-matter could not have begun to feel, perceive, think, reason, if the principle of mind had not been there behind life and substance, constituting it as its field of operation and emergent in the phenomenon of a thinking life and body: so too spirituality emerging in mind is the sign of a power which itself has founded and constituted life, mind and body and is now emerging as a spiritual being in a living and thinking body. How far this emergence will go, whether it will become dominant and transform its instrument, is a subsequent question; but what is necessary first to posit is the existence of spirit as something else than mind and greater than mind, spir-

ABANDONING WITHOUT EXCEPTION ALL DESIRES born of [selfish] will, restraining with the mind all the senses on every side,

Let him gain, little by little, tranquillity by means of reason controlled by steadiness, and, having fixed the mind on the Self, let him not think of anything else.

Whatsoever makes the wavering and unsteady mind wander away let him restrain and bring it back to the control of the Self alone,

For supreme happiness comes to the yogin whose mind is peaceful, whose passions are at rest, who is stainless and has become one with God.

Thus making the Self ever harmonized, the yogin, who has put away sin, experiences easily the infinite bliss of contact with the Eternal.

He whose Self is harmonized by *yoga* sees the Self abiding in all beings and all beings in the Self; everywhere he sees the same.

The Bhagavad-Gītā, 24-28,
quoted in A *Source Book in Indian Philosphy*, 1957.

ituality as something other than mentality and the spiritual being therefore as something distinct from the mental being. . . .

It must therefore be emphasized that spirituality is not a high intellectuality, not idealism, not an ethical turn of mind or moral purity and austerity, not religiosity or an ardent and exalted emotional fervour, not even a compound of all these excellent things; a mental belief, creed or faith, an emotional aspiration, a regulation of conduct according to a religious or ethical formula are not spiritual achievement and experience. These things are of considerable value to mind and life; they are of value to the spiritual evolution itself as preparatory movements disciplining, purifying or giving a suitable form to the nature; but they still belong to the mental evolution,—the beginning of a spiritual realization, experience, change is not yet there. Spirituality is in its essence an awakening to the inner reality of our being, to a spirit, self, soul which is other than our mind, life and body, an inner aspiration to know, to feel, to be that, to enter into contact with the greater Reality beyond and

187

pervading the universe which inhabits also our own being, to be in communion with It and union with It, and a turning, a conversion, a transformation of our whole being as a result of the aspiration, the contact, the union, a growth or waking into a new becoming or new being, a new self, a new nature. . . .

The last or highest emergence is the liberated man who has realized the Self and Spirit within him, entered into the cosmic consciousness, passed into union with the Eternal and, so far as he still accepts life and action, acts by the light and energy of the Power within him working through his human instruments of Nature. The largest formulation of this spiritual change and achievement is a total liberation of soul, mind, heart and action, a casting of them all into the sense of the cosmic Self and the Divine Reality. The spiritual evolution of the individual has then found its way and thrown up its range of Himalayan eminence and its peaks of highest nature. Beyond this height and largeness there opens only the supramental ascent or the incommunicable Transcendence. . . .

To be and to be fully is Nature's aim in us; but to be fully is to be wholly conscious of one's being: unconsciousness, half consciousness or deficient consciousness is a state of being not in possession of itself; it is existence, but not fullness of being. To be aware wholly and integrally of oneself and of all the truth of one's being is the necessary condition of true possession of existence. This self-awareness is what is meant by spiritual knowledge: the essence of spiritual knowledge is an intrinsic self-existent consciousness; all its action of knowledge, indeed all its action of any kind, must be that consciousness formulating itself. All other knowledge is consciousness oblivious of itself and striving to return to its own awareness of itself and its contents; it is self-ignorance labouring to transform itself back into self-knowledge.

To become complete in being, in consciousness of being, in force of being, in delight of being and to live in this integrated completeness is the divine living.

All being is one and to be fully is to be all that is. To be in the being of all and to include all in one's being, to be conscious of the consciousness of all, to be integrated in force with the universal force, to carry all action and experience in oneself and feel it as one's own action and experience, to feel all selves as one's own self, to feel all delight of being as one's own delight of being is a necessary condition of the integral divine living.

The plenitude of this consciousness can only be attained by realizing the identity of the individual self with the transcendent Self, the supreme Reality.

But thus to be universally in the fullness and freedom of one's universality, one must be also transcendentally. The spiritual fullness of the being is eternity; if one has not the consciousness of timeless eternal being, if one is dependent on body or embodied mind or embodied life, or dependent on this world or that world or on this condition of being or that condition of being, that is not the reality of self, not the fullness of our spiritual existence. To live only as a self of body or be only by the body is to be an ephemeral creature, subject to death and desire and pain and suffering and decay and decadence. To transcend, to exceed consciousness of body, not to be held in the body or by the body, to hold the body only as an instrument, a minor outward formation of self, is a first condition of divine living. Not to be a mind subject to ignorance and restriction of consciousness, to transcend mind and handle it as an instrument, to control it as a surface formation of self, is a second condition. To be by the self and spirit, not to depend upon life, not to be identified with it, to transcend it and control and use it as an expression and instrumentation of the self, is a third condition.

[The individual] must enter into the supreme divine Reality, feel his oneness with it, live in it, be its self-creation: all his mind, life, physicality must be converted into terms of its Supernature; all his thought, feelings, actions must be determined by it and be it, its self-formation. All this can become complete in him only when he has evolved out of the Ignorance into the Knowledge and through the Knowledge into the supreme Consciousness and its dynamis and supreme delight of existence; but some essentiality of these things and their sufficient instrumentation can come with the first spiritual change and culminate in the life of the gnostic supernature.

This realization demands a turning of the consciousness inward. The ordinary human consciousness is turned outward and sees the surface of things only. It recoils from entering the inner depths which appear dark and where it is afraid of losing itself. Yet the

entry into this obscurity, this void, this silence is only the passage
to a greater existence.

These things are impossible without an inward living; they cannot be reached by remaining in an external consciousness turned always outwards, active only or mainly on and from the surface. The individual being has to find himself, his true existence; he can only do this by going inward, by living within and from within. . . . This movement of going inward and living inward is a difficult task to lay upon the normal consciousness of the human being; yet there is no other way of self-finding. The materialistic thinker, erecting an opposition between the extrovert and the introvert, holds up the extrovert attitude for acceptance as the only safety: to go inward is to enter into darkness or emptiness or to lose the balance of the consciousness and become morbid; it is from outside that such inner life as one can construct is created, and its health is assured only by a strict reliance on its wholesome and nourishing outer sources,—the balance of the personal mind and life can only be secured by a firm support on external reality, for the material world is the sole fundamental reality. This may be true for the physical man, the born extrovert, who feels himself to be a creature of outward Nature; made by her and dependent on her, he would lose himself if he went inward: for him there is no inner being, no inner living. But the introvert of this distinction also has not the inner life; he is not a seer of the true inner self and of inner things, but the small mental man who looks superficially inside himself and sees there not his spiritual self but his life-ego, his mind-ego and becomes unhealthily preoccupied with the movements of this little pitiful dwarf creature. The idea or experience of an inner darkness when looking inwards is the first reaction of a mentality which has lived always on the surface and has no realized inner existence; it has only a constructed internal experience which depends on the outside world for the materials of its being. But to those into whose composition there has entered the power of a more inner living, the movement of going within and living within brings not a darkness or dull emptiness but an enlargement, a rush of new experience, a greater vision, a larger capacity, an extended life infinitely more real and various than the first pettiness of the life constructed for itself by our normal physical humanity, a joy of being which is larger and richer than any delight in existence that the outer vital man or the surface mental man can gain by their dynamic vital force and activity or subtlety and expansion of the mental existence. A silence, an entry into a wide or even immense or infinite emptiness is part of the inner spiritual experience; of this silence and void the physical mind has a certain fear, the small superficially active thinking or vital mind a shrinking from it or dislike,—for it confuses the silence with mental and vital incapacity and the void with cessation or non-existence: but this silence is the silence of the spirit which is the condition of a greater knowledge, power and bliss, and this emptiness is the emptying of the cup of our natural being, a liberation of it from its turbid contents so that it may be filled with the wine of God: it is the passage not into non-existence but to a greater existence. Even when the being turns towards cessation, it is a cessation not in non-existence but into some vast ineffable or spiritual being or the plunge into the incommunicable superconscience of the Absolute. . . .

In fact, this inward turning and movement is not an imprisonment in personal self, it is the first step towards a true universality; it brings to us the truth of our external as well as the truth of our internal existence. For this inner living can extend itself and embrace the universal life, it can contact, penetrate, englobe the life of all with a much greater reality and dynamic force than is in our surface consciousness at all possible. Our outmost universalization on the surface is a poor and limping endeavour,—it is a construction, a make-believe and not the real thing: for in our surface consciousness we are bound to separation of consciousness from others and wear the fetters of the ego. There our very selflessness becomes more often than not a subtle form of selfishness or turns into a larger affirmation of our ego; content with our pose of altruism, we do not see that it is a veil for the imposition of our individual self, our ideas, our mental and vital personality, our need of ego-enlargement upon the others whom we take up into our expanded orbit. So far as we really succeed in living for others, it is done by an inner spiritual force of love and sympathy; but the power and field of effectuality of this force in us are small, the psychic movement that prompts it is incomplete, its action often ignorant because there is contact of mind and heart but our being does not embrace the being of others as ourselves. An external unity with others must always be an outward joining and association of external lives with a minor inner result; the mind and heart attach their movements to this common life and the beings whom we meet there; but the common external life remains the foundation,—the inward constructed unity, or so much of it as can persist in spite of mutual ignorance and discordant egoisms, conflict of minds, conflict of hearts, conflict of vital temperaments, conflict of interests, is a partial and insecure superstructure. The spiritual consciousness, the spiritual life reverses this principle of building; it bases its action in the collective life upon an inner experience and inclusion of others in our own being, an inner sense and reality of oneness. The spiritual individual acts out of that sense of oneness which gives him immediate and direct perception of the demand of self on other self, the need of the life, the good, the work of love and sympathy that can truly be done. A realization of spiritual unity, a dynamization of the intimate consciousness of one-being, of one self in all beings, can alone found and govern by its truth the action of the divine life.

Meaning Is Found Through Overcoming Attachment to Reality

DHIRAVAMSA

Dhiravamsa is a native of Thailand who has taught the Vipassana practice of "insight meditation" throughout the world. This tradition is part of the Theravada ("path of the elders") branch of Buddhism which still flourishes in Southeast Asia. It is based on the Four Noble Truths and the Noble Eightfold Path of the Buddha, which indicate that one can overcome the selfish "craving" that causes suffering by eliminating attachment. If one is not attached to anything, one will not be mired in selfish desires which can never be satisfied. Dhiravamsa believes that one can achieve nonattachment through a method of meditation based in the Noble Eightfold Path that takes one beyond the quest for fleeting pleasure. By opening ourselves to the truth of the Buddha, the "unconditioned," one can achieve complete freedom and so end craving and attachment.

QUESTIONS

1. How does the practice of meditation lead to nonattachment, in Dhiravamsa's view?
2. What does Dhiravamsa mean by saying that true love is freedom and not attachment?
3. Why does Dhiravamsa say that thought is a "perversion" which must be overcome to obtain insight? How is this view like the Zen Buddhism of Suzuki in the previous chapter?

■　■　■

Most of us have read and learned about the ultimate goal of Buddhism, which is called Nirvana, or the unconditioned. It is something to be realised, not to be caught. Terms like reaching, arriving or attaining do not help understanding the coming to or the realisation of the ultimate goal, because we think in terms of possessing the realisation of Nirvana, or attaining to enlightenment. We think enlightenment can be caught, we must possess it, so if we do not get it we feel empty. So when we try to accumulate we will not be able to arrive at truth, or to realise Nirvana, the unconditioned. That is desire, to have, to become, or to gain something, which is the cause of suffering. The end of desire is misery or sorrow. It may give some pleasure, enjoyment, satisfaction, but all these things can change. They are not permanent. When they change we become frustrated, miserable, sorrowful.

This is because of change or because we are attached to the thing we have got. We do not want it to go away. We want it to be with us, but in fact it cannot be with us for ever. So all frustration, dissatisfaction, unhappiness, sorrow, come about because of attachment, the inner condition of man. It is not external things which make us unhappy, but our inner condition. In order to open ourselves to the unconditioned, we have to see very clearly how we are conditioned and what binds us to the world of experiences. When we learn about Buddhism we want to become knowledgeable men. If we cannot be recognised and respected we feel sorrowful and empty. We are conditioned by the desire to have and the desire to become, and so we cannot avoid suffering or disappointment. When we come to meditate we want to achieve calmness, tranquillity, serenity;

we want to cultivate insight, clarity of mind, peace within and all sorts of things, and when we cannot get what we want, we become terribly frustrated and this becomes a big psychological problem to supposed meditators.

This is one of the conditions that binds us day by day. Every thought, every feeling, every emotion is conditioned by something else. There are many associations and connections, so when there is no freedom in thinking it is very difficult for man to become liberated. We are very proud of the fact that the seeing of things as they are is the main principle in the Buddhist way of life, but we do not always succeed. Can we see all people, or all things we come across in life, as they are, without distortion? Even when we listen to someone talking about something, can we understand what he really means? In fact, people cannot understand one another very well because of their interpretation, opinions and views. We try to interpret what is said in our own way, but the speaker may mean something quite different and if we say, "This is what he means", we may be quite wrong. So interpretation and explanation can be misleading in many cases. But if we stop interpreting or explaining and look or listen to everything there is a silence between the words. In fact understanding springs up when there is silence in our minds when we are listening to something or talking about something, but if we are not fully aware in our actions we cannot catch that flow of wisdom. It is flowing all the time but it requires a very quiet mind to receive it.

In meditation practice, in fact, we do not cultivate insight at all. To meditate is to clear away all the conditions, obstructions and hindrances within us so that the inner house will become clear and clean. Then we can look through any windows we have and see everything both inside and outside very clearly, there is no obstruction.

We do not live truly in the present, in the here-and-now, because we allow day-dreaming to occupy the mind, and we know that in dreams there is no reality. The mind tends to enjoy something unreal; it does not want to go into reality because then it cannot play, it cannot entertain. In that case we may say the mind disappears. But there is another kind of disappearance of the mind in meditation. Some people have difficulty in holding the mind because when the mind becomes highly concentrated it disappears, but the disappearing of the mind does not bring about any creative energy. It is a kind of laziness similar to going to sleep. In that case the mind is conditioning itself by a kind of illusion, a deception, so people need to be very careful about going into the unconscious. There are two ways of going into the unconscious; one is through strong concentration in which there is great calmness and tranquillity of mind, but a person who cannot meditate has no clarity and lives with a very narrow outlook because his mind is not opened up. In that case we may say that the mind is hiding itself, by a trick, from its action. It requires a strong discipline and long training. The other way of going into what we call the unconscious is through the silence of the mind, but this silence is full of awareness of everything on the way, until a state is reached in which freedom is revealed without having the feeling of oneself being there. It may not be very clear, as it is a very, very big step to go into the full unconditioned.

This freedom is different from freedom as we generally understand it, because in it there is very clear understanding

---

AND THIS IS THE NOBLE Truth of Sorrow. Birth is sorrow, age is sorrow, disease is sorrow, death is sorrow; contact with the unpleasant is sorrow, separation from the pleasant is sorrow, every wish unfulfilled is sorrow—in short all the five components of individuality are sorrow.

And this is the Noble Truth of the Arising of Sorrow. It arises from craving, which leads to rebirth, which brings delight and passion, and seeks pleasure now here, now there—the craving for sensual pleasure, the craving for continued life, the craving for power.

And this is the Noble Truth of the Stopping of Sorrow. It is the complete stopping of that craving, so that no passion remains, leaving it, being emancipated from it, being released from it, giving no place to it.

And this is the Noble Truth of the Way which Leads to the Stopping of Sorrow. It is the Noble Eightfold Path—Right Views, Right Resolve, Right Speech, Right Conduct, Right Livelihood, Right Effort, Right Mindfulness, and Right Concentration.

From Saṃyutta Nikāya, 5.421
quoted in The Buddhist Tradition, 1972.

without wanting to understand, because desire is not there. It is rather difficult to put into words, but it is very meaningful when you come to it. We can see there is the freedom to be and not to be. What I speak of is different for there is no attachment to this freedom at all when you come to it, and then you come out of it because you have clear understanding. So you do not miss it, and after that you may be able to see the full Unconditioned in which the light, the very great light of clarity, is shining forth. In some traditions this is explained as the truth shining forth, but in Buddhism one may say that light has arisen as it is said in the first sermon of the Buddha. That light has no colour which may seem curious. Light as we see it has colour, but the light of wisdom has none. We call it light because it is similar to light. It is very bright and incomparable. So if we can open our minds to see all activities, all tendencies and things within us, we will see a glimpse of the Unconditioned. It is not far away. You will notice when your mind becomes a little quiet that it is free from conditions, but in that temporary freedom you can sense something coming up or some movement moving up to your conscious level. If you go deeply into that you may say you come to the unconscious, which is not quite unconscious because you have alertness and clarity of mind, perceiving something through the senses, even mental perception, but a perception which is the seeing of truth. You are not dead, yet the body becomes completely still, including the brain. But when we say there is some kind of movement coming up to the conscious level, the movement is not in the sense of moving the hand, but there is a kind of gentleness, smoothness, with nowhere for that movement to go. But we perceive it when we are completely open and free.

So how can we open ourselves up to the reality of the Unconditioned? We have to overcome something within us. The first thing is to overcome any fixed ideas we have; if you are fixed you cannot move, you cannot open yourself. You must be flexible. Fixation is a kind of death. Supposing people fix themselves along the line of Theravada Buddhism, they will say that everything said in Theravada Buddhism is right and everything said in the other schools is wrong. So that person is narrowing himself. But if we are open we are open to see all the things in all schools in all traditions, and do not fix ourselves on any one tradition. We must be free to explore and develop anything different, and to find out for ourselves. In this way we will not be sectarian. In any case, we can explore our feelings which will give us more valuable results or hopes. At the same time, not neglecting to look at other things. When one is always open, one can have a new approach all the time.

The other thing is attachment, to ideas, methods, teachers, society or anything. Attachment to anything results in holding one always in the same place so that he cannot move on to the further step. Or perhaps one will move within a circle, which is a kind of psychological imprisonment, and he may try to decorate his prison so that he can live happily. But it is still prison. If we do not have any attachments can we have anything in life? We can have anything we need, anything which is important, essential for life. Life needs something to live on, it requires some comfort in material things. You can have families, properties if you wish, but you must not be attached to your families, to your property, to anything you have. People say, "Oh, we are husband and wife and if we are not attached to one another, we do not have love." Attachment does not mean love; it breaks up love between husband and wife. Because when you are attached you try to possess, and the other one does not want to be possessed. There must be freedom for everyone, but if you are attached you cannot help possessing and then there is trouble, there is misunderstanding. If we live in freedom, freedom is love because in love there is freedom. There is a feeling of totality. There is no division or separation, although there are still two individuals. The individual is not important even though we conceive it to be so in the dualistic concept of the world. We still feel we have self-identity. But we are *whole*. When we feel we are whole, we are not divided. Some little details may not be pleasant or agreeable to everyone, or to husband and wife, but because two people have love, have *metta* and compassion, they are not divided by small differences. In this way the two people are opened up, they do not live with a narrow outlook, or according to social morality or values. This also would become an obstacle to opening up to the Unconditioned. When they say that something has a social value, they have to keep it, they refuse the new by trying to keep the old. The new cannot come to be because we are trying to keep what we have; we don't want to lose it, but if we examine it wisely, intelligently, we will see that though this is not always good, we feel secure if we still keep to the same way.

Fear arises because we don't have security and we cannot explore something completely new. We are not brave enough. Then there can be no opening up to the Unconditioned because the mind is always conditioned by morality, values, social concepts, social traditions. We have to be very simple inwardly so that we can open ourselves to everything in life. If we can overcome attachment, fears and fixed ideas, we become more and more open so that the mind will reach complete freedom. There is one verse in *Dhammapada* which says that when the mind has arrived at the Unconditioned it has achieved the complete extinction of struggle and strife in life. Before the mind comes to this we are struggling and striving all the time. But if we are more and more open, not only in outlook but to all experiences in life, we learn at every moment. We have to learn from our mistakes and from everything we come across in order to come to complete maturity. . . .

What is the main problem of human existence? We should look into situations and see them clearly—not believing what other people say, but seeing them for ourselves. Can we manage our life happily, successfully? You may answer, "Sometimes my life is happy and successful, and at other times it is miserable." There must be a problem of relationship between ourselves and what we have or do not have. Can we understand our relationship not only to people within society but to what is within us? When we have sorrows, we tend to blame situations, other people, circumstances in life—we do not look into ourselves to find the real cause. So we create another problem for ourselves which cannot be solved, because the real cause is not removed. If we can understand and manage our relationships wisely, we shall find it easier to cope with anything in life.

What is the aim of relationships, whether with people, things, or ideas? Do you desire something in return, or do you desire satisfaction? Then you will not get what you really want, because the end of desire is sorrow and dissatisfaction. We may have a kind of happiness which is fleeting, changing, and therefore unreal. But we cling to the idea of permanent happiness, although unfortunately in life happiness is always being lost, leaving the "I" weeping because it cannot maintain what it has. Perhaps what you think you are is not you. The real you, if it exists, will be very different from what you think you are. Is there such a thing inside us or outside? Within us there must be something, which cannot be reached by thought, by projection, but only by realisation.

So the moment you experience sorrow or pain, you have to put yourself the question, "Who is suffering now? Is there a sufferer? Or is there only suffering because of certain conditions?" You have to look into that and see the whole picture. When there is no sufferer, suffering is unimportant. But when there is, suffering becomes stronger and stronger, and insight cannot arise. Insight can only come the moment everything becomes quiet and still. Insight will not flow to the surface until there is tranquillity within. . . .

When you come to complete freedom, there is no identity, because in that complete freedom there is no division. If there is identity, there must be two things: complete freedom and an experiencer of the freedom. So again we come back to duality. Duality and non-duality are close together—like the front and back of the hand—but according to the idea itself they are very far apart, with a long way to go. Thoughts tell us that they are very far apart, but thought is a kind of perversion. The more we think about reality the more confused we become. It becomes more and more distorted, and we never reach reality. Thoughts are like clouds. When you are among the clouds you cannot see the clear, blue skies, but when you have gone beyond the clouds you see beautiful skies with clarity and silence. Perhaps in the initial silence there may be a sound, or something moving, but they are all parts of silence, because at that moment of being in silence the entity does not exist. When there is no entity there is no disturbance, no distraction, but complete integration and wholeness of being.

Meaning Is Found Through Uniting with the Tao

MICHAEL SASO
ON MASTER CHUANG-CH'EN TENG-YUN

Michael Saso is a Western scholar of Chinese religion who
travelled to Taiwan to study with Chuang-Ch'en Teng-Yun, a
master of the "Heavenly Master" Cheng-i sect of Taoism. The
type of Taoism Master Chuang practiced is often referred to
as "religious Taoism" in contrast with the "philosophical Taoism" of Lao Tzu and Chuang Tzu. Whereas the latter seeks
unity with the Tao through quiet contemplation and reflection, "religious" Taoists actively seek to bring themselves into
unity with the Tao through rituals and magical techniques.
The Taoist "masters" of these sects act as priests for the people by performing the elaborate rituals which harness the
power of Tao and unify human life with it. Some Western
scholars have made a stark distinction between "philosophical" and "religious" Taoism, but one should note that Master

Excerpted from Michael Saso, *The Teachings of Taoist Master Chuang*. New
Haven: Yale University Press, 1978. Copyright ©1978 by Yale University Press.
All rights reserved. Reprinted with permission.

Chuang also taught Taoist philosophy and did not view himself as practicing a "religion" separate from its teachings. The methods of "philosophical" and "religious" Taoists may differ, but the goal of unity with the Tao is the same.

For many centuries, little was known of "religious" Taoism outside of the (primarily Chinese) societies in which it is practiced, mainly due to the secrecy with which the masters guarded their esoteric knowledge of ritual techniques. Master Chuang, however, agreed to teach Saso because he believed that it was prophesied that he bring this knowledge to Western civilization. He described to him the secrets of the chiao, a ritual which reunites the elements of the world with the Tao. It is combined with a chai, a ritual which frees the souls of the dead from hell. (The belief that the dead may be reborn in many dimensions, heavens and hells, is traceable to the influence of Buddhism.) Through his knowledge of the chiao ritual, a Taoist master is able to "make the many into one," uniting with the Tao and using its power to save souls and give hope and meaning to the community.

QUESTIONS

1. Who are the "three pure ones" and with what is each associated?
2. What is the "voiding of the heart" and how does this aid the process of uniting with the Tao?
3. What rules did Master Chuang believe one had to learn before attempting to perform Taoist rituals? Summarize the philosophy behind them.

■ ■ ■

Orthodox Taoist ritual has traditionally been distinguished from the popular local rites of village magicians by a form of liturgical meditation leading to union with the Tao. The purpose of classical, orthodox ritual is threefold. For the adept, it leads to mystical union and immortality. For the men and women of the villages, it brings blessing and renewal. For the souls of the departed in the underworld, it brings salvation and release from the punishments of hell. Though innumerable local variations and styles of Taoist practices have evolved through the historic forces that wrought change in China, the basic format and purpose of orthodox ritual have remained constant to the present day. After a brief meditative hymn and entrance rite, the Taoist still begins orthodox ritual with a meditation called fa-lu for exteriorizing the spirits from his body. Next, the meditation of ritual union is conducted, during which the Taoist master ascends to the heavens and presents a memorial or grand written document before the throne of the eternal Tao. Finally, the ritual concludes with the fu-lu, or the restoration of the spirits to their places inside the microcosm. The orthodox Taoist master bases his meditation on a notion taken from the first seven chapters of the *Chuang-tzu*, where the ancient sage proposes, "The Tao dwells in the void." By "fasting in the heart" (hsin-chai) and emptying the microcosm, union with the eternal transcendent Tao is effected. . . .

Following the custom established in the Sung dynasty, when a Taoist master is hired to perform his ritual in modern Taiwan, the people of the village ordinarily call the entire festival a chiao, that is, a pure sacrifice. But concurrently with the chiao, a chai or set of ceremonies for freeing all the souls from hell is also celebrated. Thus the modern village festivals include both a chiao and a chai. Like a great symphony in which two melodic themes are developed, the Taoist performs a set of rituals whose purpose is to win blessing from heaven and union with the transcendent Tao, and at the same time celebrates another set of ceremonies whose purpose is to free the souls from hell. In the first set of rituals, which are properly called chiao, the meditations of union are performed. These meditations invariably begin with the fa-lu rite for emptying the microcosm and end with the fu-lu for restoring the spirits to their proper place. In these rituals, wine, incense, and tea are offered to the heavenly spirits, hence the word chiao used to describe them. In the second set of rituals, the Taoist reads lengthy canons of merit and litanies of repentance, in a formula which does not make use of the classical fa-lu rite of emptying. The chai ceremonies for freeing the souls end with a great sacrifice called the p'u-tu in which raw meat is used to offer to feed the souls in hell. The word chai is now used to describe these latter ceremonies, a change from the more general sense in which the word was used in the past.

Ritual Meditation Leading to Union with the Tao

According to the teachings of Master Chuang, orthodox chiao ritual is solidly based on the yin-yang five element theory of the cosmos. In a strictly religious interpretation of chapter 42 of the *Lao-tzu*, the Taoist reverses the process whereby the "Tao gave birth to the One; the One gave birth to the Two; the Two gave birth to the Three; the Three gave birth to the myriad creatures." By orthodox ritual, the Taoist "returns to the roots," that is, he "refines" or "returns" the microcosm to the state of primordial simplicity, hun-tun, in order to be united with the eternal, transcendent Tao of the Wu-wei.

The Tao is a nameless, unmoved first mover, as described in the first chapters of the *Lao-tzu*. The Tao gives birth to the One, which is interpreted to be the Tao of immanence, that is, the moved first mover, also called t'ai-chi (Great Principle) or hun-tun (primordial chaos). Primordial chaos, or t'ai-chi, is personified by religious Taoism as the first of a Taoist trinity, Yüan-shih T'ien-tsun, or Primordial Heavenly Worthy. Within the microcosm of man he stands as symbol for primordial breath, the basic life-giving substance within the body. His dwelling place is within the head of man, where he resides in an esoteric place called the Ni-wan. When called forth from within the microcosm, he always appears in a blue-green mist. In the macrocosm, he is the ruler of the highest heavens.

"The One gives birth to the Two," the next line in chapter 42 of the *Lao-tzu*, is also personified as a spirit by the religious Taoists. The second spirit, Ling-pao Heavenly Worthy, stands for the liaison spirit between heaven and earth. Thus the term "ling" refers to the half of a talisman kept in the heavens, and the "pao" to the precious half buried in the earth. Ling-pao Heavenly Worthy is the symbol for the spirit or shen in man. His rule is in the center part of the body and, when summoned forth, he appears in a yellow light.

"The Two gives birth to the Three," the next line from the verse, refers to the third of the Taoist trinity, Tao-te T'ien-tsun, who is taken to be a mystical personification of *Lao-tzu*. Tao-te Heavenly Worthy is symbolic of vital essence within man, which resides in the lower abdomen. When called forth, the "vital essence"spirit always appears in a bright white light.

Thus the Tao is seen to give birth in turn to three princi-

> **IN THE GREAT BEGINNING, THERE** was non-being. It had
> neither being nor name. The One originates from it; it has one-
> ness but not yet physical form. When things obtain it and
> come into existence, that is called virtue (which gives them
> their individual character). That which is formless is divided
> [into yin and yang], and from the very beginning going on
> without interruption is called destiny (*ming*, fate). Through
> movement and rest it produces all things. When things are
> produced in accordance with the principle (*li*) of life, there is
> physical form. When the physical form embodies and pre-
> serves the spirit so that all activities follow their own specific
> principles, that is nature. By cultivating one's nature one will
> return to virtue. When virtue is perfect, one will be one with
> the beginning. Being one with the beginning, one becomes
> vacuous (*hsü*, receptive to all), and being vacuous, one be-
> comes great. One will then be united with the sound and
> breath of things. When one is united with the sound and
> breath of things, one is then united with the universe. This
> unity is intimate and seems to be stupid and foolish. This is
> called profound and secret virtue, this is complete harmony.
>
> **Chuang Tzu, Chapter 12**
> quoted in A *Source Book in Chinese Philosophy*, 1963.

ples—breath, spirit, and vital essence. These three principles
are in the philosophic order expressed by the notions t'ai-chi,
yang, and yin. In the religious order they become three Heavenly Worthies, the "Three Pure Ones" (San-ch'ing). From the
Three Pure Ones are generated the five movers or the five elements: wood, fire, earth, metal, and water; and from the five
movers come the myriad things of nature.

The complicated process of refinement from the many to
the one, which the Taoist attempts to perform through ritual, is
difficult to describe in a brief lesson. Years of instruction from
a master are required to perfect the method. If the purpose of
orthodox ritual can be stated in a single sentence, it is perhaps
this: the Taoist, by his or her ritual, attempts to progress from
the myriad creatures, back through the process of gestation, to
an audience with the eternal, transcendent Tao. In a series of
ritual meditations, the Taoist adept empties out the myriad

spirits, until he or she stands in the state of hun-tun, or primordial emptiness. At that moment, the Tao of transcendence,
wu-wei chih Tao, comes of itself to dwell in the emptied center
of man. This process is called hsin-chai, or fasting (voiding) the
heart. Orthodox ritual is thus defined by ritual purpose.
Taoists who perform their liturgies for the purpose of union are
called orthodox. Taoists who perform their liturgies for the
sake of making a living, curing a cold, or simple exorcism, are
not. The distinction is strictly observed, and the rank given to
a Taoist at the time of ordination is determined by his or her
ability to perform the various meditations of union. . . .

Preparations for Orthodox Ritual Meditation

It was evident from the lessons of Master Chuang that he expected his sons and disciples to be familiar with the doctrines
of the *Lao-tzu* and the *Chuang-tzu*, and to meditate upon and fa-
miliarize themselves with the process of gestation and the
functioning of the cosmos described in these works. The
process of instruction was carefully planned, and I was
scolded for trying to accelerate matters to the heart of
Chuang's esoteric magic ritual. The order of instruction,
Chuang told me, would take more than ten years and could
not be accelerated without doing harm both to the disciple and
to the doctrines. The following is the traditional order of trans-
mitting the doctrines of orthodox Taoism:

1. Profession of the ten rules or vows of the Taoist novice.
2. Reception and mastery of the *Lao-tzu Tao-te Ching*.
3. Meditation and ritual of the Three Pure Ones (San-
   ch'ing).
4. Meditation and ritual of the Five Talismans (*Ling-pao
   Wu-fu*).
5. Reception and mastery of the *Yellow Court Canon*.

Only after receiving the above manuals and listening to the instructions of Master Chuang concerning the process of gestation from the Tao of transcendence, and only after understanding the workings of yin and yang, the production of the five
elements, and the other myriad details of the yin-yang five el-

ement cosmology, was mention made of the esoteric rubrics of religious Taoism.

The process of receiving the rules or vows of the Taoist novice and putting them into practice was a matter of great concern for Chuang and a source of scolding for myself as well as for his sons. I was continually reprimanded for haste, for competitiveness with my colleagues, and for attempting to introduce Chuang to other foreign scholars. The vows of esoteric transmission were binding on the master and on the disciple, and the response of the Taoist towards all outside inquirers was inevitably one of ignorance. When passing on the vows or rules of religious Taoism, Chuang sat facing the west, composed himself, and addressed us only after we had settled down to listen in quiet composure. The following are the first ten rules given to the novice:

1. Banish all hatred from the heart. Hatred, anger, and brooding cause the powers of yin to devour the inner man.
2. Be benevolent and merciful to all living things.
3. Do good to all and avoid acts which harm others.
4. Purity of heart and mind include banishing impure thoughts.
5. Both in interior thoughts and exterior acts be loyal to friends. Never speak badly of others, especially of a fellow Taoist.
6. The breath of life must be regulated; nothing should be taken in excess. Wine may not be drunk during ritual.
7. Do not try to win over others, but always yield and take the last place.
8. Do not argue or dispute, but behave always as if in the presence of spirits.
9. Put self-interest last, and never be critical of others. Life breath is injured by seeking praise or resenting blame.
10. Use the whole heart and mind to achieve equality, union, and peace.

For each of the books or rituals revealed by the master there is a set of rules, or chieh, which the disciple must follow in order to "walk in the way of the Tao." Thus, before receiving the *Ling-pao Five Talismans* the following set of rules is proposed for the disciple:

1. Do not kill, but respect all living things.
2. Do not lust after another man's wife, or any woman.
3. Do not steal or take any recompense unjustly.
4. Do not use deceit, to win one's own way.
5. Do not get drunk, and at all times act with sobriety.
6. Love all relatives, with respect and harmony. Treat all men as relatives.
7. See the good points in all men, and help their hearts to be joyful.
8. If a person is sad, help him or her to be happy and blessed.
9. Treat all others as if their desires were one's own. Never seek vengeance.
10. Work that all may attain the Tao.

The chieh or rules of the Ling-pao talismans thus teach the young disciple the attitude necessary to have in order to perform ritual for the benefit of the men and women of the community. One of the greatest fears of the masters of esoteric ritual is that the terrifying magical powers given to the novice may be used to harm and not to help men. Thus the disciple is carefully watched and tested before the secrets of esoteric ritual are revealed. The rules are summarized in the simple "three commandments" given before the meditation of union.

1. Don't forget the roots to seek the branches.
2. Don't benefit the self to the harm of others.
3. Don't get involved in things and lose the Tao.

In his final words before entrance is granted to the sacred ritual area, the master tells the disciple, "When one performs the pure chai ritual, there is no need to go to the mountains. For it is not in the mountains but within the empty center of man that the Tao is found." The purpose of the chai, therefore, is union with the eternal Tao. . . .

The chiao can be interpreted on a lower, less esoteric plane as a sending off of documents to the various deities who control the forces of nature. By the ritual perfection of the Taoist, the spirits of the cosmos are prevailed upon to grant heavenly blessing, give abundance on earth, and free the souls from hell. But on a higher, meditative plane, the chiao is interpreted as a ritual for bringing about union with the Tao. That is to say, the Taoist first unites himself to the Tao of transcendence, and then carries the petitions of the men and women of the community before the thrones of the heavenly worthies. Thus in the final definition, the highest form of esoteric Taoism is seen to be based upon the premise that the master first unites himself with the Tao and then uses his supernatural powers to save others. From his position of esoteric union, he coaxes and cajoles the spirits of the three realms (heaven, earth, and underworld) to give man blessing. All his marvelous powers come to him by reason of union with the Tao.

Meaning Is Found by Becoming a Virtuous Person

ANTONIO CUA

Antonio Cua is a scholar of Confucian ethics who, in the following viewpoint, analyzes the Confucian concept of the
"Chun Tzu" or superior moral person. This concept plays a
significant role in the writings of Confucius, as the Chun Tzu
is there described as the ideal of the virtuous person we all
should seek to be. The Chun Tzu lives by a variety of virtues:
humanity, propriety, righteousness, neutrality, honesty. Cua
describes the Confucian understanding of these qualities and
how they can be combined to form the Chun Tzu. He notes
that although no one can fulfill the ideal of the Chun Tzu, it
provides the standard at which Confucian morality aims, and
in this way it is a concept which is crucial to the Confucian
vision of life.

QUESTIONS

1. What is meant by the qualities of humanity, propriety, and
   righteousness? How are these interrelated, according to Cua?

Excerpted from Antonio Cua, "The Concept of Paradigmatic Individuals in the
Ethics of Confucius." In *Invitation to Chinese Philosophy*, Arne Naess and Alas-
tair Hannay, eds. Oslo: Universitetsforlaget, 1972. Copyright ©1972 Universitetsforlaget. Reprinted with permission.

2. How does the Chun Tzu remain flexible and so able to deal with diverse situations, in Cua's view?
3. What does Cua mean by asserting that the Chun Tzu is "a man of his words and deeds"?

■ ■ ■

The ethics of Confucius contained in the *Analects*, a major authoritative source of Chinese moral education, does not present a systematic scheme for conduct. There is a lack of an explicit and coherent ordering of moral ideas. This unsystematic character in part reflects its concern with and emphasis on the concrete and the particular. In this respect the ethics of Confucius is an ethics of flexibility that attempts to mould and adapt to the changing scenes of human life. In the words of a recent historian, 'the chief strength of Confucianism is its flexibility, a remarkable quality that enables it to resist all pressures and to face all adversities'. This quality of Confucian ethics, I believe, is best understood in terms of Confucius's notion of *chün-tzu* as a notion of a superior man who functions as a paradigmatic standard for practical morality. My aim in this essay is to inquire into the plausibility and significance of this notion as an underlying theme of Confucian ethics.

Although Confucius believed that only a *sage* (*shêng jên*), divinely inspired and intuitively wise, can envision and establish a harmonious social order, the ideal of sagehood was not regarded by him as practically attainable by ordinary moral agents. He once remarked that he could not ever hope to meet a sage (*shêng jên*), but only a *chün-tzu* (VII,25). The ideal of sagehood, in his mind, functions more like a supreme but *abstract* ideal of a perfect moral personality, as a standard of inspiration rather than as a standard of aspiration. Thus he more often discoursed on the conduct and quality of *chün-tzu* than on the nature of sagehood. In general, the notion of *chün-tzu* is a notion of a man of moral excellence, of a paradigmatic individual who sets the tone and quality of the life of ordinary moral agents. A *chün-tzu* is a man who embodies *jên* (human-heartedness) and *li* (propriety). As a guiding paradigmatic individual, every man can strive to be him rather than *Siao-jên* (inferior man). There are of course degrees of personal achievement depending on the situation, character, ability, and opportunity of moral agents. The translation of *'chün-tzu'* as 'superior man' forcefully brings out the *chün-tzu*'s superiority of moral character and aptitude. The translation of *'chün-tzu'* as 'true gentleman' focuses on *chün-tzu*'s relation with the cultural setting of his actions, his ability to satisfy, so to speak, the stylistic requirements of a form of life. A *chün-tzu*, in this sense, is an embodiment of a 'cultural life style'.

The varying remarks on *chün-tzu* in the *Analects* may be regarded as setting forth the different requirements or qualities for a life of moral excellence. A *chün-tzu* is, first of all, a man of moral virtues pervaded by an affectionate concern for *jên* or humanity. He is a man of propriety (*li*) and righteousness (*i*); of catholicity and neutrality in whom words and deeds are in harmony. The discussion that follows relates to these prominent features of the concept of *chün-tzu*.

A man of moral virtues (jên)

There are remarks of Confucius that portray *chün-tzu* as a man who possesses various virtues pervaded by the ideal of *jên* (human-heartedness). Confucius said, 'If a superior man abandon virtue (*jên*), how can he fulfil the requirements of that name? The superior man does not even for the space of a single meal act contrary to virtue (*jên*). In moments of haste, he cleaves to it. In seasons of danger, he cleaves to it' (IV,5). *Jên* is Confucius's ideal of an inclusive end that embraces the realizations of particular moral dispositions or virtues. Confucius, on one occasion responding to an inquiry about *jên*, said that a man of *jên* practices five things: 'gravity, generosity of *soul*, sincerity, liberality, and kindness'. . . .

A man of propriety (li) and righteousness (i)

Although *li* (propriety) and *i* (righteousness) are traditionally regarded as moral virtues, they received special attention in Confucian ethics. Our discussion on *jên* and particular moral virtues may be regarded as dealing with the internal aspect of *jên*-morality. The accent here is on self-cultivation rather than the outward form of conduct. As Confucius remarked, 'What the superior man seeks, is in himself. What the mean man seeks, is in others' (XV,20). *Li* and *i* relate more to the *style* and manner of moral performance. They are characteristics, so to speak, of the correctness of performance as governed by the social matrix and the appropriateness of these to concrete situations.

Confucius said, 'The superior man, extensively studying all learning, and keeping himself under the restraint of the rules of propriety (*li*), may thus likewise not overstep [the boundary] of what is right' (VI,25). This passage and many others suggest that *li*, as a body of ritual rules, functions as a restraining orbit of moral actions. *Li* appears to be the *convention* that defines the form and possibility of moral actions. In this sense, *li* defines the conventionally accepted *style* of actions, i.e. the form and possibility of moral achievement within the cultural setting, or what may be termed 'cultural lifestyle'. *Li*, unlike *jên*, does not define the nature of morality, but only the limiting form of execution of moral performance. In a more contemporary idiom, we may express this idea in terms of the *tie* or *contact* of an individual agent's actions with the cultural form of life which gives them the locus of identification and the possibility of moral achievement. An appropriate action, as conforming to the ritual requirements of *li*, may be identified as a moral action insofar as it is pervaded by a concern for *jên*. If one wants to lay more stress on the importance of *li*, then one may say that particular moral actions are partial exemplifications of a cultural lifestyle. However, without a persistent regard for *jên*, ritual observances would amount to mere formal gestures vacuous of moral essence. The *chün-tzu*'s respect for *li* or cultural lifestyle is at the same time a respect for the reality of the situation, the background and possibility that furnish the contexts for successful moral performance. . . .

The other aspect of action relates to the importance Confucius assigned to the role of the concept *i* or righteousness. 'The superior man holds righteousness (*i*) to be of highest importance' (XVIII,23). *I* is contrasted with profit (IV,16). This contrast brings out the Confucian distinction between morality and egoism. The notion of *i*, not elucidated in the *Analects*, is a difficult notion. It may be variously rendered as 'righteousness', 'right conduct', 'moral principle or standard', or 'the doing of what is right'. . . . In the language of Professor Fung, 'righteousness (*i*) means the "oughtness" of a situation. It is a categorical imperative. Everyone in society has certain things which he ought to do, and which must be done for their sake, because they are the morally right thing to do'. However, the 'oughtness' of the situation, though a characteristic of obligatory actions, has its central focus on the right act as appropriate to the particular situation confronting a moral agent. Doing what is right in a situation is not just a mere matter of conformity with moral and ritual rules, but also conformity to a *judgment* of the relevance and vindication of these in actual situations. *I* is another focus on an aspect of the concrete. If *li* is the emphasis on the contact between *jên*-morality and the cultural lifestyle, *i* is that on the contact between *jên*-morality and actual situations. Thus, the judgment of what is to be done is reserved to the moral agent. Confucius remarked, 'The superior man *in everything* considers righteousness (*i*) to be essential. He performs it according to the rules of propriety (*li*). He brings it forth in humility. He completes it with sincerity. This is indeed a superior man' (XV,17). This passage brings out the relationship of *li* and *i*. Our exposition of *i*, if it is correct, focuses on a view of the nature of moral action as an action in accordance with a judgment of the relevance of moral rules to concrete situations that occur within the setting of a cultural lifestyle.

We may sum up the significance of the preceding requirements for *chün-tzu*. A *chün-tzu* is a man of *jên*, *li*, and *i*. The concept of *jên* is the concept of an ideal of moral excellence. It is the *jên*-quality that pervades the life of a *chün-tzu*. This is the focal point of his paradigmatic function as a standard of aspiration

---

CONFUCIUS SAID, "WEALTH AND HONOR are what every man desires. But if they have been obtained in violation of moral principles, they must not be kept. Poverty and humble station are what every man dislikes. But if they can be avoided only in violation of moral principles, they must not be avoided. If a superior man departs from humanity, how can he fulfill that name? A superior man never abandons humanity even for the lapse of a single meal. In moments of haste, he acts according to it. In times of difficulty or confusion, he acts according to it."
Confucius, *Analects* 4:5
quoted in A *Source Book in Chinese Philosophy*, 1963.

for ordinary moral agents. *Jên* and other particular virtues portray the inner aspect of Confucian ethics. This focus gives us a pervasive and underlying feature of Confucian morality. The focus is on man himself and what he can morally accomplish in relation to others. This latter emphasis deals with the social and cultural setting of moral performance—the ritual context (*li*) in which human transactions occur with varying import of interests and motives. *Li* gives the moral action a locale of normative identification and an orbit of restraining conditions for the proper achievement of the moral ideal. Actions that conform to *li* requirements may be said to be in contact with the cultural lifestyle—the Confucian form of life. If *li* focuses on the *tie* of individual actions to culture, the freedom of a moral agent is radically limited in what he *can* do and accomplish. However, the restraining function of *li* defines only the *form*, not the *content*, of this freedom. The emphasis on *i* as a requirement of being a *chün-tzu* preserves a great deal of latitude in action. Just as *jên* cannot be practiced without *li*, the cultural setting, so *jên* cannot be realized without *i* or judgment of the relevance of *jên* and *li* to concrete situations of moral performance. It is *i* that establishes the contact between actions and the actual situations that confront the moral agent. Our next two sets of descriptions of *chün-tzu*, together with the present account, explain in large part this flexible and adaptable feature of Confucian ethics.

A man of catholicity and neutrality

'The superior man is broadminded and not partisan; the inferior man is partisan but not broadminded' (II,14; also VII,30). The superior man is not like an implement (II,12), 'which is intended only for a narrow and specific purpose'. Instead, 'he should have broad vision, wide interests, and sufficient ability to do many things'. He is a man of moral integrity that exemplifies itself even in the face of great emergency (VIII,8). He aims at 'the higher things or principles' (XIV,24) and is 'dignified without being proud' (XIII,26).

The above remarks on the aptitude and broadmindedness of *chün-tzu* are quite naturally expected in view of Confucius's emphasis on *jên*, *li*, and *i*. If *jên* consists in the affectionate concern, in varying degrees, for humanity, it requires from the moral agent the ability to 'know men' and sympathize with the being and predicaments of other moral agents. However, the ability to execute one's moral intentions within ritual contexts is also important. If *i* is required to give an actuating import to *jên* and *li*, then *chün-tzu* must exercise that 'secret art' that gives practical effect to his moral nature as an exemplary guide to the conduct of other agents. This theme of the contagion of the *chün-tzu*'s conduct in Confucius's thinking is perhaps best expressed in the *Chung Yung:* 'The way which the superior man pursues, reaches wide and far, and yet is secret. . . . The way of the superior man may be found, in its simple elements, in the intercourse of common men and women; but in its utmost reaches, it shines brightly through heaven and earth. . . . The superior man can find himself in no situation in which he is not himself'. Although the *chün-tzu*'s way is secret and capable of effusive influence in the lives of ordinary moral agents, he does not remain a mere spectator of human behavior, for he '*seeks to* perfect the admirable qualities of men, and does not *seek* to perfect their bad qualities' (XII,16). Being a man of *jên*, he wishes to establish his own character and also the character of others. Confucius said, 'to be able to judge *of others* by what is nigh *in ourselves;*—this may be called the art of virtue (*jên*)' (VI,28).

This 'secret way' or art of *chün-tzu* is not a mere matter of actions as intellectually determined by moral and ritual rules. If a *chün-tzu* has a natural preference for *jên*-morality, this preference does not commit him to specific courses of actions prior to a confrontation with an actual moral situation. Thus Confucius said of himself, 'I have no course for which I am predetermined, and no course against which I am predetermined' (XVIII,8). Moral actions, in concrete contexts, are not a straightforward deduction from given moral rules. The mere intellectual determination of the morality of action does not suffice in the assessment of moral performance. For the relevance of moral and ritual rules has to be assessed in concrete situations. This flexible and varying function of *i* accounts for the *neutrality* of *chün-tzu*'s attitude, or lack of commitment to specific courses of action. The actual assessment of moral and ritual rules is at the same time a way of vindicating their actual importance in human life. This act of assessment requires the neutral attitude. It is also this neutral attitude of *chün-tzu* that gives scope to the exercise of *i* in novel and abnormal situations. Thus a *chün-tzu* 'in the world, does not set his mind either for anything, or against anything: what is right (*i*) he will follow' (IV,10). He is said to be 'satisfied and composed' (VII,36) and free from anxiety, fear, and perplexities (XIV,30; XII,6). Being a man of *jên*, he is free from anxiety about acting contrary to morality; being a man of courage, he is free from fear; being a man with knowledge of human affairs, he is free from perplexities (XIV,30). His *easeful* life is more a matter of attitude and confidence in his ability to deal with difficult and varying situations, rather than an exemplification of his infallible judgment and authority. . . .

A man of his words and deeds (yen)

The neutral attitude of *chün-tzu* is related to Confucius's special emphasis on the harmony of words and deeds. If morality deals with the relations between men, as the character '*jên*' suggests, living in accordance with *jên*-morality requires the knowledge of men. And 'without knowing the *force* of words, it is impossible to know men' (XX,3). Thus the harmony of words and deeds is a frequent theme of Confucian ethics. A *chün-tzu* must act in accordance with what he professes (VIII,32). Even Confucius himself disclaimed being a *chün-tzu* in this sense. He said, 'In letters I am perhaps equal to other men, but *the character of* the superior man, carrying out in his conduct what he professes, is what I have not yet attained to' (VII,32). This doctrine of words and deeds, to borrow a phrase from Austin, may be said to be a case of 'suiting the action to the word'. This sort of action, in real life, is difficult to accomplish, not only because of the formidable strength of character required, but also because of the dynamic diversity of human situations that vary a great deal in their normative import. To preserve *chün-tzu*'s freedom to adapt to changing and varying circumstances, Confucius laid more stress on the importance of *suiting one's words to the action*. Thus Confucius remarked that a *chün-tzu* 'acts before he speaks, and afterwards speaks according to his actions' (II,12; also IV,22 and XIV,21). 'He is modest in his speech but exceeds in his actions' (XIV,29). Ideally a morally correct speech corresponds to a morally correct performance. A *chün-tzu*, therefore, does not engage in moral discourse for its own sake. He attempts to *suit* his words to actions performed. Conversely, his actions must, in other cases, conform to his words. This is particularly true of evaluative labels with which others endow him. He must live up to his title of being a *chün-tzu* (IV,5). Our present discussion is intimately related to the famous Confucian doctrine of rectification of *names* (*ching ming*), for words of honor and morality have their normative import. The names or titles of persons and their roles in society pragmatically imply certain obligatory types of actions as befitting these names. To rectify names (*ming*), or moral words, is to conform in action to the normative implications of these names.

The notion of correct speech and action is important in Confucian ethics, not only for conduct in accordance with *jên*-morality, but also for the successful execution of moral intentions within the form of a cultural lifestyle (*li*). . . . It is a *chün-tzu*, as we have previously mentioned, who is aware of the *forces of speech*. And from the standpoint of Confucian morality, a *chün-tzu* provides a moral exemplar in both his words and deeds. Suiting one's words to one's actions, of course, presupposes the satisfaction of the requirements of *jên*-morality.

In sum, the notion of *chün-tzu* is Confucius's ideal of a paradigmatic individual who functions as a guiding standard for practical conduct. In Confucius's view ordinary moral agents may not attain to sagehood (*sheng-jên*). However, they can look to a *chün-tzu* for guidance and may become a *chün-tzu* themselves. The notion of *chün-tzu*, though an exemplary model for practical conduct, is not an ideal of a perfect man, but an ideal of a *superior man* who embodies the various qualities we have discussed.

Meaning Is Found Through Discovering Spiritual Power

WALLACE BLACK ELK, INTERVIEWED BY WILLIAM S. LYON

Wallace Black Elk refers to Nick Black Elk (the Sioux holy man interviewed by John Neihardt for *Black Elk Speaks*) as his "grandfather"—but as he claims to have eleven grandfathers, the relationship is uncertain. In any case, Wallace Black Elk is a holy man in the same tradition as Nick Black Elk, and speaks out of that perspective. William S. Lyon has recorded his words, attempting to edit them as little as possible. Wallace Black Elk speaks of the spiritual power which he utilizes as a holy man, and how his "relatives"—the spirits in all things—come to help him. In truth, he does not regard himself as a "medicine man"; it is the spirits that are the "medicine people" who do the work of healing. Black Elk calls them with his Chanunpa, the sacred pipe (itself a spirit) that is used in Sioux ceremonies. With the medicine people's power, he claims one can heal the sick, protect his people

Excerpted from chapter 3 of *Black Elk: The Sacred Ways of a Lakota* by Wallace Black Elk and William S. Lyon, Ph.D. Copyright ©1990 by Wallace H. Black Elk and William S. Lyon. Reprinted by permission of HarperCollins Publishers, Inc.

from harm, and even prevent nuclear destruction. By returning to the sacred powers and using them wisely, Black Elk believes his people can find new life and purpose.

QUESTIONS

1. How does Black Elk describe the work of the "medicine
   man" who heals a sick person?
2. Why is it difficult to acquire sacred powers quickly, according to Black Elk?
3. What kinds of healing does Black Elk request from Tunkashila (the creator) in his prayer?

■ ■ ■

It takes a lot of courage to talk about these powers. It takes a
lot of courage to be a witness. Back in 1905 and 1908 some
commissioners came from Washington, D.C., to investigate the
Chanunpa. They wanted to know if it was true or not—
whether it was witchcraft or really from God. They had those
kinds of thoughts. So we do have a little piece of paper somewhere about that visit. Then they wrote laws about our using
these powers. For instance, Congress wrote a law that it was il-
legal for us to practice soul-keeping. So they wrote it that way.
"Release all those spirits. That's an order. That's a law."

But whether there's a law or no law, we could still go out
there. We don't need a piece of paper to contact those spirits. We
go out there and crawl in the stone-people-lodge. Then we send
a voice to the Creator—"Yo-ho"—and somebody responds and
comes in. Even if somebody drags me out there with no Chanunpa or anything, I could still say, "Yo-ho. I'm lost. I need
help." Then a spirit comes there and takes me some place. . . .

So I learned from the old people that those spirits that
come are my relatives. They learned that from the spirit. The
spirit told them, "This Chanunpa is your relative. The powers
of the Four Winds are your relatives. Pray to them. Talk to
them. They are your relatives. To the West, the Thunder-Beings,
they are your relatives. Send a voice out there. These are your
relatives. Look that way. These are your relatives. Look to the
North, the Buffalo Nation, the *White Buffalo-Calf Maiden*, the

Chanunpa, these are your relatives. To the East, the Elk Nation,
Black Elk, and the Elk Nation Woman that brings joy and happiness, these are your relatives. To the South, the Swan, the
two-legged spirits that bring joy and happiness, the medicine
people that bring health come from there. These are your relatives. Above you is the *Eagle Nation*. They watch, control, govern. They control the weather. They are the true meteorologists.
These are your relatives. Down to the Earth, the stone-people
are your relatives. So when you go back, tell your people that
these are all your relatives." That's what the voice said. . . .

These medicine people that come in are not just aspirin.
They are spirits. They are plants. The enemy comes in and de-
teriorates some part of the human structure like the mind,
heart, lung, bone, or blood. When you pray, whatever the
enemy deteriorated, that is where the medicine goes to recre-
ate and reform the human structure. . . .

So I was explaining how this medicine man works. This little guy goes inside and investigates everything. He sees everything. So the enemy does damage to the brain or heart or liver
or kidney or whatever. He goes there. He sees, like X ray. He
sees it, and he goes there and repairs whatever is damaged. He
recreates all the molecules, genes, organics, fibers, or whatever
the enemy damages. He recreates and reforms it. That is why
he has his name. That is why we call him Creator. So he recon-
structs the human mind and physical body. He recreates the
human spirit, so that the spirit could wear its robe and walk
with a clear mind. So that is just one medicine man at work.

When that spirit comes in, he never comes in and says,
"Office call. Ten dollars please," or, "Service call. Twenty dollars please," and like that. "What's your social security number?" "Do you have any Medicare or Medicaid?" He never
questions us like that. He just comes in and comforts and heals.
Then he leaves. So that is our medicine man.

So it's good that you hear about this medicine we have. I'm not a medicine man. Many people think that way, but that's not the way it is. The medicine is out there. Like I wear medicine. He's around here somewhere. So I say, "I need your help, my friend. I need your help." Then I fill the Chanunpa. "Hey, where are you?"

Then he comes in, "I'm right here. What do you need?"

So I tell him, "Well, this guy here needs your help." That way he gets help. The medicine man brings the help. Sometimes they bring health. So the two key words the Chanunpa carries are *help* and *health*. . . .

To get to these sacred powers you have to go through four stages. When you reach the top, the spirit will come and communicate with you. He will give you your instructions. That's the first power, and it takes four years to acquire it. Then you go another four stages to get the second power. And there's a third power and a fourth power, see? Each of them requires four years. So that is four times four years, or sixteen years, before you reach all the way through and obtain the real power. That is the first level of power. Then there is a second level of power. That also takes sixteen years. Then there is a third and fourth level of power. So you have to go on vision quest after vision quest. The spirit will give you instructions. As you go, you go deeper and deeper. Eventually, you will be there with them. When you pass the fourth level of power you will be in the hands of the Creator, and you'll be back in Grandmother's arms again. So a lot of people come to me and want this power right now. But it's not that way. I have one more vision quest to perform, and then I will have the fourth and final power. That is the impenetrable medicine. It can cure any disease known to man. So you have to have a lot of patience for this. . . .

So we rely on this medicine. We rely on these creatures, their ingenuity and powers. They even send a voice to the Creator for us, because we don't have an amplifier. We don't have a radio to send a message way up there. We may be able to send a little gadget to Mars, but we never send a voice to the Creator. We never say, "Hey, Grandfather, where are you? How are you? From up there, how do we look down here?" So we can't do that. We can't send an electrical wave up there, and five years later a message will come back. It's not that way. But over here, the Earth People say, "Yo-ho," and somebody answers back, "Yes. What do you want?" That is science. So we don't have to wait five years for some higher intelligence to send a message back.

This Chanunpa is our relative. So we're not orphans. We have Tunkashila and Grandmother here. The power is here. It is in our hands, so we have to take good care of it. I can remember how my grandmother cared for the Chanunpa. Whenever she took that Chanunpa into her arms, she always cradled it like a baby. Sometimes she would rock with the Chanunpa in her arms and sing lullabies to it and pray to it. She would pray for her grandchildren, and it always happened the way she prayed. . . .

So those are the sacred ways of the Earth People and the sacred Chanunpa. I've lived with these powers all my life. I grew up with them. They are a part of me. They're real. They're the real science and technology. But over here we just drifted away for thousands of years. Now we need to come back to our roots. We need to come back to Grandfather, the Creator, and Grandmother, the Earth, where there is life everlasting.

So I want to end here with a prayer.

"Oh, Tunkashila, Grandfather, Great Spirit, we thank you ever so much for everything. Grandmother, we thank you for the nourishment and life you give us. Tunkashila, there are all kinds of sicknesses and all kinds of viruses floating around here. Tunkashila, incurable sickness is floating around here and coming into our minds. Sometimes it comes and invades our bodies and destroys. There are pains and aches here, Tunkashila. But you are sacred. Your holy eyes see everything, Tunkashila. Let this wind blow [away] all these viruses and all these bad thoughts and bad words that come into our minds. Let it blow away piece by piece. Give us strength. Give us help and health, that way, Tunkashila. Continue to watch this sacred land and watch all of us. Continue to watch this Chanunpa and keep us from nuclear destruction. Tunkashila, I beg you and plead to you that you extend our life so that all my people will come together. Help us so we come to understand, so we keep you whole and keep you sacred. We come in a pitiful way, Tunkashila, so have mercy upon us. Have mercy on us so we have something to eat and something warm to wear this winter, Tunkashila. You're the only one who could do everything for us, Tunkashila. Help us that way. Grandmother, continue that way. Be with us, Tunkashila. You promised you'd be hovering over us all the time—you'd be in front; you'd be on both sides of us; you'd be in back of us; you'd be underneath us. Tunkashila, you promised that way. Let them understand that way, so whenever they need your help, Tunkashila, they'll look up to you. They'll ask for your help. Even if they don't ask you, Tunkashila, help them that way. So make them feel good. Make them happy. These beautiful people here, Tunkashila, keep them well that way. Ho, *mitakuye oyasin* [all my relatives]."

CHAPTER

5

What Lies Beyond Death?

Chapter Preface

Death is one of the greatest paradoxes of existence. Everyone must experience it someday, but no one knows for certain what lies beyond it. Religions have speculated about this topic, and many religions have made belief in an "afterlife" a central part of their doctrines. Some religions believe in reincarnation, and some believe we only have one life. In either case, religions may seek some final release from this world, a unity with God or the universe. The answer to the puzzle of existence, the realization of the goal of our being, may be found in this eternal life. But not all religions believe in such a goal, and so some deemphasize speculation about an afterlife, as they believe it can easily divert attention from the important things of this world. Many views are expressed here, but they share at least one characteristic—none can describe in any detail what awaits us beyond the grave.

We Cannot Know for Certain What Lies Beyond Death

EUGENE BOROWITZ

Eugene Borowitz writes from the perspective of Reform Judaism, a movement founded in nineteenth-century Germany that sought to modernize Judaism by emphasizing morality rather than traditional rituals. The early proponents of Reform Judaism claimed that Torah laws regulating ritual observance, diet, and other aspects of life were no longer relevant. The legacy of Judaism, they claimed, was in the moral teachings of the Torah—not in, for example, ancient laws proscribing working on Saturdays or eating pork. (Orthodox Judaism continued to emphasize the traditional observance of ritual law; Conservative Judaism sought a middle path between the other two movements.) Today, the Reform movement has turned back to more of the traditional rituals of Judaism, but it still remains the most "liberal" of the three major branches of Judaism in its willingness to accept new interpretations of the Bible.

Excerpted from Eugene Borowitz, *Liberal Judaism*. New York: Union of American Hebrew Congregations Press, 1984. Copyright ©1984 by Eugene B. Borowitz. Reprinted by permission of the Union of American Hebrew Congregations.

In this selection, Borowitz considers the vast diversity of Jewish beliefs about the afterlife and how these have changed over time. There is no one Jewish view that can claim to be *the* Jewish view, perhaps because Judaism has shied away from claiming certain knowledge on a topic about which the Jewish Bible says little. Borowitz indicates that many modern Jews have rejected a belief in the afterlife, and that such a belief is not essential to Judaism (as it might be said to be for Christians and Muslims). But he also holds that one can still believe God will provide a life after death, and that this belief can be part of the hope that God gives meaning to the plan of history and our lives within it.

QUESTIONS

1. What are some of the different views about death expressed in the Bible, according to Borowitz?
2. What was the rabbinic or Talmudic view of the afterlife?
3. What impact did modern scientific naturalism have on many Jews and their view of the afterlife? How does Borowitz feel the Jew should respond to naturalism?

■ ■ ■

The Bible says very little about life-after-death, concentrating almost exclusively on what God wants people to do while alive. That yielded the characteristic Jewish attitude: concentrate on this world. Had God thought it important for us to be concerned about the next world, God would have revealed some of its secrets to us. Instead, God's Torah gives us extensive direction on how to live here and now; it promises but does not emphasize or describe afterlife.

Some observers find it strange that Judaism could center itself largely on ordinary human existence and hold only marginal regard for the next world. It does not seem that odd to Jews. The Baal Shem Tov, the founder of Chasidism, epitomized our Jewish sense of balance in this regard when he said, "If I can love God here and now, why do I need to worry about the life of the world-to-come?"

A few statements in the Bible seem to rule out life-after-death. Job, fortifying his arguments against God's justice, says, "As a cloud fades away and disappears, so a person goes down to the grave and doesn't come up from it." (7:9) Many other Bible authors do mention personal survival after death. They call it "going down to Sheol" but they never give us a clear description of Sheol or of life there. Their parenthetical statements about it hardly make it attractive. They refer to it as something like a great pit under the earth, a place of darkness and silence, one where there is no prayer or praise of God. . . .

Some few places in the Bible point to a more welcome sort of afterlife. In a highly visionary chapter of Isaiah we read, "And God will destroy the covering that is thrown over all peoples and the veil that is spread over nations. He will swallow up death forever. *Adonai*, God will wipe away tears from off all faces and the reproach of His people He will take away from all the earth. *Adonai* has said it." (25:7–8) That does not explicitly say that those who had died will now live, though the vision of a revival of the dead might easily be connected to it.

Another evocative passage occurs in the psalm ascribed to Hannah, the mother of Samuel. "The Lord kills and brings to life, brings down to the grave and brings up from it." (1 Sam. 2:6) That suggests that as God causes death so God gives life after death. Perhaps, though, the verse does not describe a literal sequence but is only an extravagant appreciation of God's power to heal the gravely ill.

The Book of Daniel puts all such ambiguity to an end. It notes that, in the end-time, "many of those who sleep in the

> **AT THAT TIME MICHAEL, THE** great prince, the protector of your people, shall arise. There shall be a time of anguish, such as has never occurred since nations first came into existence. But at that time your people shall be delivered, everyone who is found written in the book. Many of those who sleep in the dust of the earth shall awake, some to everlasting life, and some to shame and everlasting contempt. Those who are wise shall shine like the brightness of the sky, and those who lead many to righteousness, like the stars forever and ever.
>
> **Daniel 12:1–3**

dust of the earth shall awaken, some to everlasting life and some to everlasting reproach and rejection. Those who are wise will shine on, bright as the sky. Those who led others to righteousness will be like stars for ever and ever." (12:2–3) Much of the rabbis' later teaching seems stated in this passage: At a distant time and in an extraordinary way, corpses return to life, are judged for their previous acts, with everlasting glory for some and complete destruction for others.

Modern scholars generally agree that the Book of Daniel is one of the latest biblical books written. It was probably composed during the Hasmonean rebellion against the Syrians, about 170 B.C.E. By then, the concept of individual life-after-death in some positive form had become an explicit theme in Jewish teaching. Since we find the historical development of ideas valuable, it would be helpful if we could clarify the passage of Jewish belief from a dismal Sheol to a gleaming eternal life. Despite a number of ingenious scholarly theories about this evolution, we simply have too little data to do much more than speculate how that transformation occurred. Whether the latest stage was a borrowing from the Persians, an ideological device to strengthen the will of the Judean rebels against the Syrians, a response to individual fear of death, an outgrowth of the classic Jewish trust in God, the inspiration of a genius, or simply the revelation of God, we cannot be certain.

The Talmudic View of the Next Life

In the period after the destruction of the Temple, 70 C.E., the doctrine of afterlife was a major and characteristic part of the Pharisees' interpretation of Judaism. Josephus reports that their opponents, the Sadducees, rejected a belief in life-after-death. The Pharisaic teaching was quite specific. The Pharisees expected a resurrection of the dead in the Days of the Messiah.

Though rabbinic literature (which almost totally reflects the Pharisees' point of view) contains many views which differ on matters of detail, we can roughly draw a composite picture of what the rabbis believed happens to us after death. God takes our souls when we die, and they enter a period of purifying punishments. (In later lore, this lasts no more than twelve months; a mourner says the *Kaddish* prayer daily only during this period.) The term *olam haba*, the world-to-come, is often applied to this status.

God then returns our souls to a heavenly "treasury" where they await the earthly coming of the Messiah. Some time after that event, the graves are opened and the bodies, made perfect and pure, arise from them. Their souls are restored to them, completing the resurrection of the dead, *techiyat hametim*.

The revived person then comes before God for a final judgment. The righteous go straight into the life of the world-to-come, the other usage of *olam haba* (a state also referred to as *atid lavo*, the future-to-come). The wicked are punished until they are purified and permitted entry into the world-to-come or else are doomed to destruction and denied the bliss of eternal life.

The Mishnah declares (San. 10:1) that all Jews have a share in the life of the world-to-come. The rabbinic attitude to non-Jews is ambivalent. One source, much quoted in later times (Tos. San. 13:2), is positive toward individual Gentiles. It rules that "the righteous people of any nation have a share in the life of the world-to-come." The general rabbinic expectation concerning "the nations" (of Gentiles) is negative, consigning them to annihilation.

To this day traditional Judaism teaches this doctrine of the afterlife. Over the centuries fantasy and folklore have decorated it with many imaginative embellishments but have not changed its basic pattern. . . .

Rabbinic Judaism contains an even greater variety of opinion on life-after-death than on most other Jewish beliefs. Rav (early third century C.E.), one of the founders of the Babylonian study style which resulted in the Talmud, taught: "The world-to-come is not like this-world-of-ours. In the world-to-come there is no eating or drinking, no procreation, no business, no envy, no hatred, and no competition. Rather, the righteous sit with crowns on their heads and bask in the splendor of God's presence." (Ber. 17a) About the same time, one of the great teachers in the Land of Israel, Rabbi Yohanan, said: "All that our prophets told us about the end-of-days concerned only the Days of the Messiah. What will happen when (after the resurrection and judgment) we go on to the world-to-come, we do not know. As Isaiah (64:3) said, 'No eye beside Yours has seen, O God, what you will do for the person who has hope in You'". . . .

How Modernity Changed
Jewish Belief About Afterlife

When the Jews emerged from the ghetto, they found all these ideas increasingly challenged by modern science. Evolution closely connected human beings with other animals. Medicine showed our life was intimately linked to specific organs and structures. More recently, the unraveling of the chemistry of genetics has lent spectacular confirmation to the intuition of several generations of scientists that life is basically chemical. If our having life means that we are a mass of fabulously intricate interrelated molecules, then death is the decisive disruption of that interaction. And there is no "us" left to survive it. Our chemicals, in their separate and changing forms, will find their way into other parts of nature. Our genetic material is carried on by our offspring, if we have any. We, individually, having been a fantastically wondrous concatenation of chemicals, come to an end when our specific chemistry loses its integration. Moreover, science denies the existence of a soul, a spiritual substance which by medieval definition is so fine it cannot be detected in any laboratory. Since the chemical theory explains life quite satisfactorily, why add unnecessary unobservable entities like the soul?

Some liberal religious thinkers have forthrightly accepted this scientific view. They have compared belief in an afterlife to other mythical matters in traditional religion, like the earth being the center of the universe. Psychology helps us understand how previous generations came to such an idea. They wished it were true, and out of their pain and anxiety they made it true. We have rejected other traditional Jewish beliefs which reflected an earlier world view. We should now also acknowledge that a mature view of reality requires us to give up the belief in personal survival after death.

Fortunately, the Jewish tradition has not emphasized life-after-death; there seem strong currents in our tradition that have largely done without it. Modern Jews, then, feel they have good Jewish warrant for denying the classic views of the afterlife. Having done so, we can emphasize the good that people need to do while they are alive and can thus intensify our sense of human responsibility. We can find long-range satisfaction in the good we have done that will survive our death and in the knowledge that the Jewish people will carry on our ideals long after we are gone.

How an Old Belief Died Out

On no other topic, I would guess, has naturalism, thinking about religion in terms of science, enjoyed a greater success. For some time now most Jews seem to me to have effectively given up belief in life-after-death. At the least, they have been more determinedly skeptical on this belief than any other.

Something of modern science's veto power in this connection may be seen in Reform Judaism's struggle to reinterpret afterlife in a modern fashion. The early nineteenth-century Reform prayer books in Europe already omitted references to the resurrection of the dead. Modern Jews could not be asked to believe that God would one day restore bodies which had disintegrated in the earth. Reincarnation, too, was utterly incompatible with their rationalism but they found the notion of the immortality of the soul congenial. . . .

Belief in such immortality of the soul faded in the mid-twentieth century. Science seemed well on its way to explaining all of life, and naturalism displaced the philosophies which proclaimed the uniqueness of the human spirit. An old Jewish belief seemed to be nearing its end.

In recent years something has changed. A different mood has been moving through much of Western culture. Science is no longer a god whose truth we blindly accept. Its benefits have serious limits, including the new problems it always seems to create for us. It knows much about facts but little about purposes or values. Science may be indispensible to our understanding of the universe, but insofar as it is unconcerned with what is good or just or loving it cannot fully describe human existence. The richness of the day-to-day reality we know ourselves to be confirms that a person is far more than laboratory measurements can show. Naturalism is no longer the obvious, undisputed way of talking about life—and of what succeeds it. . . .

Naturalism hoped to find what is truly real by reducing everything to its smallest physical constituent. The other view, mine, and I think that of Jewish tradition, sees reality most clearly in the most complex thing we know, a person. The one perspective breaks everything down to impersonal energy. The other says we see ultimate reality more clearly as we build upward from human nature to that which transcends and fulfills it. If God is the most real "thing" in the universe, then we may hope that, as we make our lives ever more closely correspond to it, we may personally share God's eternity despite our death. And knowing ourselves to be most fully human through our individuality, we trust that the God who is one will preserve our oneness and grant us personal survival after death.

Life-After-Death, a Personal Statement

That belief cannot be ruled out by saying, "You believe in life-after-death because you want that to be true. You turn your wish into an assertion of fact." Not every wish is unrelated to reality. Some motivate us to reach for what can await us. I yearn for redemptive love and social justice. My wanting them to be real does not make them false hopes even as hoping alone does not bring them into being.

Despite Marx, my desire for life after death will not desensitize me to social evil but actually will intensify my struggles in this world. Being a liberal I am dedicated to humankind's significant role in achieving God's purposes. With that sense of faith, I am unlikely to give up my activism and patiently wait for the life of the world-to-come. True, because I do not consider people the only agents of fundamental change, I will not bring a messianic enthusiasm to every immediate social struggle. But should my projects fail I will not be as dispirited as many one-time liberals have now become. Believing there is only one life, they have grown discouraged, even bitter because they were not able to bring the Messianic Age in their time. Often they now despair of human progress altogether. Why should they spend their only existence suffering continual defeats, why sacrifice their precious few years to the painful task of resisting evil?

Believers who do not expect vindication in this life alone are saved from the spiritual rot that easily sets in when humanity proves obdurate to change or malevolent in interest. They trust God to reward them in another existence for what they have suffered for God's sake in this one. They may even be strong enough to see their defeats on God's behalf as joining them to God's reality. Their lives will be fulfilled no matter what happens in this world for they have a life with God yet to come. And, trusting God, they know history will one day be redeemed by the One who will not ultimately be defeated.

I do not know much more than that, how I shall survive, what sort of judgment awaits me, or what I shall do in eternity. I am, however, inclined to think that my hope is better spoken of as resurrection rather than immortality for I do not know my self as a soul without a body but only as a psychosomatic self. Perhaps even that is more than I can honestly say, though in the use of this term I may lean upon Jewish tradition with which I share so much else. Ultimately, I trust in what I have experienced of God's generosity, so surprising and overwhelming so often in my life. In such moments I sing wholeheartedly the last stanza of the hymn *Adon Olam*, "In God's hand I place my soul both when I sleep and when I wake, and with my soul, my body. God is with me. I shall not fear."

Eternal Life with Christ in God's Kingdom Lies Beyond Death

HANS KÜNG

Hans Küng is a well-known Roman Catholic priest and theologian who has written on a great variety of theological topics. In the book from which this selection is taken, Küng examines various beliefs about life after death with the aim of providing a rationale for the Christian view. Christians do not seek to escape the world, he claims, but to transform it in the hope that they can begin to share in God's work of bringing the "Kingdom of God" into existence. Against Marx's view that hope for an afterlife diminishes the drive to change this world, Kung argues that belief in an afterlife empowers Christians to work towards a better world here and now as they anticipate the culmination of their hopes in God's kingdom.

Excerpted from Hans Küng, *Eternal Life?* translated by Edward Quinn. New York: Doubleday, 1984. Copyright ©1982 by R. Piper & Co. Verlag, Munich. Reprinted with permission.

QUESTIONS

1. What are the central characteristics of the Christian view of eternal life, according to Küng?
2. In Küng's view, what is the relationship between the Christian belief in Jesus crucified and resurrected and the Christian belief in eternal life?
3. How does Küng justify his view that belief in eternal life can lead one to work for a better world here and now?

■ ■ ■

In view of the far advanced process of intellectualizing in theology and the Church, we may perhaps learn to grasp again as a fresh opportunity the fact that the Bible describes the consummation in God with the aid of easily remembered earthly-human metaphors. We may learn perhaps what a mental impoverishment it would imply if we tried to rationalize these images out of existence or reduce them to a few concepts and ideas. Jesus himself speaks of the feast at the end of time with new wine, of the marriage, of the banquet to which all are invited, of great joy on all sides. . . . All metaphors of hope, not yet "sicklied over with the pale cast of thought.". . .

At the end of the book of Isaiah—in Third Isaiah after the Babylonian exile—we find also that great saying, which provides probably the most comprehensive announcement of the consummation, which is not by any means to be understood as escapist, antimaterial, depreciative of the body; a *new creation*, either a re-formation or a new formation of the old world, it must be understood in fact as a *"new earth and a new heaven"* and therefore as our happy homeland: "For now I create a new heaven and a new earth, and the past will not be remembered, and will come no more to men's minds. Be glad and rejoice for ever and ever for what I am creating." He goes on to say that there will no longer be any question of the infant living only a few days, that people will continue to live youthful lives, build houses, plant vines and enjoy their fruit. . . . New Creation is also described—by Jeremiah—as a "new covenant" and—by Ezekiel—as "a new heart . . . and a new spirit."

These then are the pictures for God's kingdom, for the consummation of the history of humanity by the faithful God, Creator and New Creator, taken up and augmented in the New Testament: bride and marriage feast, living water, the tree of life, the new Jerusalem, metaphors for community, love, clarity, fullness, beauty and harmony. But here at least we must remember: images are—images! They may not either be eliminated or objectified, may not be materialized. . . . In the consummation of man and the world it is a question of a new life in the *nonvisual dimensions of God* beyond our time and our space. "Who alone is immortal, whose home is in inaccessible light, whom no man has seen and no man is able to see," we read in the First Letter to Timothy. How could we identify our pictures with the reality of God? God's consummation is beyond all human experience, imagination and thought. The glory of eternal life is completely new, unsuspected and incomprehensible, unthinkable and unutterable: "the things that no eye has seen and no ear has heard, things beyond the mind of man, all that God has prepared for those who love him.". . .

Image concepts which are certainly established in the light of Scripture as a whole, but must be brought to a head in the light of Jesus of Nazareth. Hence—seen from the standpoint of the Crucified and raised from the dead—the *consummation* can be described in a dialectical movement of thought: as life, justice, freedom, love, salvation.

- A *life* into which we are taken with our whole history, however in which provisionality and mortality will be overcome by permanency and stability; a true, imperishable life in that God who proved himself in the Crucified as the living, life-bestowing God: an *eternal* life.
- A *justice* for which we are already fighting in this society, however without ever attaining it, because of the inequality, incapacity and unwillingness of human beings; a justice which—in the light of the justified Jesus—proves to be the law of his grace, which combines justice and mercy: an *all-transcending* justice.
- A *freedom* which we have already felt on earth, whose relativity however will be removed by the Absolute itself; a freedom which—as God's great gift in Jesus—has finally left behind law and morality: a *perfect* freedom.
- A *love* in which we shared already here and which we bestowed here, whose weakness and suffering however will

be transformed by divine strength and power; a love wholly and entirely filled by the God whose love has proved in Jesus to be stronger even than death: an *infinite* love.

- A *salvation* of which we have already had a hint, whose fragility and fragmentary character however will be entirely sublated into the definitive wellbeing or whobeing of God, which, in the light of the resurrection of the dead Christ, seizes the human person in all his body-soul dimensions: a *final* salvation.

All this then, as the kingdom of perfect freedom, of all-transcending justice and of infinite love, is final salvation: *eternal life*—for man and world a life without suffering and death in the fullness of a perpetual now, as in Boethius' classical definition: *interminabilis vitae simul et perfecta possessio* ("the whole and perfect possession simultaneously of interminable life"). But this classical definition of eternity is to be interpreted in a modern dialectical manner as real *life:*

- eternity understood not purely affirmatively as time continued in a linear fashion: as the consecutive *endlessness* of a pure process of unextended moments;
- eternity however not understood purely negatively, as static *negation of all time:* as pure timelessness of an unchangeable identity;
- eternity instead, understood dialectically in the light of the one raised to life, as the temporality which is "dissolved" into finality: as the perfect *power over time* of a God who, precisely as the living God, contains within himself both identity and process. Judaeo-Christian-Islamic thought (about rebirth to eternal life) and Indian thought (about rebirth and nirvana) might perhaps meet at this point.
- The real symbol of irreplaceable archetypical value for God's and therefore man's eternal life—after demythologizing by astronomy and theology—will remain *heaven:* heaven as the sign of derestriction and infinity, of the bright, light, simple, free, of the supramundane beautiful, truly never boring, but continually new, infinitely rich, of perfect bliss.

It is a question here however, not of enthusiasm out of mere blissful hope, but of a summary description as precise as possible of what eternal life can mean today. No preliminary joy however—and this must be maintained to the end—may ever permit Christians to forget the present time, the cross or the *Crucified*, which remains the great distinctive Christian feature as compared to all other hopes of immortality and ideologies of eternity. Who knows better than those who take seriously the following of the justified and the crucified Christ that life here and now is often enough a thwarted and frustrated life. Consequently we are not required to cope intellectually with the problem—highly complex in its speculative detail—of eternal life. Nor are we concerned with the individualistic-spiritualistic approach of "saving our souls." What matters is to work together with others who are living with us—out of hope for an eternal life and in commitment for a better human world—for a *practical life at the present time*, which takes its standard from Jesus the Crucified.

It is only from this standpoint that we can see the radicalness of the primitive Christian message of the Crucified and Risen. Here particularly Ernst Käsemann's comments cannot be stressed too much. The primitive Christian message "speaks of our personal hope and of the promise granted to us beyond

---

WHAT I AM SAYING, BROTHERS and sisters, is this: flesh and blood cannot inherit the kingdom of God, nor does the perishable inherit the imperishable. Listen, I will tell you a mystery! We will not all die, but we will all be changed, in a moment, in the twinkling of an eye, at the last trumpet. For the trumpet will sound, and the dead will be raised imperishable, and we will be changed. For this perishable body must put on imperishability, and this mortal body must put on immortality. When this perishable body puts on imperishability, and this mortal body puts on immortality, then the saying that is written will be fulfilled:
> "Death has been swallowed up in
>   victory."
> "Where, O death, is your
>   victory?
> "Where, O death, is your
>   sting?"

1 Corinthians 15:50-55

---

the grave. This it does in the second place and in the shadow of what is important to it beyond all measure: "God has made this Jesus both Lord and Christ," "Christ must rule," "he has paraded the Powers in public," "all should bend the knee before him." This sequence cannot be confused without everything being distorted. It is wholly and entirely un-Christian if at Easter our own wishes and hopes so come to the fore that Jesus is merely the guarantor of their fulfillment. In Christian terms our future is part of his rule, which reaches far beyond it. But because his rule remains that of the Crucified, even at Easter this is again and again opposed to our own wishes and longings. The voice of the Risen one has never been heard except as calling us to discipleship, and it does so in the words attributed in the gospel to the earthly Jesus: "He who does not take his cross upon him and follow me is not worthy of me.". . .

What does it mean to believe in a consummation in eternal life by God as he showed himself in Jesus of Nazareth?

To believe in an eternal life means—in reasonable trust, in enlightened faith, in tried and tested hope—to rely on the fact that I shall one day be fully understood, freed from guilt and definitively accepted and can be myself without fear; that my impenetrable and ambivalent existence, like the profoundly discordant history of humanity as a whole, will one day become finally transparent and the question of the meaning of history one day be finally answered. I need not then believe with Karl Marx in the kingdom of freedom only here on earth or with Friedrich Nietzsche in the eternal recurrence of the same. But neither do I have to consider history with Jacob Burckhardt in stoic-epicurean aloofness from the standpoint of a pessimistic skeptic. And still less do I need to mourn as a critic of civilization, with Oswald Spengler, the decline of the West and that of our own existence.

No, if I believe in an eternal life, then, in all modesty and all realism and without yielding to the terror of violent benefactors of the people, I can work for a better future, a better society, even a better Church, in peace, freedom and justice—and knowing that all this can only be sought and never fully realized by man.

If I believe in an eternal life, I know that this world is not the ultimate reality, conditions do not remain as they are for ever, all that exists—including both political and religious institutions—has a provisional character, the division into classes and races, poor and rich, rulers and ruled, remains temporary; the world is changing and changeable.

If I believe in an eternal life, then it is always possible to endow my life and that of others with meaning. A meaning is given to the inexorable evolution of the cosmos out of the hope that there will be a true consummation of the individual and of human society and indeed a liberation and transfiguration of creation, on which lie the shadows of transitoriness, coming about only by the glory of God himself. Only then will the conflicts and sufferings of nature be overcome and its longings fulfilled. Yes, "all joy wants eternity, wants deep, deep, deep eternity," Nietzsche's song in *Zarathustra* is here and here alone elevated. Instructed by the apostle Paul, I know that nature will then share in the glory of God: "The whole creation is eagerly waiting for God to reveal his sons (and daughters). It was not for any fault on the part of creation that it was made unable to attain its purpose, it was made so by God; but creation still retains the hope of being freed, like us, from its slavery to decadence, to enjoy the same freedom and glory as the children of God. From the beginning till now the entire creation, as we know, has been groaning in one great act of giving birth; and not only creation, but all of us who possess the first-fruits of the Spirit, we too groan inwardly as we wait for our bodies to be set free."

In belief in God, however, as he showed himself in Jesus of Nazareth, I must start out from the fact that there can be a true consummation and a true happiness of humanity only when not merely the last generation but the full number of human beings—including those who have suffered, wept and shed their blood in the past—will share in it. Not a human kingdom, but only God's kingdom is the kingdom of consummation: the kingdom of definitive salvation, of fulfilled justice, of perfect freedom, of unequivocal truth, of universal peace, of infinite love, of overflowing joy—in a word, of eternal life.

Eternal life means liberation without any new enslavement. My suffering, the suffering of man, is abolished, the death of death has occurred. It will then be the time (in [Heinrich] Heine's words) to sing "a new song, a better song." History will then have attained its goal, man's becoming man will be completed. Then, as Marx hoped, the state and the law, and also science, art and particularly theology will really have become superfluous. This will be what [Ernst] Bloch meant by "genuine transcendence," [Herbert] Marcuse's really "other dimension," the true "alternative life": No longer will "thou shalt," will morality rule, but "thou art," being. No longer will a relation established at a distance, no longer will religion determine the relationship between God and man, but the evident being-in-one of God and man, of which mysticism dreamed. No longer will the rule of Christ in the interim period, under the sign of the cross, accepted in faith, prevail in the Church, but God's rule directly and solely, for the happiness of a new humanity. Yes, God himself will rule in his kingdom, to which even Jesus Christ his Son will submit and adapt himself, in accordance with that other great saying of Paul: "And when everything is subjected to him (the Son), then the Son himself will be subject in his turn to the One who subjected all things to him, so that God may be all in all."

God all in all: I can rely on the hope that in the eschaton, in the absolutely last resort, in God's kingdom, the alienation of Creator and creature, man and nature, logos and cosmos, the division into here and hereafter, above and below, subject and object, will be abolished. God then will not merely be in everything, as he is now, but truly all in all, but—transforming everything into himself—because he gives to all a share in his eternal life in unrestricted, endless fullness. For, Paul says in the Letter to the Romans, "all that exists comes from him; all is by him and for him. To him be glory for ever."

God all in all: For me it is expressed in unsurpassed and grandiose poetic form—interweaving cosmic liturgy, nuptial celebrations and quiet happiness—on the last pages of the New Testament at the end of the book of Revelation by the seer in statements of promise and hope, with which I would like to close on eternal life: "Then I saw a new heaven and a new earth; the first heaven and the first earth had disappeared now, and there was no longer any sea (the place of chaos). I saw the holy city, and the new Jerusalem, coming down from God out of heaven, as beautiful as a bride all dressed for her husband. Then I heard a loud voice call from the throne, 'You see this city? Here God lives among men. He will make his home among them: they shall be his people, and he will be their God; his name is God-with-them. He will wipe away all tears from their eyes; there will be no more death, and no more mourning or sadness. The world of the past is gone.'" It will no longer be a life in the light of the Eternal, but the light of the Eternal will be our life and his rule our rule: "They will see him face to face, and his name will be written on their foreheads. It will never be night again and they will not need lamplight or sunlight, because the Lord God will be shining on them. They will reign for ever and ever."

VIEWPOINT

3

Eternal Bliss in the Garden of Paradise Lies Beyond Death

MUHAMMAD ZAFRULLA KHAN

As Muhammad Zafrulla Khan points out, belief in an afterlife is an essential tenet of Islam—nonetheless, no one can describe in detail the nature of this afterlife, as it differs completely from our present life in this world. The Quran sought to describe the afterlife through images of this world—it is like a garden, with streams of milk and honey—from which Christian theologians erroneously inferred that the Muslim concept of the afterlife is an unspiritual, materialistic one. Nothing could be further from the truth. As Khan shows, the Muslim view is that the soul acquires a new "body" more suited to its eternal life, and it lives with God in a manner we cannot understand. Muslims also view the belief in an afterlife as a completely rational one, as a just God will surely not allow his own creation to be destroyed. If God can create a human from a drop of sperm, is it not reasonable to believe that God can raise the dead as well?

Excerpted from "Life After Death" in *Islam: Its Meaning for Modern Man* by Muhammad Zafrulla Khan. Copyright ©1962 by Muhammad Zafrulla Khan. Reprinted by permission of HarperCollins Publishers, Inc.

Khan also discusses the nature of hell as the self-punishment of the evil soul, which reacts with pain to the afterlife because of its own diseased condition. Each individual is responsible for his or her own situation in the afterlife—the righteous shall be rewarded, and the wicked punished. But Khan also holds a belief (not the view of most Muslims) that hell will come to an end, as the punishments of the wicked are sure to purify them of their sins so they may be united with God as well. In this way, God is shown to be truly all-merciful, one who will not allow any part of creation to be lost.

QUESTIONS

1. Why does Khan believe we can better understand the afterlife by comparing it to sleep or birth?
2. How does the Quran describe hell, according to Khan?
3. How does the Quran describe heaven, according to Khan?

■ ■ ■

Life after death is a subject on which sure knowledge can be gained only through revelation. The Prophet has said: "The conditions of the life after death are such that the eye has not seen them, nor has the ear heard of them, nor can the mind of man conceive of their true reality." Even through revelation man can acquire knowledge of the life after death only in the language of symbol and metaphor. All illustration of the conditions of that life can be by way of similitude only.

Man's life on earth is not in itself a perfect whole: it is incomplete; it lacks fulfillment. Too often it seems to come to an end like a snapped ribbon, leaving loose ends flapping idly. If there is nothing to follow, the co-ordination of values in this life would have little meaning and, indeed, would become almost impossible. There would be no accountability and consequently no responsibility. More than that, there would be no consummation of the deepest yearnings of the human soul. Such realization as is possible in this life is only a twilight experience.

Islam insists on belief in the life after death. There are several matters of belief which Islam regards as essential, but be-

EVERY MAN'S FATE [2187]

We have fastened
On his own neck:
On the Day of Judgment
We shall bring out
For him a scroll,
Which he will see
Spread open.[2188]
(It will be said to him:)
"Read thine (own) record:
Sufficient is thy soul
This day to make out
An account against thee."[2189] . . .
If any do wish
For the transitory things
(Of this life), We readily [2196]
Grant them—such things
As We will, to such persons
As We will : in the end
Have We provided Hell
For them : they will burn
Therein, disgraced and rejected.[2197]
Those who do wish
For the (things of) the Hereafter,[2198]
And strive therefor
With all due striving,
And have Faith,—[2199]
They are the ones
Whose striving is acceptable
(To God).

Quran, Surah 17.13–14, 18–19

lief in the life after death is concomitant with belief in the Existence of God (5:70). Failing belief in the life after death there is no faith at all. The absence of such belief is almost a negation of, and inconsistent with, belief in a Wise Creator.

Too often has man been apt to say: "There is no life other than our present life. We were without life and now we live; but we shall not be raised again" (23:38). "Man says: 'What!

When I am dead shall I be brought forth alive?' Does not man remember that We created him before, when he was naught?" (19:67–68). Man, and indeed the whole universe, has been brought into being from a state of nothingness. It is idle to contend that inasmuch as our observation merely confirms that man dies and his *body* disintegrates, therefore his personality and his existence come to a final end with death. Man's very coming into existence is proof that there is the possibility of continuation. When the fact of man's having been brought into existence through a long process is viewed against the existence of a Wise and All-Powerful Creator, the conclusion is inevitable that man was created for a purpose, and the fulfillment of that purpose demands a continuation of life.

"They say: 'When we shall have become bones and broken particles shall we be really raised up as a new creation?' Say: 'Be ye stones or iron or some created thing which appears hardest in your minds, even then shall you be raised up.' Then will they ask: 'Who shall restore us to life?' Say: 'He Who created you the first time.' They will then shake their heads at thee and say: 'When will it be?' Say: 'Maybe it is nigh. It will be at the time when He will call you.' And then you will respond praising Him, and you will think that you have tarried but a little while" (17:50–53).

It is a misconception that a continuation of life beyond this life must involve the assembly of a dead body's bones and particles after everything has disintegrated and decomposed, so as to reconstitute the body. The body, which is developed for terrestrial existence, is fashioned for the conditions of this life. Life after death cannot and does not mean that the dead will be reassembled and reconstituted upon the earth. Even if that were possible, the earth could not hold a billionth fraction of them. Consequently, the decomposition and disintegration of the human body is completely irrelevant to the possibility of life after death.

The Quran draws attention to the phenomena of sleep and dreams to illustrate that man is capable of undergoing experiences and receiving impressions without physical participation in space and time. These experiences being part of this life, the connection between the soul and the body is no doubt maintained while the experiences last; though their physical co-relations are transformed. There is, as it were, complete realization that the total organism, body and soul, is participating in them. The Quran states: "Allah takes souls unto Himself at death, and during their sleep the souls of those who do not die. Then He retains those on which He has passed a decree of death, and sends the others back for a named period. Therein are Signs for those who reflect" (39:43). The admonition to reflect over the Signs which this phenomenon draws attention to is a clear indication that man can derive an understanding of the nature and reactions of the soul and its condition after death by pondering over his experiences during sleep. . . .

The Quran invites attention to physical birth into this life for the purpose of illustrating the process of rebirth through which the soul passes after death:

"Does not man see that We have created him from a mere drop of seed? Yet behold, he is given to constant arguing. He coins similitudes for Us and forgets the process of his own creation. He says: 'Who can quicken the bones when they are decayed?' Say: 'He Who created them the first time will quicken them; and He knows every kind of creation full well, He who produces for you fire out of the green tree, and behold, you kindle from it. Has not He Who created the heavens and the earth power to create the like of them?' Yea, and He is indeed the Supreme Creator, All-Knowing" (36:78–82). Attention is here drawn to the process of man's own creation for the purpose of this life. The flesh, the bones, the muscles, the blood, the brain, and indeed all the faculties and the whole complicated and yet wonderfully coordinated machinery of the human body constituting a complete microcosm is all potentially contained in less than a millionth part of a drop of fluid. The Wise Creator knows what He is doing. In accord with the manifold provisions that He has already made, the drop of fluid in due course experiences a new creation at birth and matures into an intelligent human being, capable of the highest attainments in every field of life. The center of the whole process is the soul. The body is an essential part for the purpose of life in the conditions of this world. Up to a point, the soul and the body together constitute a unit and are indissoluble; then dissolution comes and that is the end of life upon earth, but that is not the end of life itself. At death the functions of the body come to an end, and except for considerations of decency and respect for the dead, it is immaterial how the body be disposed of. The soul then enters upon a process of rebirth, during the course of which it acquires a new frame, and the result is another organism for the purposes of the new life. Thus "the bones are quickened," but they are quickened out of the soul itself. "He knows every kind of creation full well" indicates that this "quickening of the bones" will be a new kind of creation. The Wise and All-Powerful Creator Who created man from an insignificant drop of fluid and created the whole universe for the fulfillment of the purpose of human life has power to endow the human soul with the capacity to develop into a new organism; and He has power to transport the soul into another universe in which it may find its complete fulfillment. . . .

It is obvious that the conditions of the life after death, though capable of being expressed to some degree in terms of human speech, have not the same character as the conditions of this life. Compared with the conditions of this life, they are purely spiritual, and yet they are so manifested that they are felt and experienced and realized with far greater intensity than are the conditions of this life in the course of existence here. It is not possible with our present faculties to realize the true nature of the conditions of the life after death. All that is possible is to attempt some approximate, intuitive understanding of them. As the Prophet has said, it is not possible for the mind of man to conceive of the true reality of these conditions. The Quran states: "No soul knows what bliss is kept hidden for it as a reward for its good works" (32:18).

A study of the Quran reveals that each human being through his or her conduct during this life develops certain qualities or defects in the soul which render it capable of the appreciation and enjoyment of the conditions of the life after death or which cause it to react painfully to those conditions. We see, for instance, that a healthy organism reacts agreeably to the conditions of this life and finds joy and happiness in them. A defective or diseased organism reacts painfully to those conditions of this life which affect it. For instance, the light of the sun, refreshing to healthy eyes and a great source of delight on account of the facilities it provides for human intercourse and the performance of daily tasks and occupations, and the beauties that it reveals, becomes a source of intense pain and discomfort to one with sore eyes, so much so that if they are not quickly shielded from the bright rays of the sun they may suffer permanent injury and even loss of sight. The same applies in respect of the other senses: hearing, smell, taste, touch, sense of heat and cold, and the muscular sense.

Similar is the case with the spiritual senses. The reactions of the soul in the life hereafter will be governed by the condition in which it enters upon that life. A diseased soul will react painfully, very painfully, to the conditions of the life after death. It may suffer indescribable tortures, according to the degree to which its faculties have become diseased during its life on earth. A healthy soul will react joyfully to all the conditions of the life to come. "We call to witness the soul and its perfect proportioning. He revealed to it what is wrong for it and what is right for it. The one indeed will surely prosper who purifies the soul, and the one who corrupts it will be ruined" (91:8–11).

The same concept is expressed in a different manner. "Verily, he who comes to his Lord a sinner, for him is hell; he shall neither die therein nor live" (20:75). This means that he who enters upon the life after death with a diseased soul will have to face prolonged suffering, from which he will not be able to obtain release through complete extinction, for the soul is immortal, and does not suffer extinction; nor will he be, during this period of suffering, in the full enjoyment of life, for his existence will be only a series of miseries and torments. "But he who comes to Him as a believer, having acted righteously, for such are the highest ranks: Gardens of Eternity, beneath which streams flow; they will abide therein forever. That is the recompense of those who keep themselves pure: (20:76–77). Those who keep their souls pure, that is, those who develop their spiritual faculties in this life into a state of purity which is the state of perfect health for the soul, will experience spiritual reactions that are blissful, the intensity of the reactions depending upon the degree of attunement achieved by the soul in this life. . . .

The Quran explains that all human action leaves an impress upon the soul and that the soul when it enters upon the life to come carries the sum total of this impress with it, and reacts in that life accordingly. The record of a person's acts and their consequences will be presented to him, as in an open book, and he will be told to read his book and to follow the course that it lays down for him. His reactions will be determined by his record. He will himself render an account of the manner in which he spent his life on earth and that very account will constitute his reward or his punishment. "Every man's works have We fastened to his neck; and on the day of resurrection We shall place before him a book which he will find wide open. It will be said to him: 'Read thy book; sufficient is thine own soul this day as a reckoner against thee.' He who follows the right way follows it only for the good of his own soul; and he who goes astray, goes astray only to his own loss. No bearer of burden shall bear the burden of another" (17:14–16). . . .

It is emphasized that the consciousness of living every moment of one's life in the sight of God is the most effective deterrent against wrongdoing and the most potent incentive toward righteous action. Those who live their lives in the full consciousness of being in the sight of God every moment shall enter upon the new life in perfect spiritual health and all their reactions will be joyful. "Those who fear their Lord will be conducted to the Garden in groups, until, when they approach it, and its gates are opened, its keepers will say to them: 'Peace be upon you; you have attained to the state of bliss, so enter it, abiding therein.' They will say: 'All praise belongs to Allah; who has fulfilled His promise to us, and has bestowed upon us this vast region for an inheritance, permitting us to make our abode in the Garden wherever we please.' How excellent, then, is the reward of the righteous workers" (39:74–75). . . .

"The similitude of the Garden promised to the righteous is: Therein are streams of water which corrupt not; and streams of milk of which the taste changes not; and streams of wine, a delight to those who drink, and streams of pure honey. In it will they have all kinds of fruit, and forgiveness from their Lord" (47:16). The verse begins by saying that this is a similitude of the Garden promised to the righteous. The streams and their contents signify certain spiritual qualities of conditions. For instance, water signifies prosperity of every kind; milk signifies knowledge of Divine attributes; wine signifies man's love for God (which is why we often hear of a person being drunk or intoxicated with joy or with love of a person or of God); and honey signifies the Grace and Mercy of God. . . .

One important question in connection with the conditions of the life after death is whether they will be permanent and everlasting or will come to an end. The Quran teaches that while the rewards and joys experienced in the life after death will be everlasting and ever intensifying, the pains and torments will come to an end; all mankind will ultimately find admission to the Grace and Mercy of God. We have been told that mankind has been created for the purpose of becoming the manifestations of God's attributes (51:57). That being the Divine purpose, it follows that it must be fulfilled in respect of everyone. God says: "I will inflict My punishment on whom I will; but My Mercy encompasses all things" (7:157). Indeed, mankind has been created for the fulfillment of God's Mercy (11:120). When pain, punishment, and torment will have achieved their purpose, which is curative, and is in itself a manifestation of God's Mercy, Divine Mercy will then enable each human being to react joyfully to the conditions of the life after death.

The Prophet has said that a time will come when hell will be empty, and the cool breezes of God's Mercy will blow through it. Duration in the Hereafter is within God's knowledge alone and he alone knows how long any particular condition will last. It is common experience that periods of joy and happiness seem to race by, while moments of pain and anxiety appear unending. Pain and torment will appear long, for the torment suffered under the operation of Divine law will be severely felt, and no alleviation of it may be in sight. But eternity is infinite, and in each case a stage will be reached when torment will cease, pain will disappear, and all will be joy. As the experience of pain and punishment will be corrective and reformatory, each succeeding stage will bring an amelioration, but so long as the process is incomplete, the over-all reaction will continue to be painful. The Quran states that the punishment of evildoers will appear to be unending, but it will in fact be terminated when God wills (11:108). The joys of the life after death are also subject to God's Will, but with respect to those, God's Will has been announced; they are a "gift that shall not be cut off" (11:109). For the righteous there is an "unending reward" (95:7).

Thus there will be continuous progress for all in the life after death. Those under sentence will work out their sentence, not as a penance, but as a curative process designed to cure the soul of the defects and disorders accumulated in its life upon earth and to bring it into a state of purity and health in which it can react with joy and pleasure to the conditions of the life after death. The righteous will be continuously praying for, and seeking the perfection of, their light (66:9). They will be greeted by their Lord with: "O, soul at peace, return to thy Lord; thou well pleased with Him, and He well pleased with thee. So enter thou among My chosen servants, and enter thou My Garden" (89:28–31). In these words the righteous are told that because of their unending quest for knowledge of the attributes of God—that they may become perfect manifestations of those attributes—heaven is a state of being in which there is continuous progress and continuous action. Because the attributes of God are without limit, man's seeking to become the perfect manifestation of God's attributes will be endless.

VIEWPOINT

Dissolution into the One Lies Beyond Death

SARVEPALLI RADHAKRISHNAN

Sarvepalli Radhakrishnan (1888-1975) was educated in Western as well as Indian philosophy, and probably did more than anyone to increase the respectability of Hindu thought outside of India. A major scholar of Hinduism and author of many books and translations of Hindu classics, he also found time to serve as vice president of India from 1952 to 1962 and president of India from 1962 to 1967. His lifework was based in the effort to achieve a universal community of humanity, and his philosophy was based in the belief that all religions are striving for the same goal of unity with the Divine.

In this selection, Radhakrishnan explains Hindu beliefs regarding life after death. Everyone experiences many lives on this earth as each is reborn in the cycle of life and death known as "saṁsāra." One tries to end this cycle and obtain release from rebirth or "moksha" by a combination of good works (karma) and knowledge (vidya). Good deeds bring one closer to moksha and unity with Brahman, but it is finally knowledge and understanding of the oneness of reality which brings release. When all have obtained this knowledge, the universe becomes truly one and "lapses into the Absolute," which is beyond expression.

Excerpted from Sarvepalli Radhakrishnan, *Selected Writings on Philosophy, Religion, and Culture*, edited by Robert A. McDermott. New York: Dutton, 1970.

QUESTIONS

1. In what sense is the Hindu conception of eternal life beyond both heaven and hell, according to Radhakrishnan?
2. What are some of the different conceptions of moksha that Radhakrishnan describes?
3. Why does Radhakrishnan believe that knowledge is more important than good works in achieving moksha?

■ ■ ■

Until we negate the ego and get fixed in the Divine Ground we are bound to the endless procession of events called *saṁsāra*. The principle which governs this world of becoming is called *karma*. There are moral and spiritual laws as well as physical laws. If we neglect the laws of health, we injure our health; if we neglect the laws of morality, we wreck our higher life. Any rational conception of the universe, any spiritual conception of God requires us to recognise the utter and unquestionable supremacy of law in shaping our conduct and character.

The law of *karma* is not external to the individual. The judge is not without but within. The law by which virtue brings its triumph and ill-doing its retribution is the unfolding of the law of our being. The world order is a reflection of the Divine Mind. The Vedic gods were regarded as the maintainers of the order, *ṛta* of the world. They were the guardians of *ṛta*. God, for the Śvetāśvatara Upaniṣad, is the ordainer of *karma*, *karmādhyakṣaḥ*, God is law as well as love. His love is through law. The working of *karma* is wholly dispassionate, just, neither cruel nor merciful. Though we cannot escape from the workings of this principle, there is hope, for if man is what he has made himself, he may make himself what he will. Even the soul in the lowest condition need not abandon all hope. If we miss the right path, we are not doomed to an eternity of suffering. There are other existences by which we can grow into the knowledge of the Infinite Spirit with the complete assurance that we will ultimately arrive there. If there is a fundamental difference between Christianity and Hinduism, it is said that it consists in this, that while the Hindu to whatever school he belongs believes in a succession of lives, the Christian believes that 'it is appointed to men once to die, but after this the judgment'.

Belief in rebirth has persisted, at any rate, from the time of the Upaniṣads. It is a natural development from the views of the Vedas and the *Brāhmaṇas* and receives articulate expression in the Upaniṣads. After mentioning the dispersal of the members of the human body at death—the eye of man goes to the sun, the breath to the wind, speech to fire, the mind to the moon, the ear to the quarters of heaven, the body to the earth, the soul to the ether, the hair to the plants and trees, the blood and seed to the waters—Yājñavalkya is asked as to what remains of the individual. He takes the questioner apart, discusses with him in secret about the nature of work. In truth, a man becomes good by good works and evil by evil works. Our lives incarnate our characters.

The future of the soul is not finally determined by what it has felt, thought, and done in this one earthly life. The soul has chances of acquiring merit and advancing to life eternal. Until the union with the timeless Reality is attained, there will be some form of life or other, which will give scope to the individual soul to acquire enlightenment and attain life eternal. Even as non-being is only an abstract lower limit of the existential order, absolute evil is also such a lower limit. Nonbeing, if it existed in itself diametrically opposed to being, would be completely destroyed. Such non-being is nonexistent. Therefore as every existent thing has the form of the Divine, it has also the promise of good.

The Upaniṣads give us detailed descriptions of the manner in which a man dies and is born again. The transition is illustrated by certain examples. As a grasshopper, when it has come to the end of a blade of grass, finds another place of support, and then draws itself towards it, similarly this self, after reaching the end of this body, finds another place of support and then draws himself towards it. As a goldsmith, after taking a piece of gold, gives it another, newer and more beautiful shape, similarly does this self, after having thrown off this body, and dispelled ignorance, take another, newer and more beautiful form, whether it be of the manes, or demigods or gods or of Prajā pati or Brahmā or of any other beings. These passages bring out several aspects of the theory of rebirth. The soul finds out its future body before it leaves the present one. The soul is creative in the sense that it creates a body. At every

> **FROM THE REALM OF** Brahmā downwards, all worlds are subject to return to rebirth, but on reaching Me, O Son of Kuntī (Arjuna), there is no return to birth again.
>
> Those who know that the day of Brahmā is of the duration of a thousand ages and that the night of Brahmā is a thousand ages long—they are the knowers of day and night.
>
> At the coming of day, all manifested things come forth from the unmanifested, and at the coming of night they merge in that same, called the unmanifested.
>
> This very same multitude of existences arising again and again merges helplessly at the coming of night, O Pārtha (Arjuna), and streams forth into being at the coming of day.
>
> But beyond this unmanifested, there is yet another Unmanifested Eternal Being who does not perish even when all existences perish.
>
> This Unmanifested is called the Imperishable. Him they speak of as the Supreme Status. Those who attain to Him return not. That is My supreme abode.
>
> **The Bhagavad-Gītā Chapter 8, 16-21**
> quoted in A *Source Book in Indian Philosophy*, 1957.

change of body, the soul takes a newer form. The state of each existence of the soul is conditioned and determined by its knowledge (*vidyā*), its conduct (*karma*) in the previous existence. From the Bṛhad-āraṇyaka Upaniṣad it appears that all the organs accompany the departing soul, which enters into the *saṁjñāna* and becomes possessed of knowledge and consciousness *vijñāna*. The results of learning and conduct cling to the soul.

The ignorant, the unenlightened go after death to sunless demoniac regions. The good are said to go up to regions which are sorrowless, through the air, sun, and moon. The Chāndogya Upaniṣad speaks of two ways open to mortals, the bright and the dark, the way of the gods and the way of the fathers. Those who practise penance and faith enter the path of light, and they never return to the cycle of human existence. Those who are only ethical, performing works of public utility, travel by the path of smoke, dwell in the world of the fathers till the time comes for them to fall down, then they are born again according to their deserts. The descriptions may be fictitious, but the principle of the ascent and the descent of the soul is what the Upaniṣads insist on. Beautiful characters attain covetable births and ugly ones miserable births. Heaven and hell belong to the world of time.

Rebirth is the lot of man until he obtains true knowledge. By virtuous acts he furthers his evolution. The reward of goodness is to grow in goodness. The reward of growing in purity of heart is to gain a clearer vision of reality. Knowledge of reality leads to salvation. . . .

The fact that the individual consciousness has for its essential reality the Universal Self implies the possibility that every human being can rend the veil of separateness and gain recognition of his true nature and oneness with all beings. The Upaniṣads develop this character of life eternal.

In the Ṛg Veda, what is aimed at is length of days on earth and life in the world of heaven in the company of gods. In the Brāhmaṇas, the performers of various rites are promised the reward of community of being, companionship, and fellowship with the gods. When the Absolute Brahman was recognised, the gods became intermediaries through whose influence the end of unity with the Absolute is obtained. When Brahman and Ātman are identified, the highest goal is declared to be unity with the Self. Deliverance is different from existence in svarga or paradise. The latter is a part of the manifested world. The soul may live there for ages and yet return to earth, an heir to its deeds. Deliverance, on the other hand, is a state of permanent union with the Highest Self. Life in paradise is a prolongation of self-centred life, while life eternal is liberation from it. While the former is time extended, the latter is time transcended.

Enlightenment does not mean a departure in space to a new abode. Arrival and departure have no meaning in the context of liberation. The passages where the soul is said to go by the veins to the rays of the sun and to the sun or from the moon through the worlds of fire, wind, Varuṇa, Indra, and Prajā pati, to Brahman speak of the soul on the pathway to perfection. The Chāndogya Upaniṣad states that the soul of the emancipated, at death, goes out by the hundred and first vein through the crown of the head, fire, wind, and sun to Brahman.

He who knows Brahman becomes Brahman. Perfection is

a state of mind, not contingent on change of time or place. It is an experience of the present, not a prophecy of the future. Temporal distinctions do not apply to it, but if any temporal terms are to be used, they will be words like 'now', 'presently', 'When all desires that dwell in the human heart are cast away, then a mortal becomes immortal and (even) here he attaineth to Brahman'. Freedom is not a future state on whose coming we wait in expectation. It is life in the spirit, in God who is the foundation and power of life.

Is *mokṣa* or liberation life with the Supreme Person whom we love and worship in this life? Is it personal immortality with absolute likeness to God in the world of Brahmā? Is it an impersonal absorption in the Divine Transcendent? All these views are to be found in the Upaniṣads. There are four aspects of release distinguished as *sāmīpya* or intimacy with the divine, *sārūpya* or *sādharmya*, similarity of nature with the divine, reflecting his glory, *sālokya* or conscious co-existence with the divine in the same world, and *sāyujya* or communion with the divine bordering on identity.

There are certain general characteristics of the state of *mokṣa* or freedom. It is conceived as freedom from subjection to time. As birth and death are the symbols of time, life eternal or *mokṣa* is liberation from births and deaths. It is the fourth state of consciousness beyond the three worlds, what the *Bhagavadgītā* calls *paramam brahma* or *brahma-nirvāṇa*. It is freedom from subjection to the law of *karma*. The deeds, good or bad, of the released cease to have any effect on him. Even as a horse shakes its mane, the liberated soul shakes off his sin; even as the moon comes out entire after having suffered an eclipse from *Rāhu*, so does the liberated individual free himself from mortal bondage. His works consume themselves like a reed stalk in the fire. As water does not stop on the lotus leaf, works do not cling to him. Works have a meaning only for a self-centred individual. Liberation is the destruction of bondage, which is the product of ignorance. Ignorance is destroyed by knowledge and not by works. Freedom is not a created entity; it is the result of recognition.

Knowledge takes us to the place where desire is at rest, *a-kāma*, where all desires are fulfilled, *āpta-kāma*, where the self is the only desire, *ātma-kāma*. He who knows himself to be all can have no desire. When the Supreme is seen, the knots of the heart are cut asunder, the doubts of the intellect are dispelled and the effects of our actions are destroyed. There can be no sorrow or pain or fear when there is no other. The freed soul is like a blind man who has gained his sight, a sick man made whole. He cannot have any doubt for he is full and abiding knowledge. He attains the highest bliss for which a feeble analogy is married happiness. He can attain any world he may seek. . . .

Brahma-loka is the widest possible integration of cosmic experience, the farthest limit of manifested being. Brahmā is the soul that ensouls this great dwelling. He is the true life of every being. He endures during the whole period of the cosmos. Beyond it there is nothing in the manifested world. It is not the eternal beyond the empirical. It is the farthest limit of manifestation. When the world receives its consummation, when it is delivered from time to eternity, then there is the flight of the alone to the Alone. The plan of God for the world, which was before creation, is carried out, for He is the beginning and the end of the world. The Cosmic Lord has his exteriorised existence and his interior life. When he turns outward the cosmos is evolved; when he turns his attention inward, the cosmos retreats into latency and the manifested world terminates. When the world is redeemed, the Supreme Lord becomes the Absolute One, alone, and knows nothing else.

In the *Brahma-loka* the liberated individuals present to each other as one. They are manifold in the cosmic process. Their consciousness of the Supreme which is lodged in the *buddhi* is one and not divided among the bodily forms. This identical consciousness is associated with different bodies. This manifoldness does not take away from the unity of the divine being. Until the final return of the whole universe into the Absolute, until the purpose of God before the creation is carried out, the individuals, freed from bondage to matter, will retain their distinctiveness without being sundered by boundaries. When the two poles of being are reconciled, when all individuals rise above the plane of quality, with its ego sense, struggling aspiration, and imperfect love, the world lapses into the Absolute.

Indescribable Nirvana Lies Beyond Death

SANGHARAKSHITA

Sangharakshita is a Theravada Buddhist monk who has lived and studied in India and who now teaches in England. His extensive knowledge of the whole Buddhist tradition is reflected in his writings, in which he explains both the commonalities and the differences among the branches of Buddhism. In this section of his *Survey of Buddhism*, he writes about the Buddhist view of Nirvāna.

The concept of Nirvāna is one of the most difficult of Buddhist concepts to explain. It is the goal that the Buddhist seeks, an overcoming of suffering and selfishness which is usually interpreted as escape from the cycle of reincarnation. But what happens to one who reaches this goal, as the Buddha (or "Tathāgata") was said to have done? Buddhists have always rejected "eternalism" (the belief that there is an eternal "soul" that lives on after escaping rebirth) as well as "annihilationism" (the belief that the person ceases to exist or is annihilated). Nirvāna is neither existence nor non-existence; nor is it both, nor is it neither! Part of the difficulty in describing Nirvāna lies in the fact that Buddhists do not believe that there

Excerpted from Sangharakshita, *A Survey of Buddhism*, 6th ed. rev. London: Tharpa Publications, 1987. Reprinted by permission of Windhorse Publications, Birmingham, England.

is any phenomenon (or "dharma") that endures through time, not even our selves. What we call a self is just a constantly changing collection of states of consciousness, ideas, and feelings. There is in a human no self either to become immortal, or to cease to exist. Sangharakshita attempts to clarify this difficult doctrine, although as he points out, the only true way to understand what happens to a Buddha is to become one.

QUESTIONS

1. According to Sangharakshita, how is Nirvāna described negatively (by what it is not) and how is it described positively (by what it is)?
2. How did the Buddha answer those who assert the doctrine of annihilationism?
3. Why does Sangharakshita claim that the Buddha was not ignorant of the true nature of Nirvāna, in spite of its indefinability?

■ ■ ■

Although the state of perfection attained by following the Path is said to be ineffable, it is referred to in the Scriptures by a bewilderingly rich variety of names. The best known of these in the West is Nirvāna, from the root *vā*, meaning to blow, and the prefix *nir*, out or off. Its Pāli equivalent *nibbāna* is made up of the negative particle *ni* and *vana* meaning selfish desire or craving. Hence the traditional explanations of Nirvāna as the 'blowing out' of the fires of greed, hatred and delusion and as the state wherein the thirst for sensuous experience, for continued existence, and even for non-existence is altogether absent. Notwithstanding these etymologies, however, the goal of Buddhism is far from being a purely negative state, a metaphysical and psychological zero wherein individuality disappears, as some of the older orientalists maintained that the Buddhists believed. What does not in reality exist cannot be said to cease to exist: all that is extinguished is the false assumption of an individual being distinct from and independent of the psychophysical processes of which it is composed. Positive descriptions of Nirvāna are in fact of no less frequent occurrence in the Scriptures than negative ones, though in both cases it must be borne in mind that these are not so much definitions in the logical sense as conceptual-cum-verbal signposts pointing in the direction of a realization which leaves them far behind. . . .

At the outset of our enquiry we are confronted by what at first sight appears an insurmountable obstacle. In common with other teachings of the kind loosely described as 'mystical,' Buddhism solemnly affirms that the Ultimate Experience is beyond the reach of speech, and that words are powerless to describe it. In fact it cannot even be thought about; for the entire cessation of all thought-constructions, including even the distinction—so fundamental to existence in the phenomenal world—between 'self' and 'not-self,' is the principal condition of its attainment. The ineffability, not only of Truth (a word sufficiently colourless for our present purpose), but also of the Tathāgata, the One by whom Truth has been attained, is a topic upon which Buddhist literature of all schools tends to expatiate at a length which might seem to the uninitiated not altogether appropriate. Says an early Buddhist text:

> Since a Tathāgata, even when actually present, is incomprehensible, it is inept to say of him—of the Uttermost Person, the Supernal Person, the Attainer of the Supernal—that after dying the Tathāgata is, or is not, or both is and is not, or neither is nor is not.
> (*Saṁyutta-Nikāya*, III. 118. Horner's translation)

The condition of an Enlightened One after the death of the physical body seems to have been a question about which the Buddha's contemporaries were deeply concerned. The Buddha, however, declared it to be one of the 'undetermined questions' (*avyākrtavastūni*), that is to say, a question which could not be answered by means of any form of logical predication. The condition of the Tathāgata after death is incomprehensible because even during life his nature cannot be fathomed by the intellect. He is not to be measured, any more than the waters of the mighty ocean are, or the infinite expanses of the sky. The Master's reply to Upasiva, who had asked whether one who had attained the goal was non-existent or whether he enjoyed a perpetuity of bliss, makes it quite clear that this incomprehensibility, far from being peculiar to a Buddha, in the full traditional sense of that term, is a characteristic shared by all who have realized the Truth. It also states the reason why nothing can be affirmed or denied of an Enlightened One:

> There is no measuring of man,
> Won to the goal, whereby they'ld say
> His measure's so: that's not for him;
> When all conditions are removed,
> All ways of telling are removed.
> (*Sutta-Nipāta, 1076*. E.M. Hare's translation)

'Words cannot describe the unconditioned,' as the translator tersely paraphrases the last two lines of the stanza.

The Sanskrit texts of the Mahāyāna schools, which are on the whole of much later date than the Pāli Scriptures from which we have quoted, continue to affirm the same truth. That Nirvāna is inexpressible (*nisprapañca*) is the first of the eight points of agreement between the various conceptions of this most exalted state. . . . During the centuries which elapsed between the compilation of the Pāli Canon and the composition of the Sanskrit *sūtras* which embody the fully developed Mahāyāna doctrine, a shift of emphasis had, however, taken place. It was not the inexpressibility of Nirvāna, or even of the Enlightened Man, that was now so much affirmed, as the indefinability of the real nature of things, which was declared to be uniformly identical with voidness (*śūnyata*). . . . What formerly had been applicable to a strictly limited number of cases was now expanded into a universal law. Inexpressibility was no longer a special characteristic of Nirvāna. All *dharmas* (things or phenomena in general) were unthinkable and indefinable in their essential nature, and therefore Nirvāna, as well as the Buddhas and Bodhisattvas, and whatever else might be named, being *dharmas* were unthinkable and indefinable too. . . .

The Buddha himself and his immediate disciples appear, at least in the Pāli Scriptures, to have been more concerned with the delineation of the Path than with descriptions of the Goal; though it is untrue to say, as people sometimes do, that when questioned about the nature of Nirvāna the Buddha invariably remained silent. The texts dealing with this subject may not seem very numerous when compared with those treating of other topics, but they are much more plentiful than is generally supposed, and certainly sufficient to give us a tolerably adequate account of what the limitations of language compel us to refer to as the Buddha's 'conception' of Nirvāna. In a well-known and oft-quoted text the Blessed One declares:

> There is, monks, the stage where there is neither earth nor water nor fire nor wind nor the stage of the infinity of space nor the stage of the infinity of consciousness nor the stage of neither consciousness nor non-consciousness; neither this world nor the other world nor sun and moon. There, monks, I say there is neither coming nor going nor staying nor passing away nor arising. Without support or going on or basis is it. This indeed is the end of pain.
>
> There is, monks, an unborn, an unbecome, an unmade, an uncompounded; if, monks, there were not here this unborn, unbecome, unmade, uncompounded, there would not here be an escape from the born, the become, the made, the compounded. But because there is an unborn, an unbecome, an unmade, an uncompounded, therefore, there is an escape from the born, the become, the made, the compounded.
>
> (Udāna, VIII. 1 and 3. Thomas's translation)

Even in the absence of other texts the second part of this quotation is sufficient evidence for the fact that though Nirvāna is a conceptually negative state, in the sense that no attribute can be predicated of it, nevertheless inasmuch as it constitutes the very basis of the possibility of emancipation from phenomenal existence it may be described as spiritually positive, in the sense of being the definite goal of the religious life. . . .

That Nirvāna, or an Enlightened One, or the essential nature of all *dharmas*, was beyond the reach of all possible predications, that it was not any object denoted by any word in any language, appeared to some uncomprehending critics equivalent to a declaration of nihilism. Overlooking the fact that not only positive but also negative terms had been rejected as inadequate, such persons maintained that Nirvāna was a state of absolute annihilation, and that a man who had attained Nirvāna was no longer in any sense of the word existent. . . .

The Pāli word for nihilism is *ucchedadiṭṭhi*, the belief or 'view' that after death the soul or life-principle is annihilated. At the time of the Buddha this belief existed in two forms, one of which was the doctrine taught by Pakudha, Ajita Kesa-

> **"REVEREND NĀGASENA,"** SAID THE KING, "does the Buddha still exist?"
>
> "Yes, your Majesty, he does."
>
> "Then is it possible to point out the Buddha as being here or there?"
>
> "The Lord has passed completely away in Nirvāna, so that nothing is left which could lead to the formation of another being. And so he cannot be pointed out as being here or there."
>
> "Give me an illustration."
>
> "What would your Majesty say—if a great fire were blazing, would it be possible to point to a flame which had gone out and say that it was here or there?"
>
> "No, your Reverence, the flame is extinguished, it can't be detected."
>
> "In just the same way, your Majesty, the Lord has passed away in Nirvāna. . . . He can only be pointed out in the body of his doctrine, for it was he who taught it."
>
> **From _Milindapañha_**
> quoted in _The Buddhist Tradition_, 1972.

Kambalin and other teachers, the other a doctrine attributed to the Buddha himself by his enemies and, on one occasion at least, by the more obtuse among his own disciples. According to Ajita, the vital principle (_jīva_) was identical with the physical body (_sarīra_), at the death of which both the foolish and the wise were 'cut off' (the literal meaning of the verbal root whence _ucchedadiṭṭhi_ derives) and destroyed. This wrong belief the Buddha rejected in terms of the strongest condemnation, teaching instead the doctrine of the Middle Way which avoids the two extremes of nihilism (_ucchedadiṭṭhi_) and eternalism (_sassatadiṭṭhi_). . . .

The second kind of _ucchedadiṭṭhi_, which was the annihilation doctrine wrongfully attributed to the Buddha, maintains that after death a Tathāgata, or released person, no longer exists. The condition of an Enlightened One was declared to be unthinkable even during his lifetime, and whether after the dissolution of his physical body either, or both, or neither of the terms existent and non-existent could be applied to him was stated to be one of the four undetermined questions (*avyākrtavastūni*) to which no answer ought to be made. Though the view that after death the Tathāgata no longer exists is thus unequivocally rejected, both disciples and non-disciples sometimes insisted in deducing from the Buddha's position a completely nihilistic conclusion. We are told that the monk Yamaka, for example, had formed such an evil view as this, that he understood the doctrine as taught by the Lord to be 'that a monk in whom the āsavas are destroyed at the dissolution of the body is cut off and destroyed and does not exist after death.' Śāriputra, who had taken him to task for his misconception of the Buddha's teaching, counters his argument by forcing him to admit that a Tathāgata, or released person, being neither identical with nor different from, the aggregates of body, feeling, perception, karma-formations and consciousness either individually or collectively, is even in this very life 'not to be apprehended in truth and reality.' Having granted that the condition of the Tathāgata is unthinkable during life, Yamaka has no alternative but to admit that it is equally unthinkable after death, and that negative predications are as much out of the question as positive ones.

A similar case is that of the wanderer Vacchagotta. Approaching the Buddha, he enquires whether or not he is of the view that the universe is eternal, that the universe is finite, that the vital principle is identical with the body, and that the Tathāgata exists after death. Nor are the two remaining forms of predication recognized by Indian logic, namely, the both affirmative and negative and the neither affirmative nor negative, forgotten by the industrious inquirer, who seems to have been anxious to get to the bottom of the matter and have it settled one way or another once and for all. But the Buddha refuses to accept any of them, and Vacchagotta therefore asks what danger he sees in such views that he thus entirely avoids them. The reply he gets is in principle pragmatic. The Buddha refers to each doctrine in turn, and after describing it as 'a view, a thicket of views, a wilderness, jungle, tangle, fetter of views, full of pain, vexation, trouble and distress,' declares that it 'does not tend to aversion, absence of passion, cessation, tranquillity, higher knowledge, enlightenment, Nirvāna.'

Having exhausted all possible views on the four problems which he had raised, Vacchagotta is left no alternative but to ask the Buddha whether he even has any view. He is answered by an emphatic negative and a succinct summary of the Doctrine: the Tathāgata has seen the body, sensation, perception, the karma-formations and consciousness, and he has seen their origin and disappearance; a released person is released upon the complete abandonment of 'all imaginary and confused leanings to conceit in a self or in anything belonging to a self.' Vacchagotta is quick to put another question: Where is the monk who is thus released reborn? But the Buddha retorts that to say that he is reborn does not fit the case. Neither does it fit the case to say that he is not reborn, or that he both is and is not reborn, or that he neither is nor is not reborn. . . .

The texts do not anywhere suggest that the Buddha did not know the answers to the undetermined questions. This does not imply that the correct answer was to be found among the four possible modes of stating each question, for the Buddha had unambiguously rejected each and every one of them as out of the question. Rather does it draw attention to the fact that his knowledge was of an altogether transcendental kind, and that the questions concerned, being by their very nature not susceptible to logical treatment, could be 'answered' only by ascending to a supra-logical spiritual 'plane' where they simply did not arise. As far as the fourth undetermined question, at least, was concerned, this plane was identical with the object with which the question itself dealt. The question concerning the nature of the Tathāgata, and his condition after death, was to be answered by becoming a Tathāgata oneself. That the Buddha, far from being an agnostic, was possessed of full spiritual knowledge and transcendental wisdom, is indicated, not only by the title by which he is most often referred to, but also . . . by the whole trend of his Teaching, which throughout insists that Enlightenment is the true goal of human life.

The Cycle of Continual Change Lies Beyond Death

DENG MING-DAO AND KWAN SAIHUNG

Deng Ming-Dao's book *The Wandering Taoist* is the story of Kwan Saihung, the only member of the Taoist Zhengyi-Huashan sect living outside of China. This sect seeks unity with Tao through separation from the world, meditation, and a discipline of body and mind involving exercise, herbal regimens, and breath training. In this selection, Saihung recounts some of the teachings on death which he received at the Huashan monastery. The Huashan Taoists speak of immortality as a goal, but not as an escape from the ceaseless changing of reality—rather, becoming one with the Tao and its cyclical fluctuations is precisely the way to immortality. In Saihung's view, one must accept death as just another change in the sequence and so be able to flow with the change. This acceptance of change allows one to obtain "immortality," not as an isolated individual but as a part of a larger whole. One who is united with Tao cannot be destroyed.

QUESTIONS

1. What examples from nature does Saihung give to explain the cycles of Tao?
2. Why should the Taoist not be afraid of death, according to Saihung?
3. How does harmonizing with the cycles of nature help one to obtain unity with the Tao and "perhaps even immortality," in Saihung's view?

■ ■ ■

Everything is cyclical. . . . The world follows the seasons. The seasons—spring, summer, fall, and winter—follow one another.

The animals live in harmony with the seasons. In spring, they mate. In summer, they bear their young. In autumn, they nurture their young and prepare for winter. In winter, they either maintain stillness or migrate, but everything is aimed at survival. Rodents burrow. Turtles and bears hibernate. The weak die.

Each year, you should also follow the seasons. Spring is the time for new growth, movement, exercise, and fresh activity. Summer is the time to release your vigor fully, to work on endeavors begun. Autumn is a time of harvest but also of preparation for winter. Winter is a time when nothing moves. Everything withdraws into the earth or dies. That is when you should withdraw into yourself and meditate.

The course of your life will also follow the patterns of the seasons. [First] you are in the spring of your life. You must go forward, bursting like the buds on the trees. You must act any way you feel. You're a child and if you didn't act mischievous or playful, you wouldn't be normal. But as you grow older, remember that the spring is also the optimum time to plant the seeds of your future.

In the summer of your life, be a strong, proud, and able youth. Cultivate yourself, make achievements, explore, leave nothing undone that should be started. Do everything, satisfy all the emotions, but do so with moderation and within the context of your philosophy. Whether you must sometimes be active or retreating, shining or veiled, good or even evil, you must

CHUANG TZU'S WIFE DIED AND Hui Tzu went to offer his condolence. He found Chuang Tzu squatting on the ground and singing, beating on an earthen bowl. He said, "Someone has lived with you, raised children for you and now she has aged and died. Is it not enough that you should not shed any tear? But now you sing and beat the bowl. Is this not too much?"

"No," replied Chuang Tzu. "When she died, how could I help being affected? But as I think the matter over, I realize that originally she had no life; and not only no life, she had no form; not only no form, she had no material force (ch'i). In the limbo of existence and non-existence, there was transformation and the material force was evolved. The material force was transformed to be form, form was transformed to become life, and now birth has transformed to become death. This is like the rotation of the four seasons, spring, summer, fall, and winter. Now she lies asleep in the great house (the universe). For me to go about weeping and wailing would be to show my ignorance of destiny. Therefore I desist."

Chuang Tzu, Chapter 18
Quoted in A *Source Book in Chinese Philosophy*, 1963.

come forth and do great things in the summer of your life.

In autumn, you will reap what you have sown. Once you're in middle age, you will have set your life's course. The consequences of your earlier acts and decisions will begin to appear. How important it is to reach this stage with no regrets! This should be the time you begin to slow down, to teach others, collect your rewards, and make preparations for old age.

Old age is winter. You become still. Your hair becomes ice and snow. You meditate, contemplate life's meaning, and prepare for death. . . .

Many men are afraid of death because they are ignorant of what it is and when it will come. They think death is an ending. It isn't. It is a transformation. Life does not cease. It goes in cycles like the seasons. . . .

You've seen death. You've seen fallen trees, withered wildflowers, corpses of animals in the snows. But have they all ceased to exist? Is death to be a simple fall into immobility and decay? Whether it is a person or animal, the fact is that death is only the casting off of a shell.

What you are, what I am, what the animals are, is something intangible, indestructible, formless—a collection of ancestral memories mixed with traces of the past cosmos. We are spirits, and each individual spirit has existed from the very beginning and will continue hurtling through space, changing and evolving, into infinity.

What you know to be animals were not always animals and will not always remain animals. They are only taking this shell during this lifetime. They are spirits who have come into this world to learn things that are important to them as individuals, and to achieve a divine purpose. But when they come to earth they need a shield, a shell, a body. The body is not the true individual. It is only a vessel. When it is time to go on to another reality, the bodies that have been the vessels are discarded and the spirit goes on.

You cannot wear two sets of clothing. You cannot stay in one building and simultaneously enter another. The shell that is your body must be used up. It will get worn, broken, destroyed. But the spirit is never destroyed, and there is no need to be frightened.

Men are also afraid because they do not know when death will come. This is just one of the curses the gods have placed on humanity. As punishment for man's perversity and evil, the gods blocked the knowledge of death's approach.

The animals know it, though. They know when death is approaching because they are in constant communion with the gods. But the gods no longer speak with men. In our sorrow and ignorance, our arrogance and vanity, we are the only creatures on earth who live out of communion with the higher levels. Only by living a pure life can we lift this curse from ourselves.

So don't be afraid of death. . . . Rather, be prepared for its coming, know its approach, and seek the knowledge in this lifetime that will guide you to a higher reality in the next. Then, at the moment of death, you will cast off your body fearlessly and enter into the next cycle. . . .

All that matters to a Taoist is that one is in harmony with nature. In one's character, one is like heaven and earth, as bright as the sun and the moon, as orderly as the four seasons.

When one has attained Tao, one can even precede heaven, but heaven will not act in opposition, for one will act only as

273

heaven would have at the time. One is not destroyed because one harmoniously follows only the cyclic motion of the Tao, avoiding the aggressive, extravagant expenditures of energy. Efforts to achieve strength and power may lead to short-term success, but such excessiveness ultimately results in an early death.

The *Tao Te Ching* clearly states that when things reach the pinnacle of their strength, they begin to grow old. Therefore, excessive strength is contrary to Tao, and what is contrary to Tao will come to a speedy end.

Thus one seeks not to build up one's own power, but to unite with Tao. One is not aggressive and mighty, but rather humble and peaceful. One seeks not to go the way of other men but rather to follow the cycles of nature. Only then can one know renewal and rejuvenation. Through returning and going forth, expansion and contraction, one knows infinity and perhaps even immortality. For at that point, one is wholly integrated with the Tao.

What Lies Beyond Death Should Not Concern Us

Okada Takehiko, Interviewed by Rodney Taylor

Rodney Taylor decided to interview Okada Takehiko because he had been described as a perfect example of a "living Confucian." What this means is that Okada's Confucianism is central to his life, as he is devoted to a form of Confucian contemplation akin to the Buddhist practice of Zen. But Okada also expresses his religiosity in his beliefs about morality, human nature, and death. He expresses well the Confucian belief that one should not be overly concerned about death—one should be concerned about this life, and seek to improve it for all. He does not speculate about what lies beyond the grave, but instead speaks of the dead with reverence and remembrance in keeping with the rituals of Confucianism. The way one honors the memory of the dead reflects how one lives here and now, as one's recollection of the dead shows what one values in the living.

Excerpted from Rodney L. Taylor, *The Confucian Way of Contemplation*. Columbia: University of South Carolina Press, 1988. Copyright ©1988 by University of South Carolina. Reprinted with permission.

The following selection is comprised of Okada's own words as recorded by Taylor.

QUESTIONS

1. How does the memory of his teacher affect Okada Takehiko and his views on the afterlife?
2. How does Okada describe the relationship between life and death?
3. What is Okada's view on "respect for life"? How does this relate to his views on death?

■ ■ ■

Let me turn to the topic of the personality of my teacher. He always worried about my health because I was so weak. Whenever I talked with him about my family problems he listened very considerately. His personality had the humaneness of the famous Neo-Confucians Chou Tun-i and Ch'eng Hao. I myself felt that I was in the warm breeze of spring when I was in his presence. I felt easy and carefree when I was returning home from my teacher's house, as the Ch'eng brothers reported when they left Chou Tun-i. My teacher was physically very strong and this permitted him to study very hard. There was no way I could put anywhere near the time or energy into study because of my health. I certainly never worried about my teacher's health, and then suddenly he was diagnosed as having stomach cancer. I feel so terribly sorry whenever I think about it, even now. He asked me at one point if after he was dead I would read the first chapter of the *Doctrine of the Mean* during the funeral service. And so, I read the first chapter of the *Doctrine of the Mean* and tears and sobs filled my eyes and face. I was even thinking of leaving Fukuoka, the place where I had devoted myself to my teacher who now had died. Before he died he gave me an ink stone as something to remember him by, an ink stone from the Sung dynasty. In addition, I also received pieces of calligraphy and many books belonging to Kusumoto Tanzan, my teacher's grandfather. This made me feel all the more committed to bringing Neo-Confucianism to society, for I was now a person who had had a great teacher who died. Because of this sense of responsibility, I organized the publication of a series of volumes on Neo-Confucianism.

When I recall all these people there really is no word with which I can thank them, my parents, my eldest brother, the person who supported me to go to university, and my teacher Dr. Kusumoto. Whenever I would complete a book I would express my gratitude to them by offering the book in front of their photograph or memorial tablet, burning incense and then pressing my hands together in prayer. . . .

If those people whom I love, my wife, my parents or other relatives, die, then a deep grief arises in my heart, naturally. The law of the universe, however, is that those who are born will die; this we must believe. As a matter of fact those who have died still exist. They exist in my heart, and I shall never forget them. For example, when my teacher died, I suffered deeply and painfully. I want to think that when I myself die and go to an afterlife, I shall see my teacher again and I shall read books with him and study under him once again. Whether there actually is an afterlife or not, my teacher lives on in my heart. In a similar way my parents, my brothers and sisters, they all live on in my heart. And, of course, I remember my former wife every now and then, though I don't talk about it with my current wife!

In the Confucian tradition life and death are complementary to each other. The *Book of Changes* suggests this complementary nature, and most Confucians would think this way. Of course, over and above that, many would feel that the souls of the dead can continue to have a relationship with the living.

"THE ANCIENTS HAD THE SAYING 'Dead but immortal.' What does it mean?". . .

There was a former great officer of Lu by the name of Tsang Wen-chung. After his death his words remain established. This is what the ancient saying means. I have heard that the best course is to establish virtue, the next best is to establish achievement, and still the next best is to establish words. When these are not abandoned with time, it may be called immortality.

Tso Chuan, Duke Hsiang, 24th year
quoted in A *Source Book in Chinese Philosophy*, 1963.

For that reason, ancestor worship has played a major role.

From my own point of view, the relation of life and death is that of cause and effect. Because something is born, it will die. This is simply the law of the universe. Now if I know that I am going to die, then I would simply say I am following that principle. In my heart I would worry, of course, about my family, about society and the state. I guess too that I would be saying to the dead, "I'm coming to see you!" I would be thinking this way until my actual death. The actual question of the existence of an afterlife is unsolvable and endless. In my own heart I would entertain this particular question in the following way. If I have done something good or beneficial during my lifetime, then the people whom I have had contact with in the world might remember some small thing I have done or said and they might receive some small benefit from this. Even if it were true that there were an afterlife, my response would be nothing more than the hope that the living would derive some good, some benefit, from something I might have said or done.

The universe, of course, has a purpose and human beings exist in this universe with purpose. In fact the universe would be meaningless without human beings, since the universe exists together with the human mind; the human mind is a reflection of the mind of the universe. . . .

I still remember Confucius' own words, "We don't yet know about life," how could we thereby know what is going to happen in the future? It is obvious that everyone is born and everyone must die, but it seems ridiculous to think about death while we are still living. Humankind came to exist on this earth and it might disappear one day. That is a fact, and yet I am still opposed to thinking about the end of the world. The only point that might be useful is to raise the issue of the potential danger of the destruction of the world in order to make humanity realize the inherent importance of life itself. The nuclear threat has posed this as a real problem. To counter this we need to stress the importance of respect for human life more than the development of science. In practice, however, it does not develop itself in this way. This is regretful. Yet still we want to make that attempt to stress the importance of respect for life, especially to scientists and politicians. . . .

The important point is the issue of the common survival of humanity. We need to reach out to overcome differences and

> **11:11. CHI-LU (TZU-LU) ASKED ABOUT** serving the spiritual beings. Confucius said, "If we are not yet able to serve man, how can we serve spiritual beings?" "I venture to ask about death." Confucius said, "If we do not yet know about life, how can we know about death?"
>
> **Confucius, Analects 11:11**
> quoted in A *Source Book of Chinese Philosophy*, 1963.

conflicts, to seek a oneness with others. This is the only means available. The West has focused upon analytic philosophy and science, the East upon the integration and wholeness of things. Both of these perspectives are indispensable. Until quite recently it seemed that the analytic Western model prevailed in the world. But we should not forget the Eastern method, the experience of the wholeness of things. Otherwise the Western analytic approach could bring about the destruction of human society. On the other hand, only to focus upon the Eastern model might result in the stopping of the scientific and technological development of civilization. Both are essential. Confucianism expresses this perspective, for it accepts the Western analytic model but also builds upon an Eastern model of the wholeness of things. To Confucianism, respect for human life and human dignity is the central issue.

VIEWPOINT

8

Life with the Ancestors Lies Beyond Death

VINE DELORIA JR.

Vine Deloria Jr. is a scholar of Sioux heritage who has studied both Western and Native American thought and culture. As a practicing lawyer, he fights for Native American rights, and is also a professor of Native American Studies. He has concluded that Western beliefs (and Christianity in particular) have been destructive not only to Native Americans but to other societies and nature itself. In his book *God Is Red*, Deloria defends Native American religious beliefs (using examples from many tribes, the Sioux among them) and rejects the corresponding Christian beliefs. Whereas Christians seem to fear death (he claims), Native Americans view it as a natural continuation of life. They do not speculate in great detail about life after death, but tend to speak of unity with their ancestors in a spirit-world or unity with nature and their land. They do not seek to escape this world but believe that the dead remain in this world in a sense, as they are part of the community which endures. In this way, according to Deloria, Native Americans show that death is not to be feared but accepted as a natural change.

Excerpted from *God Is Red* by Vine Deloria Jr., by permission of Fulcrum Publishing, Inc. 350 Indiana St., #350, Golden, CO 80401, (800) 992-9208.

1. How do Native American views on death indicate their understanding of nature, in Deloria's view?
2. Why is it so important to Native Americans that they are buried on their own land, according to Deloria?
3. Why does Deloria believe that Native Americans are able to confront death without feelings of guilt or inadequacy?

■　■　■

W hen we examine American Indian tribal religions, we find a notable absence of the fear of death. Burial mounds indicate a belief that life after death was a continuation of the life already experienced. Personal possessions, familiar tools and weapons, cooking utensils, and quite frequently food were placed near the body so that it would be sustained in the next life. It was not contemplated that the soul would have to account for misdeeds and lapses from a previously established ethical norm. All of that concern was expressed while the individual was alive. Some tribes viewed entrance into the next life as almost a mechanical process to which everyone was subject, a natural cosmic process to which all things were bound.

Many Indians perceived not only that the next life was a continuation of the present mode of existence but also that the souls of people often remained in various places where they had died or suffered traumatic events. People visiting the Sand Creek location where the Cheyennes were massacred under Colonel Chivington have told me that they can hear the cries of the women and children who are still living near this dreaded place. Indians receiving bones from museums for reburial tell about spirits of the departed speaking to them during the reburial ceremonies and thanking them for helping to get their bones from the museums so they can rest in the Mother Earth. Some decades ago I attended a burial in a Christian cemetery at Mission, South Dakota. After the body was in the grave and the several mourners were still standing at the grave, an old woman stepped forward and put an orange on the grave. The Episcopal priest who had conducted the service rushed over and took the orange away, saying, "When do you think the departed will come and eat this orange?" One of the Sioux men standing there said, "When the soul comes to smell the flowers!" No one said anything after that.

The Indian ability to deal with death was a result of the much larger context in which Indians understood life. Human beings were an integral part of the natural world and in death they contributed their bodies to become the dust that nourished the plants and animals that had fed people during their lifetime. Because people saw the tribal community and the family as a continuing unity regardless of circumstance, death became simply another transitional event in a much longer scheme of life. Some tribes made up medicine bundles containing bits of hair of the deceased, flesh or claws of the animals and birds most closely related to the family, and other intimate things of the deceased. This bundle was kept in the family dwelling for a year after the death and treated as if the person was still present with the family. In that way the trauma of losing the person was extended over a period of time and people could be comforted that, while the deceased was not visibly present, he or she was spiritually and emotionally present.

Most tribes were very reluctant to surrender their homelands to the whites because they knew that their ancestors were still spiritually alive on the land, and they were fearful that the whites would not honor the ancestors and the lands in the proper manner. If life was to mean anything at all, it had to demonstrate a certain continuity over the generations and this unity transcended death. At a treaty-signing session in the Illinois country in 1821, the Potawatomi chief, Metea, spoke of this continuity as the basic reason for his reluctance to cede the tribal lands.

A long time has passed since first we came upon our lands, and our people have all sunk into their graves. They had sense. We are all young and foolish, and do not wish to do anything that they would not approve, were they living. We are fearful we shall offend their spirits if we sell our lands; and we are fearful we shall offend you if we do not sell them. This has caused us great perplexity of thought, because we have counselled among ourselves, and do not know how we can part with our lands.

My father, our country was given us by the Great Spirit, who gave it to us to hunt upon, to make our cornfields upon, to live upon, and to make our beds upon when we die.

This idea of identity and continuity of life lay behind the posture of many of the tribes as they approached the whites. It could be said to be a more fundamental reason than any other for the Indian resistance to white invasions of tribal land a century ago and even today. Young Chief Joseph, the famous Nez Percé leader, remained at peace with the white settlers until they began to invade his valley. When he was finally forced to fight to protect himself, he recalled the promise he had made to his father as the older Joseph lay dying.

My son, my body is returning to my mother earth, and my spirit is going very soon to see the Great Spirit Chief. When I am gone, think of your country. You are the chief of these people. They look to you to guide them. Always remember that your father never sold his country.

You must stop your ears whenever you are asked to sign a treaty selling your home. A few more years and the white men will be all around you. They have their eyes on this land. My son, never forget my dying words. This country holds your father's body. Never sell the bones of your father and your mother.

Some people have regarded this speech of the older Joseph as merely symbolic of Indian religion, but we must recall that for tribal people symbolism is not the communicative image of Westerners but the expression of a reality that Westerners often refuse to acknowledge. This conception of land as holding the bodies of the tribe in a basic sense pervaded tribal religions across the country. It testified in a stronger sense to the underlying unity of the Indian conception of the universe as a life system in which everything had its part.

It is doubtful, however, if any of the tribal religions considered life after death to be radically changed from the life they were living. Chief Seattle, on signing the Treaty of Medicine Creek in 1854, gave a famous speech in which he summarized his beliefs about the nature of the lands his tribe had given up. If ever an Indian could have been said to have anticipated D. H. Lawrence, Albert Camus, and William Carlos Williams, Seattle's speech would certainly merit first consideration. In it he distinguished between tribal beliefs and the attitude of the Christians who were taking control of the land—at least in a legal sense.

To us the ashes of our ancestors are sacred and their resting place is hallowed ground. You wander far from the graves of your ancestors and seemingly without regret. . . .

Your dead cease to love you and the land of their nativity as soon as they pass the portals of the tomb and wander way beyond the stars. They are soon forgotten and never return. Our dead never forget the beautiful world that gave them being. . . .

Every part of this soil is sacred in the estimation of my people. Every hillside, every valley, every plain and grove, has been hallowed by some sad or happy event in days long vanished. The very dust upon which you now stand responds more lovingly to their footsteps than to yours, because it is rich with the blood of our ancestors and our bare feet are conscious of the sympathetic touch. Even the little children who lived here and rejoiced here for a brief season will love these somber solitudes and at eventide they greet shadowy returning spirits. And when the last Red Man shall have perished, and the memory of my tribe shall have become a myth among the White Men, these shores will swarm with the invisible dead of my tribe, and when your children's children think themselves alone in the field, the store, the shop, upon the highway, or in the silence of the pathless woods, they will not be alone. At night when the streets of your cities and villages are silent and you think them deserted, they will throng with the returning hosts that once filled and still love this beautiful land. The White Man will never be alone.

Let him be just and deal kindly with my people, for the dead are not powerless. Dead, did I say? There is no death, only a change of worlds.

Again we see the fundamental conception of life as a continuing unity involving land and people. One might be tempted to suggest that as land is held by the community, the psychic unity of all the worlds is made real. We are not faced with formless and homeless spirits in this idea but with an ordered and purposeful creation in which death merely marks a passage from one form of experience to another. Rather than fearing death, tribal religions see it as an affirmation of life's reality. . . .

It is probably in the idea of the death song, which was found in many of the tribal religions, that the idea of death can adequately be understood. The death song was a special song sung as a man faced certain death. Often it taunted his enemies who were in the act of killing him. More often it acted as a bene-

> **GOOD THUNDER NOW TOOK ONE** of my arms, Kicking Bear
> the other, and we began to dance. The song we sang was like this:
> "Who do you think he is that comes?
> It is one who seeks his mother!"
> It was what the dead would sing when entering the other
> world and looking for their relatives who had gone there before
> them.
>
> **From Black Elk Speaks, 1972**

dictory statement by the individual to summarize and conclude his time of existence. Rather than being a feverish preparation for death it was the final affirmation of the meaning of individual existence, for it glorified the personal integrity of the person. It individualized his tribal membership in a manner bringing credit and meaning to his life as a tribal member. . . .

The singular aspect of Indian tribal religions was that almost universally they produced people unafraid of death. It was not simply the status of warrior in the tribal life that created a fearlessness of death. Rather the integrity of communal life did not create an artificial sense of personal identity that had to be protected and preserved at all costs. . . .

Some tribes had special ceremonies to be used in conjunction with the dead. The Lakota, or Sioux, for example, had a ceremony in which the sacred pipe was used, and the souls of the recently departed were kept with the tribal community to be purified and eventually released. In a tragic interference with the tribal religion, the government banned this ceremony in the 1890s, causing a great trauma among the people. . . .

In general we could say that the afterlife was not of overwhelming concern to people of the tribal religions. Vague references to the lands of the spirits, descriptions of the Milky Way as the path over which souls traveled, and concern for the departed spirits remaining, which was prevented in some tribes by burning of personal possessions, probably indicated distinct beliefs of certain tribes. No highly articulated or developed theories of the afterlife were ever necessary, and certainly none projected a life radically different than that experienced on Earth. . . .

It is in the face of death that Indian tribal religions have

285

their magnificence. Big Elk, an Omaha chief, delivered a funeral oration in 1815 at the death of Black Buffalo, a fellow Omaha, and counseled his fellow chiefs as follows:

> Do not grieve. Misfortunes will happen to the wisest and best of men. Death will come and always out of season. It is the command of the Great Spirit, and all nations and people must obey. What is past and cannot be prevented should not be grieved for. . . . Misfortunes do not flourish particularly in our path. They grow everywhere.

While death is truly a saddening event for people of tribal religious traditions, it is an event with which every person and nation is faced and not an arbitrary, capricious exercise of divine wrath. Even today this attitude persists in Indian societies, and the natural grief occurring with the loss of a loved one is rarely translated into personal feelings of guilt, inadequacy, or sin, which appear to plague Westerners. The community regroups and continues to exist; while individuals are lonely, they are not alone.

GLOSSARY

advaitic Literally, to be "one without a second" (in Sanskrit, the language of the Hindu **Vedas**). This attribute describes **Brahman**, the one reality in all things, which is ultimately the only reality.

a priori Literally, "prior to" (in Latin). Used to refer to that which is postulated prior to something else; e.g., an idea believed to be in the mind prior to and apart from learned experiences and so not based in experience (such as mathematical concepts).

Analects The most central texts attributed to Confucius.

an sich Literally, "in itself" (in German). Refers to something as it exists apart from our perceptions of it. See also **Ding an sich**.

asavas In Buddhism, the selfish cravings that cause people to suffer and that bind them to the world.

atman The inner soul or self of a person, in Hinduism. Because all are one, there is ultimately only one "Self," which is also **Brahman**.

bourgeoisie The middle class of property owners who control capitalist society, in the Marxist view.

Brahman Hindu term for the only reality that truly exists; the sacred; all are Brahman and one in their inner essence. See also **advaitic** and **atman**.

Buddha An enlightened one, in Buddhism; one who has "woken up" to the truth of Buddhism. Often refers to the founder of Buddhism, Siddhartha Gautama, but not only to him. See also **Tathagata**.

chai The ritual performed by Taoist priests that frees the souls of the dead from "hell" or "purgatory." Closely associated with the ritual of **Chiao**.

chanunpa The sacred pipe used in Lakota Sioux religion, viewed as a spirit that can bring other spirits to a ceremony.

ch'i The life energy of a person, in Chinese philosophy.

Chiao The Taoist ritual that seeks to unite one with the Tao by a process of self-emptying and manipulation of cosmic powers. See also **chai**.

Chun Tzu The superior person whom one aims to become, in Confucian moral philosophy.

cosmogony A view of how the world came to be; a creation story.

dharma Also *dhamma*. This term has several meanings. (1) In Buddhism, it may refer to the truth or teaching of the Buddha (The Dharma) or (2) phenomenal objects, things as we perceive them to exist (dharmas); (3) in Hinduism, the term refers to the moral order of the universe or (4) an individual's place in this order, his or her moral duty, role, or destiny.

287

Ding an sich "Thing in itself" (in German). In Immanuel Kant's philosophy, this notion referred to objects as they exist apart from our perceptions of them. See also **noumena**.

doxology Praise of God.

empirical Experiential; based on our experience of the world perceived through our senses, in contrast to **a priori** knowledge.

eros Greek word for a love that desires to acquire and unite with its object; the creative drive to obtain a desired aim.

eschatological Pertaining to the *eschaton* (Greek: "last things"), the end of the world, including (in Christian thought) the final judgment and resurrection of the dead.

exclusivism The belief that truth is found in one religious tradition alone that forms the exclusive basis for the correct understanding of God, the world, humanity, etc.

fides implicita "Implicit faith" (in Latin). In Roman Catholic theology, the term refers to a faith in God or Christ that may not be consciously recognized or fully developed but that can nonetheless be sufficient for salvation.

fiqh Interpretation of the Law, in Islam; the expert who engages in such interpretation is known as a *Faqih* (plural: *Fuqaha*). See also **Shari'ah**.

Hadiths Reports of things Muhammad said that were not divine revelations, but his own personal opinions. See also **Sunnah; Shari'ah**.

halakhah The way of life prescribed by the **Torah** and **Talmud**, accepted by Orthodox Judaism as including adherence to 613 commandments relating to every aspect of life.

Hinayana "The Lesser Vehicle" (in Sanskrit). **Mahayana** Buddhists sometimes referred to **Theravada** Buddhists by this derogatory label.

homo religiosus Literally, "religious man" (in Latin). Used to refer to the basic nature of humans as religious beings.

i The Confucian virtue of justice or righteousness.

impersonae John Hick's term for nonpersonal concepts of the sacred, as those expressed in Hindu or Taoist religion.

inclusivism The belief that, while one religion alone contains the norm by which religious truth should be evaluated, other religions may participate in this truth to a lesser extent and so be at least partially "true."

jen The Confucian virtue of benevolence or humanity.

justification In Christian theology, the process whereby the sinner comes to be regarded as just or righteous in God's eyes, and thus saved. Based in God's forgiveness of sins and human faith in the power of Jesus' death to take away sin.

Ka'bah The central shrine of Islam, located in Mecca.

karma In Hinduism, one's karma, or deeds, can influence one's journey towards salvation; specifically, good deeds can cause one to be reborn with a better status, and evil or selfish deeds can cause one to be reborn with a lower status.

Lakota One of the group of tribes that make up the Sioux peoples.

li The Confucian virtue of propriety; honoring one's elders and ancestors, acting with respect for tradition and in accordance with rituals and customs of Chinese religion.

Mahayana "The Greater Vehicle" (in Sanskrit). The branch of Buddhism practiced mainly in China and Japan that claims to make salvation possible for all beings. Directed against **Theravada** Buddhism, which Mahayana Buddhists derided as "**Hinayana**" ("The Lesser Vehicle").

midrash In rabbinic Judaism, an interpretation that adds to or embellishes a biblical story.

Mishnah The oldest part of the **Talmud**, which provides rabbinic interpretations of the **Torah**.

Mitakuye Oyasin "All my relations" (in Lakota Sioux). Used to refer to the spirits of all things.

moksha Hindu term for the escape or liberation from **samsara** (the rebirth cycle). Upon obtaining moksha, one is no longer reborn but united with **Brahman**.

monotheism Belief in one god.

mysterium tremendum Literally, "great mystery" (in Latin). Rudolf Otto's term for that to which all religions point.

nihilism The belief in nothing; not believing in anything.

nirvana also *nibbana*. The goal of Buddhism, the extinction of self; literally, "to blow out," as a candle.

noumena Things that exist outside our ability to perceive them; the unknowable aspect of reality that transcends our knowledge. Singular: *noumenon*. See also **phenomena**; **Ding an sich**.

numinous Rudolf Otto's term for the "holy" that is experienced by all religions.

personae John Hick's term for the personal forms of the sacred expressed, for example, in Jewish, Christian, or Muslim concepts of God.

phenomena Things as we perceive them, as they are understood by us to be, in distinction from the nature of things in themselves. See also **noumena**; **Ding an sich**.

pluralism In distinction from **exclusivism** and **inclusivism**, pluralism holds that no one religion contains the norm for truth and that several religions may contain truth.

polytheism Belief in many gods.

proletariat Karl Marx's term for the urban working class, which he believed would seize power from the capitalists.

pro nobis "For us" (in Latin). Used in Christian theology to refer to what God does for our sakes or for the sake of our salvation.

samsara Hindu term for the cycle of births and deaths, rebirth, or reincarnation, from which Hindus seek to escape. See also **moksha**.

seder The ritual meal celebrated as part of the Jewish holiday of Passover, which commemorates the rescue of the Israelites from Egyptian slavery.

Shari'ah Muslim law, based on the **Quran** and **Hadiths** of Muhammad.

sheol Hebrew word used in Jewish scriptures to refer to the place of the dead. Sheol was not really a place of punishment like "hell" but a shadowy form of pseudo-existence (like Hades in Greek mythology).

shirk The sin of associating a created thing with God, in Islam; idolatry or worship of worldly things; worship of other gods besides the One God.

shunyata Also *sunyata*. Emptiness, the Void; the understanding of **nirvana** put forth by some Buddhists, especially in the **Zen** tradition. Beyond both existence and nonexistence as normally understood.

soteriological Of or pertaining to salvation; e.g., finding grace, meaning, fulfillment, etc.

Sunnah The traditions of the prophet Muhammad found in the Quran and **Hadiths**. The basis for Muslim law (**Shari'ah**).

syncretism A tendency to combine several religious beliefs together without regard to their diverse origins.

Talmud Rabbinic texts that interpret the **Torah** and its divine commandments to Israel.

Tao (pronounced "dow") Chinese for "the Way," a central concept in Taoism referring to the mysterious power behind all existence with which the Taoist seeks harmony.

Tao te Ching *The Way and Its Power*; the Taoist classic by Lao Tzu.

Tathagata One who has obtained release from suffering and selfishness, in Buddhism; a Buddha; one who has attained enlightenment regarding Truth.

tawhid The Muslim doctrine of unity; the belief that there is only one God.

theanthropocosmic Raimundo Panikkar's term for the interrelation of God (Greek: *theos*), humanity (*anthropos*), and world (*cosmos*).

theodicy The justification of God; usually an explanation of why evil exists, if God is supposed to be all-good and all-powerful.

Theravada "Path of the Elders." Branch of Buddhism practiced mainly in Southeast Asia that emphasizes the Four Noble Truths and the Noble Eightfold Path of the Buddha. See also **Mahayana**.

Torah The first five books of the Jewish Bible, containing God's commandments to Israel and the story of Israel's origins. The basis for Jewish ritual and moral law as interpreted by rabbinic Judaism in the **Talmud**.

Tunkashila Lakota Sioux word for the Creator, personified as male.

Upanishads Hindu scriptures composed 600-200 B.C.E. that developed the philosophy of classical Hinduism through such central concepts as **Brahman, atman, moksha, samsara**.

Vedas Hymns to the gods comprising the earliest Hindu scriptures, dating from 1500-1000 B.C.E. The term *Vedas* also sometimes refers to the larger set of Hindu scriptures which includes the Vedas, the Brahmanas (1000-800 B.C.E.), and the **Upanishads** (600-200 B.C.E.)

vidya Hindu term for the spiritual knowledge that, along with works, or **karma**, helps one toward **moksha**. Specifically, knowledge that one's **atman** is **Brahman** leads to the knowledge that all are one.

qi Another spelling of **ch'i**.

Quran Also *Koran*. The holy scriptures of Islam, composed of revelations to the prophet Muhammad.

wakan "Sacred" (in Lakota Sioux). All things are wakan in Lakota philosophy and religion.

Wakan Tanka "The Great Mystery" (in Lakota Sioux). Sometimes translated as "Great Spirit," Wakan Tanka is the basis of all that is sacred (**wakan**).

Weltanschauung "worldview" (in German); a philosophy through which one understands the world and one's place in it.

yang The active force associated with light, heat, day, sun, etc., in Taoism; always to be balanced with **yin**.

yin The passive force associated with dark, cold, night, moon, etc., in Taoism; always to be balanced with **yang**.

yogin A practitioner of yoga, a discipline, or "Way" to salvation, in Hinduism. Yoga involves physical as well as spiritual and mental discipline and can include meditation, good works, and devotion to gods and goddesses.

Zen Branch of **Mahayana** Buddhism that emphasizes a certain form of meditation. Zen has no real doctrine or creed, only a method for achieving enlightenment through experiencing **shunyata**.

FOR FURTHER DISCUSSION

Chapter 1

1. Reflect on the various definitions of religion found in this chapter and evaluate each. Are these good definitions? Why or why not? Do they include your own religious experiences and those of other people you know? Which do you like best and why?
2. How do you define religion? Write down characteristics you think the concept "religion" should include. Does this constitute a good definition? Why or why not? Is it broad enough without being too broad?
3. Are any of the characteristics of your definition similar to those of the definitions found in this chapter? Reflect on why you chose the characteristics you did. Why did you not include certain aspects that may be found in the other definitions?
4. Some of the viewpoints in this chapter seriously criticize religion as a destructive and negative phenomenon while others give a more positive assessment of it. Is religion a good thing? Why or why not? Do you view it as something positive or something negative? Explain. In what cases might it be something good, and in what cases something bad (for individuals, societies, etc.)?
5. Given the fact that definitions of religions often include an evaluation of religion as good or bad, do you think it is possible to have a definition of religion that avoids this? Can a definition of religion be neutral or value free, one that refrains from making value judgements? Are any of the definitions in this chapter value free? (Is Tillich's? Otto's?) Can you come up with a value-free definition?

Chapter 2

1. How do you view other religions? Which of the positions in this chapter do you find most convincing? Why?
2. What are the advantages and disadvantages of each approach found in this chapter? Are some too narrow, others too broad? Why? Can one find an approach that preserves the uniqueness of one's own religion while recognizing the value of others?

Chapters 3, 4, 5

1. Consider how the eight religious traditions approach each of the three questions posed in these chapters. Can you find similarities in the way certain religions answer a particular question? What are the important differences?
2. In each chapter, which view is closest to your own? Why? What do you like about it?
3. Pick a view very different from your own. Even though this is not your view, can you understand how someone could find meaning in this view? Why or why not?
4. Consider the viewpoints expressed by the three representatives of each tradition cited in chapters 3, 4, and 5. Are there significant differences among, for example, the three Buddhists? the three Christians? etc. To what extent do they agree with each other? To what extent do their views diverge? Do you believe their differences can be reconciled? Why or why not? What are the commonalities in their views that cause them all to be members of the same religion?
5. Consider whether the authors of the selections could be considered exclusivists, inclusivists, or pluralists (in regard to the issues of chapter 2). Do they give any indication of whether they believe truth is found in their religious tradition alone? Do they believe it is found elsewhere? Explain.

Suggestions for Further Reading

Chapter 1

D. Mackenzie Brown, *Ultimate Concern: Tillich in Dialogue*. New York: Harper & Row, 1965. Conversations with Tillich from a 1963 seminar on his theology. Tillich replies to questions about Judaism, Buddhism, and secularism, among other topics.

Mircea Eliade, *Patterns in Comparative Religion*, trans. Rosemary Sheed. New York: New American Library, 1958. A study of the "sacred" in the history of religion. An extremely influential scholar, especially in his analysis of how religions symbolically bring "life" out of "death."

Ludwig Feuerbach, *The Essence of Christianity*, trans. George Eliot. New York: Harper & Row, 1957. This book influenced Marx and Freud through its proposal that the concept of God is simply a projection of human desires and ideals onto an imaginary subject. A classic atheistic work.

Victor E. Frankl, *The Unconscious God*. New York: Simon & Schuster, 1975. Frankl counters Freud's assertion that religion is a mental disease by affirming that the concept of God is essential to a healthy psychological life.

Sigmund Freud, *The Future of an Illusion*, trans. James Strachey. New York: W. W. Norton & Co., Inc., 1961. Freud here develops his criticisms of religion as an "illusion" produced by psychological projection and human insecurity.

William James, *The Varieties of Religious Experience*. New York: New American Library, 1958. James distinguishes healthy religious experience from unhealthy religious experience, and so provides a psychological assessment of religion as something which can be either positive or negative from a "pragmatic" perspective.

C. G. Jung, *Psychology and Religion*. New Haven: Yale University Press, 1938. Jung analyzes religion as a set of symbols and "archetypes" which exist in human consciousness. A sympathetic assessment of religion from a major psychological theorist.

Abraham H. Maslow, *Religion, Values, and Peak Experiences*. New York: Viking Press, 1970. Maslow's "hierarchy of needs" presents the notion that life involves not only material necessities, but also spiritual necessities, and so religion is a crucial part of a healthy human existence.

D. Z. Phillips, *Religion Without Explanation*. Oxford: Basil Blackwell, 1976. A modern philosopher of religion attacks the reductionist notion that religion is a "fiction" through a critique of Hume, Freud, and Feuerbach.

Jean-Paul Sartre, *Being and Nothingness,* trans. Hazel E. Barnes. New York: Washington Square Press, 1956. The most thorough development of Sartre's philosophy, based on an analysis of human consciousness, the world, and human freedom.

Friedrich Schleiermacher, *On Religion: Speeches to Its Cultured Despisers,* trans. John Oman. New York: Harper & Row, 1958. An early work of the great Protestant theologian in which he first proposed that religion is primarily a matter of "feeling" rather than knowing or doing.

Ninian Smart, *Beyond Ideology: Religion and the Future of Western Civilization.* San Francisco: Harper & Row, 1981. Smart develops his understanding of religion by comparing Christianity, other religions, and secularism.

_____, *The Phenomenon of Religion.* London: Macmillan, 1973. Smart here considers how one "explores" religion as a phenomenon, analyzing the notion of "myth" and tensions between religion and science.

Jonathan Z. Smith, *Imagining Religion.* Chicago: University of Chicago Press, 1982. Smith considers a variety of religious phenomena, "from Babylon to Jonestown," as a way of uncovering what is distinctive about them.

Frederick J. Streng, *Understanding Religious Man.* Belmont, CA: Dickenson Pub. Co., Inc., 1969. An introduction to the "phenomenological" analysis of religion, which includes discussion of ways of being religious (e.g., harmony with law, or spiritual freedom) and modes of human awareness used to express religious meaning (art, reason, communal identity).

Paul Tillich, *The Courage to Be.* New Haven: Yale University Press, 1952. Tillich here develops the existential notion that religion involves a courageous commitment to life in the midst of uncertainty about questions of meaning.

Joachim Wach, *The Comparative Study of Religion.* New York: Columbia University Press, 1958. A "phenomenological" analysis of religious experience as it is expressed through thought, action, and social forms.

CHAPTER 2

Norman Anderson, *Christianity and World Religions: The Challenge of Pluralism.* Downers Grove, IL: Inter-Varsity Press, 1984. Anderson defends the uniqueness of Christianity as the only way to salvation, expressing an "exclusivist" evangelical position.

Carl E. Braaten, *No Other Gospel!* Minneapolis: Fortress Press, 1992. Braaten defends the idea that the final truth is found in Christianity alone, but accepts the possibility that other religions may "reflect" this truth to a lesser extent.

John B. Cobb Jr., *Beyond Dialogue: Toward a Mutual Transformation of*

Christianity and Buddhism. Philadelphia: Fortress Press, 1982. Cobb considers what Buddhists and Christians might learn from each other, and argues that often their claims do not so much conflict as complement each other.

Kenneth Cracknell, *Towards a New Relationship: Christians and People of Other Faiths.* London: Epworth Press, 1986. Cracknell offers an understanding of how God might be working through non-Christian communities of faith.

Kenneth Cragg, *The Christ and the Faiths.* Philadelphia: Westminster Press, 1986. A consideration of how Muslims, Jews, Hindus, and Buddhists might see Christian claims contributing to their own understanding of truth.

William V. Crockett and James G. Sigountos, eds., *Through No Fault of Their Own? The Fate of Those Who Have Never Heard.* Grand Rapids, MI: Baker Book House, 1991. Conservative evangelicals consider the eternal destiny of non-Christians, and whether saving truth can be found outside Christ.

Donald G. Dawe and John B. Carman, eds., *Christian Faith in a Religiously Pluralistic World.* Maryknoll, NY: Orbis Books, 1978. Representatives of Christianity, Buddhism, Hinduism, Judaism, and Islam discuss pluralism and particularity.

Gavin D'Costa, *Theology and Religious Pluralism: The Challenge of Other Religions.* Oxford: Basil Blackwell, 1986. D'Costa defends and updates the "inclusivist" view of Karl Rahner that Christians ought to view their own claims as normative for all religious truth-claims.

_____, ed., *Christian Uniqueness Reconsidered: The Myth of a Pluralistic Theology of Religions.* Maryknoll, NY: Orbis Books, 1990. A variety of scholars attack the "pluralism" of Hick, Knitter, et al., usually to argue for an "inclusivist" understanding of the uniqueness of Christian truth.

John Hick, *God and the Universe of Faiths: Essays in the Philosophy of Religion.* London: Macmillan, 1973. One of Hick's first ventures into the theology of religions contains essays outlining his early views on the subject.

_____, *God Has Many Names: Britain's New Religious Pluralism.* London: Macmillan, 1980. Although Hick considers Great Britain, his remarks are relevant to any country which contains diverse religious traditions. The title says it all.

_____, ed., *Truth and Dialogue in World Religions: Conflicting Truth-Claims.* Philadelphia: Westminster, 1974. Essays from several scholars on how to deal with the differences that exist among religious claims.

W. A. Visser't Hooft, *No Other Name.* Philadelphia: Westminster Press, 1963. Hooft attacks the "syncretistic" tendency to reconcile diverse religious beliefs and ignore the differences, proposing instead that Christianity should seek the unity of Christians of diverse cultures.

Paul F. Knitter, *No Other Name? A Critical Survey of Christian Attitudes Toward the World Religions.* Maryknoll, NY: Orbis Books, 1985. An excellent introduction to a wide variety of approaches to other religions, including Knitter's own, which he calls a "theocentric" (god-centered) variety of "pluralism."

Paul F. Knitter and John Hick, eds., *The Myth of Christian Uniqueness: Toward a Pluralistic Theology of Religions.* Maryknoll, NY: Orbis Books, 1987. Essays from a variety of contemporary scholars who challenge the traditional notion that Christianity alone has "The Truth." Many of the authors defend the "pluralist" position quite well.

Hendrik Kraemer, *Religion and the Christian Faith.* Philadelphia: Westminster Press, 1956. Kraemer defends the conservative evangelical understanding of the Christian "mission" to the non-Christian world.

Hans Küng et al., *Christianity and the World Religions: Paths of Dialogue with Islam, Hinduism, and Buddhism,* trans. Peter Heinegg. Garden City, NY: Doubleday, 1986. The famous Roman Catholic theologian responds to representatives of three religions, looking for what they might learn from Christianity and vice versa.

Stephen Neill, *Christian Faith and Other Faiths.* London: Oxford University Press, 1961. Neill promotes the need for a Christian dialogue with other religions which maintains Christian identity. He considers several traditional religions as well as modern atheistic existentialism.

Lesslie Newbigin, *The Finality of Christ.* Richmond, VA: John Knox Press, 1969. Newbigin defends the idea that conversion to Christ is essential, for the Christian revelation is the "final" truth.

Schubert Ogden, *Is There Only One True Religion or Are There Many?* Dallas: Southern Methodist University Press, 1992. This philosophical theologian argues that one cannot logically be an exclusivist or an inclusivist, but one need not be a pluralist, either; Christians can assert that their religion is true, but it is possible that others are true as well.

Willard G. Oxtoby, *The Meaning of Other Faiths.* Philadelphia: Westminster Press, 1983. Clear, succinct introduction to the various approaches to other religions, from the Bible and traditional church views to modern pluralism and evangelicalism.

Raimundo Panikkar, *The Cosmotheandric Experience,* ed. Scott Eastham. Maryknoll, NY: Orbis Books, 1993. Panikkar analyzes the interaction of World, God, and Humanity, and how religious experience expresses this.

_____, *The Unknown Christ of Hinduism,* rev. ed. Maryknoll, NY: Orbis Books, 1981. Panikkar proposes that Christ is also revealed through Hinduism, although in a different way.

Alan Race, *Christians and Religious Pluralism*. Maryknoll, NY: Orbis Books, 1983. Race analyzes approaches to religion through the now well-known categories of "exclusivism," "inclusivism," and "pluralism."

Karl Rahner, "Anonymous Christianity and the Missionary Task of the Church" in *Theological Investigations*, Vol. 12. New York: Seabury Press, 1974. Another famous essay by Rahner on how Christians should view the followers of other religions.

Frithjof Schuon, *The Transcendental Unity of Religions*. New York: Harper & Row, 1975. Schuon proposes that while "exoteric" believers always identify truth with the external form of their own religions, "esoteric" believers look for the mystical core of all religions that is the same. He favors the latter approach.

Wilfred Cantwell Smith, *The Meaning and End of Religion*. New York: New American Library, 1964. Smith proposes "faith" as a category which reaches across the boundaries of religious communities, in spite of their differences.

_____, *Religious Diversity*, ed. Willard G. Oxtoby. New York: Harper & Row, 1976. More essays by Smith on various religions and the connections that exist among them.

_____, *Toward a World Theology*. Philadelphia: Westminster Press, 1981. Smith develops a theology of comparative religions by analyzing how the faiths of different peoples save them from alienation and despair.

Donald K. Swearer, *Dialogue: The Key to Understanding Other Religions*. Philadelphia: Westminster Press, 1977. Swearer develops the notion that the interchange of ideas among religions can lead to better understanding and mutual enrichment.

Leonard Swidler, ed., *Toward a Universal Theology of Religion*. Maryknoll, NY: Orbis Books, 1988. Essays from religious scholars of various traditions debate the nature of religious truth in a pluralistic world.

Paul Tillich, *The Future of Religions*, ed. Jerald C. Brauer. New York: Harper & Row, 1966. This includes some of Tillich's final lectures in which he began to develop a theology of world religions that acknowledged that truth may exist in more than one tradition.

CHAPTERS 3, 4, 5

On Judaism

Rudolph Brasch, *The Judaic Heritage: Its Teachings, Philosophy, and Symbols*. New York: David McKay Co., 1969.

Steven Katz, *Jewish Ideas and Concepts*. New York: Schocken Books, 1977.

Harold Kushner, *To Life! A Celebration of Jewish Being and Thinking*. Boston: Little, Brown, 1993.

Bernard Martin, *A History of Judaism*. Vol. 2: *Europe and the New World*. New York: Basic Books, 1974.

Jacob Neusner, *The Life of Torah: Readings in the Jewish Religious Experience*. Belmont, CA: Wadsworth, 1974.

Jacob Neusner, *The Way of Torah: An Introduction to Judaism*. 5th ed. Belmont, CA: Wadsworth, 1993.

Robert M. Seltzer, *Jewish People, Jewish Thought: The Jewish Experience in History*. New York: Macmillan, 1980.

Phillip Sigal, *Judaism: The Evolution of a Faith*. Grand Rapids, MI: Eerdmans, 1988.

Daniel Jeremy Silver, *A History of Judaism*. Vol. 1: *From Abraham to Maimonides*. New York: Basic Books, 1974.

Milton Steinberg, *Basic Judaism*. New York: Harcourt Brace Jovanovich, 1965.

Leo Trepp, *Judaism: Development and Life*. 3rd ed. Belmont, CA: Wadsworth, 1982.

Herman Wouk, *This Is My God: The Jewish Way of Life*. New York: Doubleday, 1970.

On Christianity

Kurt Aland, *A History of Christianity*. 2 vols. Translated by James L. Schaaf. Philadelphia: Fortress Press, 1985.

Geoffrey Bromiley, *Historical Theology*. Grand Rapids, MI: Eerdmans, 1978.

A. Daniel Frankforter, *A History of the Christian Movement: The Development of Christian Institutions*. Chicago: Nelson-Hall, 1978.

Paul Johnson, *A History of Christianity*. London: Weidenfeld & Nicolson, 1976.

Howard Clark Kee, *Christianity: A Social and Cultural History*. New York: Macmillan, 1991.

Kenneth Scott Latourette, *A History of Christianity*. Rev. ed. 2 vols. New York: Harper, 1975.

Clyde Leonard Manschreck, *A History of Christianity in the World*. 2nd ed. Englewood Cliffs, NJ: Prentice-Hall, 1985.

Martin E. Marty, *A Short History of Christianity*. New York: Meridian Books, 1959.

John McManners, ed., *The Oxford Illustrated History of Christianity*. New York: Oxford University Press, 1990.

Jaroslav Pelikan, *The Christian Tradition*. 5 vols. Chicago: University of Chicago Press, 1971-1989.

Stephen Reynolds, *The Christian Religious Tradition*. Belmont, CA: Wadsworth, 1977.

Williston Walker et al., *A History of the Christian Church*. New York: Charles Scribner's Sons, 1985.

On Islam

Peter Clarke, ed., *The World's Religions: Islam*. London: Routledge, 1990.

Kenneth Cragg and R. Marston Speight, *The House of Islam*. 3rd ed. Belmont, CA: Wadsworth, 1988.

Kenneth Cragg and R. Marston Speight, *Islam from Within: Anthology of a Religion*. Belmont, CA: Wadsworth, 1980.

Victor Danner, *The Islamic Tradition*. Amity, NY: Amity House, 1988.

John L. Esposito, *Islam: The Straight Path*. New York: Oxford University Press, 1988.

Seyyed Hossein Nasr, *Ideals and Realities of Islam*. San Francisco: Harper, 1989.

F.E. Peters, *A Reader on Classical Islam*. Princeton, NJ: Princeton University Press, 1994.

Fazlur Rahman, *Islam*. 2nd ed. Chicago: University of Chicago Press, 1979.

Andrew Rippin, *Muslims: Their Religious Beliefs and Practices*. 2 vols. New York: Routledge, 1990-1993.

Andrew Rippin and Jan Knappert, eds. and trans., *Textual Sources for the Study of Islam*. Manchester, UK: Manchester University Press, 1986.

John Sabini, *Islam: A Primer*. Rev. ed. Washington, DC: Middle East Editorial Associates, 1990.

Frithjof Schuon, *Understanding Islam*. London: George Allen & Unwin, 1976.

Wilfred Cantwell Smith, *On Understanding Islam: Selected Studies*. New York: Mouton, 1981.

John Alden Williams, ed., *Islam*. New York: G. Braziller, 1961.

On Hinduism

A.L. Basham, *The Origins and Development of Classical Hinduism*. Kenneth G. Zysked. Boston: Beacon Press, 1989.

A.L. Basham, *The Sacred Cow: The Evolution of Classical Hinduism*. Kenneth G. Zysked. London: Sydney Rider, 1990.

Sarasvati Chennakesavan, *A Critical Study of Hinduism*. New York:

Asia Publishing House, 1974.

A.L. Herman, *A Brief Introduction to Hinduism: Religion, Philosophy, and Ways of Liberation*. Boulder, CO: Westview Press, 1991.

Thomas J. Hopkins, *The Hindu Religious Tradition*. Belmont, CA: Wadsworth, 1971.

David Kinsley, *Hinduism: A Cultural Perspective*. Englewood Cliffs, NJ: Prentice-Hall, 1982.

Klaus Klostermaier, *A Survey of Hinduism*. Albany, NY: SUNY Press, 1989.

Wendy Doniger O'Flaherty, trans., *Hindu Myths: A Sourcebook*. Baltimore: Penguin, 1975.

Sarvepalli Radhakrishnan, trans., *The Principal Upanishads*. London: Allen & Unwin, 1953.

Sarvepalli Radhakrishnan and Charles A. Moore, eds., *A Sourcebook in Indian Philosophy*. Princeton, NJ: Princeton University Press, 1957.

Louis Renou, *Hinduism*. New York: G. Braziller, 1961.

Herbert H. Stroup, *Like a Great River: An Introduction to Hinduism*. New York: Harper & Row, 1972.

Heinrich Zimmer, *The Philosophies of India*. Princeton, NJ: Princeton University Press, 1969.

On Buddhism

Samuel Bercholz and Sherab Chodzin Kohn, eds., *Entering the Stream: An Introduction to the Buddha and His Teachings*. Boston: Shambhala, 1993.

Stephen Beyer, *The Buddhist Experience: Sources and Interpretations*. Belmont, CA: Wadsworth, 1974.

Kenneth K.S. Ch'en, *Buddhism: The Light of Asia*. Woodbury, NY: Barron's Educational Series, 1968.

Edward Conze, *Buddhist Scriptures*. Baltimore: Penguin, 1959.

Edward Conze, *A Short History of Buddhism*. London: George Allen & Unwin, 1980.

Richard Corless, *The Vision of Buddhism: The Space Under the Tree*. New York: Paragon House, 1989.

William T. De Bary, ed., *The Buddhist Tradition in India, China, and Japan*. New York: Vintage Books, 1972.

Dorothy C. Donath, *Buddhism for the West*. New York: Julian Press, 1971.

Nolan Pliny Jacobson, *Understanding Buddhism*. Carbondale: Southern

Illinois University Press, 1986.

David J. Kalupahana, *A History of Buddhist Philosophy: Continuities and Discontinuities.* Honolulu: University of Hawaii Press, 1992.

Richard H. Robinson and Willard L. Johnson, *The Buddhist Religion.* 3rd ed. Belmont, CA: Wadsworth, 1982.

John Snelling, *The Buddhist Handbook: A Complete Guide to Buddhist Teaching, Practice, History, and Schools.* London: Century, 1987.

On Taoism

Thomas F. Cleary, *The Essential Tao: An Initiation into the Heart of Taoism Through the Authentic Tao te Ching and the Inner Teachings of the Chuang Tzu.* San Francisco: Harper, 1992.

Herrlee G. Creel, *What Is Taoism? and Other Studies in Chinese Cultural History.* Chicago: University of Chicago Press, 1970.

Benjamin Hoff, *The Tao of Pooh.* New York: Dutton, 1982.

Max Kaltenmark, *Lao Tzu and Taoism.* Stanford, CA: Stanford University Press, 1969.

Michael LaFargue, *The Tao of the Tao te Ching.* Albany, NY: SUNY Press, 1992.

Da Liu, *The Tao and Chinese Culture.* New York: Schocken Books, 1979.

Henry Maspero, *Taoism and Chinese Religion.* Amherst: University of Massachusetts Press, 1981.

Arthur Waley, *The Way and Its Power: A Study of the Tao te Ching and Its Place in Chinese Thought.* New York: Grove Press, 1958.

On Confucianism

Chu Chai, *Confucianism.* Woodbury, NY: Barron's Educational Series, 1973.

Chung-ying Cheng, *New Dimensions of Confucian and Neo-Confucian Philosophy.* Albany, NY: SUNY Press, 1991.

Herrlee G. Creel, *Confucius: The Man and the Myth.* New York: Harper, 1960.

Raymond S. Dawson, *Confucius.* New York: Oxford University Press, 1981.

William T. de Bary, *The Trouble with Confucianism.* Cambridge, MA: Harvard University Press, 1991.

Herbert Fingarette, *Confucius: The Secular as Sacred.* New York: Harper & Row, 1972.

D.C. Lau, *Mencius.* New York: Penguin, 1970.

Liu Wu-Chi, *A Short History of Confucian Philosophy.* New York: Dell, 1955.

William McNaughton, ed., *The Confucian Vision.* Ann Arbor: University of Michigan Press, 1974.

Tu Wei-Ming, *Confucian Thought: Selfhood as Creative Transformation.* Albany, NY: SUNY Press, 1985.

Arthur Waley, *The Analects of Confucius.* New York: Random House, 1989.

Arthur F. Wright, ed., *The Confucian Persuasion.* Stanford, CA: Stanford University Press, 1960.

Arthur F. Wright and Denis Twitchett, eds., *Confucian Personalities.* Stanford, CA: Stanford University Press, 1962.

On Chinese Religion in General

Wing-Tsit Chan, ed., *A Sourcebook in Chinese Philosophy.* Princeton, NJ: Princeton University Press, 1963.

Herrlee G. Creel, *Chinese Thought: From Confucius to Mao Tse-Tung.* Chicago: University of Chicago Press, 1953.

Fung Yu-Lan, *A Short History of Chinese Philosophy.* Princeton, NJ: Princeton University Press, 1966.

Christian Jochim, *Chinese Religions: A Cultural Perspective.* Englewood Cliffs, NJ: Prentice-Hall, 1986.

Charles A. Moore, ed., *The Chinese Mind: Essentials of Chinese Philosophy and Culture.* Honolulu: East-West Center Press, 1967.

Daniel L. Overmyer, *Religions of China: The World as a Living System.* San Francisco: Harper, 1986.

Benjamin I. Schwartz, *The World of Thought in Ancient China.* Cambridge, MA: Belknap Press, 1985.

Lawrence G. Thompson, *Chinese Religion: An Introduction.* 4th ed. Belmont, CA: Wadsworth, 1989.

Lawrence G. Thompson, *The Chinese Way in Religion.* Belmont, CA: Wadsworth, 1973.

C.K. Yang, *Religion in Chinese Society.* Berkeley: University of California Press, 1967.

On Sioux Religion

Joseph Epes Brown, ed., *The Sacred Pipe: Black Elk's Account of the Seven Rites of the Oglala Sioux.* Norman: University of Oklahoma Press, 1953.

Raymond J. DeMallie, ed., *The Sixth Grandfather: Black Elk's Teachings*

Given to John G. Neihardt. Lincoln: University of Nebraska Press, 1984.

Raymond J. DeMallie and Douglas R. Parks, eds., *Sioux Indian Religion: Tradition and Innovation*. Norman: University of Oklahoma Press, 1987.

Archie Fire Lame Deer and Richard Erdoes, *Gift of Power: The Life and Teachings of a Lakota Medicine Man*. Santa Fe, NM: Bear & Co., 1992.

James LaPointe, *Legends of the Lakota*. San Francisco: Indian Historian Press, 1976.

Thomas H. Lewis, *The Medicine Men: Oglala Sioux Ceremony and Healing*. Lincoln: University of Nebraska Press, 1990.

William K. Powers, *Oglala Religion*. Lincoln: University of Nebraska Press, 1975.

William K. Powers, *Yuwipi: Vision and Experience in Oglala Ritual*. Lincoln: University of Nebraska Press, 1982.

Omer C. Stewart, *Peyote Religion: A History*. Norman: University of Oklahoma Press, 1987.

James R. Walker, *Lakota Belief and Ritual*. Raymond J. DeMallie and Elaine A. Jahner, eds. Lincoln: University of Nebraska Press, 1980.

James R. Walker, *Lakota Myth*. Elaine A. Jahner, ed. Lincoln: University of Nebraska Press, 1983.

On Native American Religion in General

Joseph Epes Brown, *The Spiritual Legacy of the American Indian*. New York: Crossroad, 1989.

Denise Lardner Carmody and John Tully Carmody, *Native American Religions: An Introduction*. New York: Paulist Press, 1993.

Sam Gill, *Native American Religions: An Introduction*. Belmont, CA: Wadsworth, 1982.

Sam Gill, *Native American Traditions: Sources and Interpretations*. Belmont, CA: Wadsworth, 1983.

Ake Hultkrantz, *The Religions of the American Indians*. Berkeley: University of California Press, 1979.

Index